SIMMO
THE WHOLE TRUTH

Best Wishes
'Simmo'

SIMMO
THE WHOLE TRUTH

By MALCOLM SIMMONS

With Tony McDonald

First published in June 2006 by
Retro Speedway
Tel: 01708 734 502
www.retro-speedway.com

©Copyright Retro Speedway & Malcolm Simmons

All rights reserved.
Without limiting the rights under copyright reserved above, no part of this publication may be reproduced, stored in or introduced into a retrieval system, or, transmitted, in any form or by any means (electronic, mechanical, photocopying, recording or otherwise) without the prior written permission of the copyright owner of this book.

Printed by Biddles Ltd, King's Lynn, Norfolk

Distributed by Retro Speedway
103 Douglas Road, Hornchurch, Essex, RM11 1AW, England
Email: editorial@retro-speedway.com

Set in Times Roman

ISBN 0-9551176-2-3

Cover photography by Mike Patrick & Alf Weedon/Retro Speedway

PHOTOGRAPHIC ACKNOWLEDGEMENTS
A number of the photographs used in this book have been kindly donated by Malcolm Simmons, and every attempt has been made to correctly identify the individual source. In this respect, we would like to thank the following:
Alf Weedon, Mike Patrick (Speedway Star), John Somerville (courtesy of the Wright Wood and Trevor Meeks collections), Dave Fairbrother (Speedway Star), Ken Carpenter, John Hipkiss, the late Don Ringrow, Chris Convine, Gordon Elsworth and B.R. Nicholls.
And anybody else whose pictures we have unfortunately not been able to credit.
The views expressed in this book are those of Malcolm Simmons
and not necessarily those of the publisher.

I would like to dedicate this book to June, who was filled with horror when she read some parts of it . . . and very proud when she read others. She has turned my life around and, but for her, I wouldn't be the person I am today.

Contents

Introduction	Malcolm Simmons	9
Forewords	Ivan Mauger MBE OBE	13
	Barry Briggs MBE	16
	John Berry	19
Chapter 1	Born to ride	23
Chapter 2	Grass roots	28
Chapter 3	Treble champions	36
Chapter 4	To Russia with blood	49
Chapter 5	The inside story	58
Chapter 6	Fond farewell to our shining Star	72
Chapter 7	Bettsy…and why I had to leave	86
Chapter 8	The new blue-eyed boy	98
Chapter 9	Turning up the heat – 1976-77	114
Chapter 10	England pride	140
Chapter 11	Hung out to dry	174
Chapter 12	Do me a favour	184
Chapter 13	Back on track	194
Chapter 14	Swindon shame	207
Chapter 15	Flying high again	212
Chapter 16	Who's the fraudster?	218
Chapter 17	England fears	227
Chapter 18	Love and tears	238
	Simmo: Speedway Honours & Milestones	250
	Index	251

Acknowledgements

Thanks must go to the following people, for many different reasons:

Tony Mac, for his coaxing
June, for just being June
Dad, for the beginning and the end
The late Maurice Littlechild
Charles, Jim, Jack and Dawn Knott
Weslake Engineering
Ted Laessing
Ivan Mauger MBE OBE
Barry Briggs MBE
John Berry
Chris MacDonald
Ray and Tom Palmer
Roy Francis
John Wilson
Les and Christine
Andy and Jackie
David and Christine
Ken and Linda
Dave, Carol and family
John and Pauline
And especially after Spain . . . Graham and Pat,
whom we couldn't have done without.
These are what true friends are all about.

Publishers Tony McDonald and Susie Muir, of Retro Speedway, would particularly like to thank the following for their help and enthusiasm in making this book possible:
  Malcolm and June; John Berry; Richard Clark; Martin Rogers; John Somerville; Mike Patrick; and Bryn Williams.
  And finally, Marios Flourentzou, for the cover design and production.

Introduction
By Malcolm Simmons

I GUESS the title of this book will cause quite a few people who have known me to head somewhat anxiously straight for the index section, to see if they've got a name-check! My publisher originally suggested simply *Simmo*, but it was my idea to add *The Whole Truth* line.

I've tried to present this as a most open and honest account of my life and career as a sports motorcyclist and I imagine that some aspects of it will shock and amaze many people while, at the same time, probably dismay a number of others.

As one who has never deliberately ducked a serious question from a journalist, even if my strongly held views are not shared or liked by the majority, it won't stop me voicing them. I wanted to tell my story the way it really is, or as candidly as possible within legal limits! I'm not telling all for the money – unfortunately, where speedway books are concerned, there's very little in it financially.

There are an increasing number of speedway books on the market now, though, several of them focusing on that memorable 70s and 80s period when I was at my peak as a top England international, World No.2 and British League star. John Berry's Confessions of a Speedway Promoter is the best of those I've read but, outspoken and forthright though he is, I still think John could have been even more controversial in recalling what speedway was like back then, when he and I worked together as England team manager and captain.

In the mid-70s, England ruled the speedway world but can you honestly imagine another day soon when this country will have two of its riders standing proudly on top of the World Championship (Grand Prix) rostrum, as Peter Collins and I did in Katowice 30 years ago? I've got some strong views on the reasons why England (or should that be Great Britain?) is lagging behind the rest of the world and the way modern speedway is run – and it won't make very comfortable reading for today's BSPA members.

Here, I will reveal the truth about race-fixing. Yes, it really did go on and I was involved in a number of instances where money changed hands and favours were done and returned. My revelations may irritate those who prefer us to believe that our sport has always been squeaky-clean but after you've read this, you will see that it has not always been the case.

One of my biggest regrets – and I have plenty – is the manner of my unseemly departure from Poole in 1980, when I was sacked for 'throwing' a race. For the first

Introduction

time, I can honestly say that it's true . . . I didn't try to win that infamous race in the best pairs meeting that signalled the end of six otherwise happy years with the Pirates. But there was a lot more to it than that, as you'll find out . . .

Not that I recall such events with an air of boastful arrogance. I truly believe that no-one's reputation will come under closer scrutiny from the telling of these stories than my own, and I admit my behaviour in my last meeting for Swindon, in particular, still makes me feel guilty and a little ashamed of it some 21 years later.

I know some die-hard speedway purists will not welcome all my comments and observations and I've been warned to expect a backlash from some people. I can only repeat that it is not my intention to upset anybody, but to tell the truth as I see it.

Writing this book has also caused me to question and scrutinise my own part in many of my past problems and misdemeanours . . . and reach the conclusion that I've been very much my own worst enemy at various times. I had to face a few home truths when I sat down with Backtrack magazine's Tony McDonald and his tape recorder at the Kent home I share with my long-term partner and soul mate, June. When confronted with my 'colourful' past, I knew I had to be as honest and critical of myself as I have been of others – there wasn't a probing question or contentious issue left unanswered – and I hope that this also comes across clearly over the following pages.

I've found discussing some of the more personal issues of my past a bit sad and yet therapeutic. I've tried to address issues that I've never faced up to or even discussed in any depth with anybody apart from June before. My lonely childhood; the break up of my parent's marriage; the part I played in my own divorce from Sandra and the fall-out from that; and how my 82-year-old father and I have finally, and thankfully, been reconciled after more than 20 years apart. That happy reunion came about just last year thanks to June. I know very well just how much she has done to put my life on the straight and narrow, and how much I must thank her for bringing us the happiness we share today.

Rumours in speedway have been rife for years about my various brushes with the law and, again, these are unhappy episodes in my life that cannot be swept under the carpet any longer. It still frightens me today to recall the six hellish months I spent in prison as a 22-year-old who was still serving time inside when my only child, Lisa, was born.

The whole truth? Well, almost. There are still one or two things, mainly involving other people, that I just won't reveal or speak about – either because I cannot prove in a court of law that these events took place, or I am not prepared to divulge the details of some sexual encounters that involved my former colleagues. I'm a bit old school in that I still observe that age-old male motto: 'What goes on tour, stays on tour'. I certainly wouldn't wish to unnecessarily damage marriages or personal relationships, some of which have survived longer than my first marriage did. Phew . . . I can almost hear the sigh of relief echoing across England and the rest of Europe!

It was my choice to ask Ivan Mauger, Barry Briggs and John Berry to contribute their own forewords to this book and I'd like to thank all three for immediately agreeing to help. Ivan is quite simply the most professional and successful speedway rider I've ever known. Briggo is an old mate who wasn't far behind his fellow New Zealand legend at winning all the sport's major honours. And John is, without doubt, the best team manager I've ever ridden for. Ivan, Briggo and John all feature fairly prominently at various stages in my story, as do many other former heroes of the golden era I enjoyed in speedway.

My life and speedway career has been a roller coaster journey right from the beginning and I'm sure there are a few more interesting

June and I returned from our Spanish 'holiday' injured. 'What an amateur!' she told me, for crashing a 50cc scooter.

twists and turns to come yet. I celebrated my 60th birthday in March, and I'm still working five or six days a week repairing wheels to earn my living, but there is still nothing I love more than to get on a bike and ride competitively, albeit in trials events held up and down the country. In fact, when Tony and I first got together to write the first few chapters earlier this year, I could hardly move after crashing and breaking a rib at a trials meeting the previous weekend!

I've got an incurable lung disease now – nothing too serious, but enough to make me give up grasstrack racing a couple of years ago because I simply got out of breath after just two laps. Another regret: I wish I'd never smoked!

If I could, I'd still be riding both grasstrack and speedway today and I know I'll never lose my life-long love of bikes.

Having said that, I didn't love it much when June and I were unceremoniously knocked off our 50cc scooter while taking a pleasure ride on our recent week's holiday in Spain. June broke her arm in the fall and I busted two ribs. Some holiday!

Many thanks for buying my book – I hope you enjoy it.

Malcolm Simmons
West Kingsdown, Kent
May 2006

Foreword 1
By Ivan Mauger OBE MBE

MALCOLM Simmons, in the words of a Kinks song from way back when, always was a bit of a 'dedicated follower of fashion', so we should not be surprised that he is putting pen to paper.

Speedway books, and especially those by riders from another time, are quite the thing these days. And nobody will be in any doubt that Simmo has a few stories to tell.

He featured in many headline-making activities, and during the 70s certainly was one of the outstanding riders in the world even if a silver medal in the 1976 World Final at Katowice – which Peter Collins won – was as good as it got for him.

Malcolm, though, does have a handsome collection of FIM gold medals. Four times he was a World Team Cup winner (in 1973, 1974, 1975 and 1977) and but for one of the all-time contentious refereeing decisions at Vojens in 1979, he should have added to the three World Pairs titles he won – with a different partner each time.

We were throwing Simmo and Michael Lee into the air as the pairs champions until – after a delay which seemed like 10 minutes – the local timekeeper/judge and referee Tore Kittilsen decided that Hans Nielsen had just nicked second place from Poland's Edward Jancarz which meant Denmark, and not the English boys, topped the score chart.

But Malcolm had plenty to celebrate in the years when officialdom decided it was time to rid the Great Britain team of its colonial influence. The first such occasion was at Wembley in 1973, when the all-English quartet of Ray Wilson, PC, Simmo and his long-time King's Lynn sparring partner Terry Betts won the World Team Cup.

Before then, for years, Briggo, Ronnie Moore and I had been regulars in the competition. After a lot of heartaches, we flew the flag with a breakthrough win in 1968, at Wembley, followed famously at Wroclaw in 1971 (when Barry, Jim Airey and I did our bit as 'World Cup Willie' raced to a maximum) and then at Olching the following year, I was the lone colonial.

Bettsy and John Louis made their WTC debut that day, and with Simmo just one of several British riders improving fast, there was a push for an all-English team. At this stage Malcolm probably was not yet at his peak – although he'd been around since 1963, the year I came back to ride in the Provincial League.

In his early years he obviously was a very talented motorcyclist, stylish and safe,

SIMMO

England v Rest of the World at Hackney, 1978.

"He always seemed to be a bit of an artful dodger, a lovable rogue and maybe closer in spirit and attitude to some of the cavalier types of an earlier era"

quick and clever. Of course, it takes more than that to be a champion and he was kind enough to credit me with helping to change his mindset after we had some conversations in Perth when we were both racing at Con Migro's Claremont track in the early 70s.

It was after he moved to Poole, in 1975, that Simmo's star really began to rise. As an acknowledged No.1 in his own right, he blossomed, his confidence soared, and around this time you would have to say he was very close to the highest honours. On his day he could beat anybody, anywhere and make it all look ridiculously easy.

At a time when any one of half a dozen English riders were there or thereabouts, when it came to consistency of performance, day in, day out, he was often regarded as being the pick of the crop. The fans of Peter Collins, John Louis, Dave Jessup, Michael Lee and the rest were always ready to argue the point.

The fact Simmo didn't make much of an impact on the individual World Championship is an argument against rating him in quite the same league. But with the greatest of respect to all the rest, I would put him up alongside most, maybe almost all of them, as a rider and an opponent to be respected.

His performance in Poland in 1976 underlines what people say about nobody remembering a runner-up. PC took all the accolades that afternoon in Katowice but Malcolm, to this day, regards it as the day 'his' crack at individual glory slipped away from him.

However, those team wins count for plenty and so too the pairs successes achieved in 1976 with Louis, 1977 with PC and 1978 with Gordon Kennett. When it came to the time-honoured art of team-riding, Simmo was just the perfect partner, always aware of what was going on and what was needed.

His critics may suggest that this wasn't always the case in a 25-year career which had as many twists and turns and bumps as a ride round Brough Park in my early days there. Nobody doubted Simmo's talent but it was his ability to settle down and avoid distractions which was in question. He always seemed to be a bit of an artful dodger, a lovable rogue and maybe closer in spirit and attitude to some of the cavalier types of an earlier era.

Foreword

But he was a thoroughly modern man when the sport moved up a gear in the mid-70s, immediately in tune with the demands of new technology. If there was one thing which always impressed me about him, from his earliest days right through to his farewell years, it was his presentation – arriving at meetings with well prepared bikes, a clean car and neatly dressed .

When I'm talking to young riders nowadays, I always stress to them the importance of such things. This is something I have strong views on and it is one of the lessons that I enforce on my Academy pupils, and one that too many current GP stars seem to overlook in their role as the sport's top ambassadors. Malcolm, though, was a shining example of his time who invariably appeared as the best turned-out rider on parade, his equipment a sparkling tribute to his professionalism.

Through tough times, good times and right up to the present day, Simmo remains a motorcycling enthusiast. He loves it. He was a terrific grasstrack rider before he made his mark in speedway, and brilliant in trials as well. In recent years I have been proud to follow his success in Classic Longtrack events in Europe, where he has been riding one of my ex-grasstrack bikes now owned by my long-time friend Chris MacDonald. In fact, Malcolm is one of those guys you could put on anything and he would look good.

His book, I suspect, will mirror the Malcolm Simmons I have known for more than 40 years – plenty of dash and style, some forceful opinions expressed, a bit of controversy here and there. And shining through it all, no doubt, will be the enthusiasm of a man who, warts and all, has been one of speedway's best-loved personalities.

World Final maestro and the new boy on the block line up at Wembley in 1975.

Foreword 2
By Barry Briggs MBE

MALCOLM Simmons was one of the most talented speedway riders of our generation and if only he'd decided much earlier in his career that he was going to become World Champion, then I'm sure he could have achieved it.

Simmo reminds me a bit of my fellow countryman Ronnie Moore. Ronnie was more naturally talented than either Ivan or myself, but he never really worked at it and was only very determined to win the world title earlier in his career. He did win the World Championship twice but Ivan and I wanted it more than Ronnie did. Simmo was, like Ronnie, a smooth stylist and should have won more titles than he did. If I had to choose between somebody with natural talent and somebody else who wants it badly, I figure I'd take the bloke who wants.

I was aware of Simmo's tremendous talent from an early stage in his career, when he was still learning the ropes as a young kid with West Ham and I was riding for Swindon.

The trouble with Simmo was that he was never quite as dedicated to the task as he should have been, and sometimes I got the feeling that he had another agenda – maybe a grasstrack meeting to go to somewhere or other the next day. He just didn't seem to care that much about it and wanted an easy time of it. The speedway world didn't really get to know just how good he was until much later in his career.

He was still very successful but I think he could have been even bigger than he was, which is saying something considering he was World No.2 and a top England international for the best part of a decade. He certainly had a lot of natural talent but you need a bit more than that to go all the way to the top.

His career never really took off until he got away from the shadow of Terry Betts, who was *the* big personality at King's Lynn, and joined Poole in 1975. That was a very good move for Malcolm and he was brilliant for the Pirates and England around that time. He went very close to winning the big one in Katowice in 1976 but Simmo was 30-years-old by then and it turned out to be Peter Collins' day instead. Simmo was so close to winning the speedway World Championship but I don't think it was

> **"The great thing about Simmo is that he would ride you hard but he always remained fair. He knew what he was doing on a bike and always left his opponents just enough room"**

Foreword

Briggo was still going strong for Hull in 1976, as he shows in this duel with Exeter's Kevin Holden. One of the most tragic moments of my career came the following year when Kevin was killed riding for Poole.

the most important thing in his life.

It's a measure of how much I rate Simmo as a great all round motorcyclist that, when I had the UK franchise for the American-made Carlisle tyre in 1982, he was the first British-based rider I asked to test the new tyre for me. Malcolm was an obvious choice for me, because he has such a good feel and touch on any motorcycle. He knew what was going on with a speedway bike and he gave me excellent feedback. I still maintain that the Carlisle was the best tyre ever made for speedway – they were consistent.

Even last year, when I was developing a new dirt deflector, I asked Simmo to try it for me on English grasstracks, because I value his opinion above many, many others. If I had any new product to test and develop, Simmo is the first bloke I'd go to. He still knows what's what.

When my son, Tony, was trying to make his mark in the British League for Reading, before serious injuries halted his career, he learned a lot just from racing against Simmo and he had some of his best-ever races with Malcolm. The great thing about Simmo is that he would ride you hard, but he always remained fair. He knew what he was doing and always left his opponents just enough room.

It's been said before that Simmo could be his own worst enemy at times and could be irresponsible. But he's never let me down in all the time I've known him and I consider him a good mate today.

I'm sure Simmo will say plenty in his book that won't please everyone but I'm a bit like him when it comes to saying what I think. I'm probably not the most popular man in speedway either but I don't really care about that – and I'm sure Simmo feels the same way about himself. You've just got to treat your friends, and the people who are good to you, well. Just treat people for what they are.

SIMMO

I've always found Simmo great to get on with it. We have a laugh together because we understand each other. He might be a bit different but nobody's perfect and I've had bugger all trouble with him – and vice-versa.

Simmo was really good for speedway – he had a nice style and his equipment was always clean and in fantastic condition.

I'm pleased to see that he is still competing today in trials events. People have probably said the same to him as what they've said to me in the past – that we should quit while we're at the top – but that's a lot of bullshit. I saw Simmo racing on grasstrack a couple of years ago. OK, so he wasn't winning races by then, but he was still enjoying himself and that's the main thing. You only have one life, so don't do things simply to please others. That's my philosophy and I'm sure it's been Malcolm's too.

Malcolm Simmons has always been his own person – and some of his previous problems were created by himself – but at the end of the day, all that matters is that he does his own thing and continues to ride for his own satisfaction.

He's all right is old Simmo.

Briggo thinking of something else I can test for him.

Foreword 3
By John Berry

ONE of my less endearing features is a demeanour that makes Sir Alex Ferguson look like a cuddly Teddy Bear. I'd like to announce this apparent personality bypass is purely imaginary.

I'd like to, but in all honesty, I can't.

Just to complete the picture, under the veneer I'm pretty much a goody-two-shoes to go with it. I simply don't have the 'flair' to wander too far from the straight and narrow no matter how much I think I can. As a consequence, my alter-ego, which is always kept strapped down and unable to fight its way to the surface, has to satisfy itself by encouraging me to be drawn towards people who are far more able to show a bit of 'character'.

Australians have a single word for such 'free flying' types. They call them 'ockers'. An ocker is one who retains his defiant disrespect towards conformity well past adolescence. He doesn't need excessive amounts of falling down water to loosen his inhibitions, nor is he too bothered about possible reprisals arising from what society might regard as irresponsibility. He gets on and has fun, and to hell with the consequences.

My life has been littered with such people, both in and away from speedway. I used to use them to fire the bullets I enjoyed making whilst I hid behind their coat-tails. In return, I have often been able to act as something of a bit of a stabiliser for them, helping them from allowing their free spirits to get too far out of line and often managing to prevent a certain amount of self-inflicted damage. They would cover for my weaknesses and in return I would try to protect them from themselves.

Simmo was one of those people.

Malcolm Simmons is actually younger than me, which feels strange inasmuch as I used to see him racing for West Ham when I was still a schoolboy. More than telling you I was reluctant to join the working ranks, it lets you know that Malcolm was a speedway prodigy, which was something of a rarity in the days when you could have any colour leathers you wanted as long as they were black. Speedway riders were men rather than jockeys in those days, when the nearest you got to toiletries for males were Old Spice and Brylcream.

Early in his speedway career Malcolm got caught on the wrong side of the law. Just about all of us did silly things in our teenage years but most of us got away with it. Simmo just didn't know when to stop pushing his luck and finally it ran out.

Anyway, that is Malcolm's story to tell. All I will say is that from then on, he became famous for two things: The first was being a very talented speedway rider; and the second was for developing something of a bad boy image.

Stories abounded, many true I suspect, and I daresay a few perhaps becoming embellished with the re-telling. Perhaps I am just a trusting soul but the worst problem I had with Malcolm was his constant refusal to honour bookings he had accepted to ride in big meetings at Ipswich. Other than that, he has never done me any wrong. Not that I know of, anyway!

I cannot say I had got to know the man in great depth early on in his career, but it seemed clear, in the areas that counted for me, he was as solid as a rock. There was never a doubt about his riding talent, but as I became involved on the international scene I began to find out there was more to Malcolm Simmons, the person.

He has a quick brain, and like myself, doesn't suffer fools gladly. His dry sense of humour matches my own and despite his irresponsible image, he was proud to represent his country and took the honour seriously. Far more seriously, it must be said, than some of his peers, who measured success purely in financial terms.

Despite the intensity of his commitment to the cause, though, there was always just a spark of potential misadventure in Malcolm's eyes. I wouldn't have wanted it any other way. That was what made the man who he was.

When the England captaincy came along in 1977, and much against the advice of one or two more senior promoters, I decided he was the natural choice . . . just so long as he stayed inside the boundaries.

> **"Despite his irresponsible image, he was proud to represent his country and took the honour seriously. Far more seriously than some of his peers, who measured success purely in financial terms"**

And that is exactly what I said to him when I offered him the position. I told him there would be no second chance, that I had stuck my own neck out and that any tiniest straying from the path of righteousness would be enough.

It never happened. Oh yes, he lived up to his 'ocker' image here and there. We had many a laugh, and maybe even sometimes stepped outside what might be considered the perfect way to behave, but never to the detriment of the England team or the England cause.

Throughout his and my time together as a partnership, England enjoyed a great deal of success and was much respected throughout the speedway world. The England team was made up of a great bunch of responsible riders and I was proud to be associated with them. Irreverent, Malcolm might have been, but nobody stood straighter or prouder when the British National Anthem was being played.

September 1977, Wroclaw in Poland. England was expected to win the World Team Cup Final. Simmo had been troubled by a sore shoulder – the legacy of a grasstrack crash that worsened when he fell again at the British Final. I kept in touch with him by telephone. Come the time to travel, he assured me the shoulder he had injured was good to go. He and his mechanic, Ken Beckett, who was a tremendous character and influence himself, were a powerful component of the team and I was delighted and relieved they could make it.

Until the practice session on the day before the meeting.

Foreword

It became immediately clear then that Malcolm's shoulder was nowhere near as repaired as he would have had me believe. In short, the pain was too great for him to ride properly at full speed. Sheepishly, he admitted he had known the shoulder would be a risk but he had been desperate to be there.

Now riding for England was not quite done on an honorary basis, but the financial return, compared to the cost in time and money of preparation and the loss of potential earnings to be gained elsewhere, was not huge. It definitely wasn't the money that had caused Simmo to gamble on his fitness but the desire to wear the England colours.

I grumbled at him, as any team manager would, but quietly I was proud of his determination. We took a second gamble. We sought out the Polish doctor at the event and asked his advice. He checked the shoulder and said he would be happy to give Simmo a pain-killing injection before the meeting the next day.

I wasn't present when the injection was given but Malcolm was grey when he came back. The doctor had jiggled the hypodermic all around the offending area, spraying liberal amounts of novocaine into the muscles. The procedure had caused Simmo to all but faint but the consequence was even worse. Just like the lip of someone being prepared for a root canal filling, he had no feeling in his entire shoulder or upper arm area. We never did work out if the doctor was genuinely trying to help or was a saboteur!

Malcolm did try to ride but it was just not on. The reserve, John Davis, took his later rides and did well, as did the other three team members. England won at a canter, despite some machine problems. I had my easiest team managing afternoon ever whilst Simmo, desperate to ensure an England victory to make up for his bad gamble, begged, cursed and cajoled his team-mates into covering for his own error.

As I say, I could easily have correctly accused him of a lack of professionalism but I felt then, as I do now, proud of him for his desperation.

On the other side of the coin, through a long series of circumstances, Malcolm found himself with Gordon Kennett as his partner in the 1978 World Pairs Final, again in Poland. If ever there was a one-man show, this was it. Gordon, naive and way out of his depth at this level, was carried along by Simmo's sheer professionalism and brilliance. Malcolm scored 15 to Gordon's nine and beat Ivan Mauger in a run-off for the title. I was moved to give a rare speech in defence of my riders at the post-meeting banquet when the FIM Steward suggested the second placed country, New Zealand, represented by Mauger (12) and Larry Ross (12), had actually been the Best Pair, although I understood clearly the point being made. For me, notwithstanding his 1976 achievements, that pairs final, and the preceding semi-final in Hungary, were Simmo's finest hours.

I note that recently Malcolm and the veteran grasstrack organisation in Germany had a falling out. Relying on the press reports and reading between the lines, it seems that, even at 60, Simmo was taking his participation in the glorified exhibition events far too seriously. That is the nature of the man. That is what the general public does not see or would find it difficult to believe.

Even before the times of obsession with health and fitness, Malcolm was looking

On parade at Debrecen, Hungary, before the 1978 World Pairs semi-final with John Berry and Gordon Kennett. With those flares John's wearing, it's a good job it wasn't windy.

after his body with diet supplements and exercise. He was meticulous with his professionalism and preparation of equipment, both racing and personal.

At one stage after his retirement from riding, he threw his cap into the ring for the England manager's job. Perhaps he might have needed a boring, old fart like me to hold his coat for him and keep an eye on the admin, but I have no doubt he would have been brilliant at the speedway part of the job.

Malcolm is one of those once-in-a-lifetime people I simply seemed to understand. Somehow, we clicked, and I like to think we had a great time working together. I am proud that he asked me to write a few words for him. I'd love to catch up and shake his hand once again someday . . . although I'll make sure to count my fingers carefully afterwards!

Post Script:

I've now read the book draft. It will no doubt be billed as a shocking exposé of speedway during the time Malcolm was riding. Even with the careful guiding hand of Tony McDonald, Simmo goes further than any others have done in telling it like it was.

Having said that, it is not speedway that becomes totally exposed so much as Malcolm himself. I understand now what it must be like to be a psychiatrist, listening as a patient bares his soul. There were times I was uncomfortable reading the chapters. There were times I was even embarrassed for him. This is Simmo in the raw, an X-ray rather than a pen picture.

For all of his faults and foibles, you will not fail to appreciate how much he has allowed us a chance to look through the windows of his world.

1 BORN TO RIDE

I WAS born on March 20, 1946, at the Pembury Hospital, near Tunbridge Wells, Kent, the county where I have lived for most of my life. I was an only child – my parents didn't want any more after me!

My father, Tony, worked as a foreman, repairing lorries for British Road Services, a large company which had depots all over south-east England. He loved motorcycles and rode grasstrack for a long time before and after I was born. Considering he used the same bike in a race meeting that he had ridden to get to the track, and he was up against others who had help from outside sponsors, I believe he was fairly successful.

He was evidently a very good sidecar racer, too, and would like to have ridden full-time, but didn't have enough money to turn his hobby into a profession. My father excelled in the passenger role and it was a measure of his ability that Jack Surtees, the father of former world motor racing champion John, asked him to be his passenger when Jack rode sidecars on the European tour circuit. It would have been a big and exciting adventure for him but my mother wouldn't give my father her blessing to take up Jack's tempting offer.

But mother couldn't do anything to stop me riding a Vespa on the road while still under-age. She rode it to work each day but before she got up in the mornings, I'd be awake even earlier to do my paper round on it . . . and then quickly return it to the shed, ready for her use, before she had realised that I'd even been out on it.

My earliest childhood memories are of me riding on the back of my father's Velocette motorcycle and sidecar outfit. I had my own little seat behind his saddle and we were strapped together by a belt. I'd hang on to him for dear life while my mother, Margaret, rode along in the sidecar. One day we were on our way to his mum and dad, Mabel and Jack's house, at Tonbridge when we broke down near Hadlow. It meant my father had to go all the way back to where we lived, at Gillingham, by bus, to get the part he needed to repair the thing, while my mother and I stayed with the bike until he returned to fix it. I could only have been around four or five-years-old at the time but, for some reason, that experience has stuck in my memory.

Until my parents could afford their first house, we lived firstly with dad's parents for a couple of years and then spent roughly the same time living with my other grandparents, Bill and Nan (I don't know her first name).

I was fairly bright at school – Featherby Road infants and juniors in Gillingham – but I didn't like going there much and never pushed myself to achieve anything. I didn't mind the traditional sports of football, cricket and running. I was left footed and had football trials for Kent schoolboys but I gave up the game after being knocked over in one game and breaking my collarbone. I occasionally watched our

23

nearest professional team, Gillingham, as a kid but I decided football was too dangerous and didn't really want to play it again!

At school, it was the practical lessons that I enjoyed most. I was once given permission to skip lessons to build a catamaran for use by the pupils, and which we later sailed along the River Medway.

When I was about 11, we moved from Gillingham to Rainham, where I attended Orchard Street secondary modern. I failed my eleven-plus exam and, as I said, never really applied myself at school.

I was 14 when my parents parted. In those days, divorce was almost looked upon as a sin, and it was certainly very rare at that time. Unlike today, when they reckon one in three marriages ends in divorce, back in the late 50s and early 60s husbands and wives tended to stay together for better or worse.

It was a horrible situation for me to be in, though, and I'll never forget the day that mother left us after asking me to make what was a heartbreaking choice between either packing up and leaving with her, or staying with my father. She had initially left on the spur of the moment but returned to the house a few days later to tie up loose ends and to find out what I wanted to do.

> "It was a very difficult and emotional scene. I know that my father and I were both in tears and I don't think my mother was so hard that she didn't cry as well"

The three of us sat together in the living room discussing what to do and, as you can imagine, it was a very difficult and emotional scene. I know that my father and I were both in tears and I don't think my mother was so hard that she didn't cry a little as well.

But when she gave me her ultimatum, my answer was straight and immediate. I was riding motorbikes by then, in my first year of racing, and as much as I loved my mother, I felt naturally drawn towards my father, mainly I suppose because of our shared love of bikes. Whether my decision to stay with him was based purely on bikes and his influence in that respect, I don't know. Another contributory factor in choosing to stay with father is that she was the one who had left us.

Once I told her that I would be staying with my father, she didn't try and put any pressure on me to leave him and join her. I know that father did all he could, though, to get her to stay but she had made up her mind to go. It was a very sad time and I didn't see her again for a couple of years. I think she would have wanted to see me regularly but I didn't wish to talk to or see her. I felt rejected, I guess, and I didn't want to see my father hurt any more by arranging to see her behind his back. My loyalty then was to him.

It was an acrimonious split, although, looking back now, perhaps not a total surprise. When I was as young as seven or eight, I can remember her saying that she would stay at home until I was 14 and then she'd leave. And it wasn't something that she said just once either. She had clearly made up her mind long before they broke up and was true to her word. I think she considered that, by the age of 14, I'd be more or less able to look after myself.

I can't say she was a bad mother to me, because she wasn't. When I was a little kid,

I'd run home from school to a cooked dinner. It was always on the table waiting for me, as my father's meals were ready waiting for him.

She looked after me while he was out working from six-thirty in the morning until seven at night. He also worked at weekends, so I didn't see much of him. As far as I was concerned, she was a good mother and a good wife – I wasn't aware that things were not good between my parents until the day she left.

I never saw their divorce coming. I had a girlfriend at the time, I was enjoying the thrill of my first motor bike and became too wrapped up in myself to think about the state of their marriage. I certainly never thought about what she had said years earlier, about her planning to leave, but, unbeknown to me, their marriage problems had been obviously ongoing for a long time.

After she left the home, with father still working all hours possible, I was very fortunate that we had lovely next-door neighbours in Gwen and Fred Andrews, who always took me in after school and fed me. I'd sit down to eat dinner with their daughters, Wendy and Sue, almost every day, and the family treated me like one of their own. My father was out a lot of the time, combining his day job at BRS with part-time private work fixing cars, so I was very grateful to the Andrews for taking care of me at a time when I needed it.

I think my parents broke up because they simply didn't get on. Mother is not around to defend herself today but my view now of their divorce is that she wanted more out of life than my father could give her. He simply didn't have enough money to provide the better lifestyle she wanted. One example of her trying to keep up with the Jones's was when some friends of theirs, who were quite well off, invited mum and dad to their villa in the south of France. But mum wasn't content for them to drive down there in the car they had, so she made my dad go out and buy a newer and better model. It still wasn't good enough for her, though – the paint-work was a bit iffy, so she told my dad she wasn't prepared to travel in it unless he re-sprayed

The Roger brothers – Cyril, Bob and Bert – at New Cross in the late 40s.

Despite problems at home, grasstrack racing would always put the smile back on my face.

the bodywork. He did what she asked, which was quite an achievement since they were travelling the next day and the paint must still have been a bit tacky as they drove aboard the cross-Channel ferry.

It appears that my father did everything he could for her but it was never going to be enough. To tell the truth, and I'll come to this later, my father and I fell out later on and we've only got back in contact with each other fairly recently after 20 years. We've been talking to each other again and one of the things we spoke about was the name I called him by. He was definitely 'Dad' to me in my very young days but as the years went by we drifted apart. Not that far apart for me to call him 'Tony', but enough for 'Dad' to become a more formalised 'Father'. I don't think I knew what to call him for the best, it felt awkward, so I tended to skirt around it and just spoke to him without using a name. It was strange to even have to think about what to call him but that's how we'd become.

Part of our reconciliation has been to reflect on the painful time when he and mother split. He told me that she left him with debts of around £18,000, which is a hefty amount today but it was a hell of a lot to cope with in the early 60s. For a bloke who worked hard to earn his living as a foreman in a garage, that must have been a massive burden to him. I don't know how those debts escalated to that extreme level but it was probably just a case of my parents living beyond their means. They always had a nice car – for instance, I can recall father coming home with a Hillman Minx that was just 12 months old. In 1954, that was unheard of for most men of his means.

He explained to me recently that while he had been content to live in Gillingham, my mother wanted them to better themselves with a bigger place at Rainham, so they moved there. It was more than they could afford to do but they still did it.

Born to ride

Mother didn't go out to work until I went to senior school and she began a job at a local chemist, and I think it was around this time that she met the man she went to live with after splitting from my father. It seems that father always did all he could to try and please her, no matter what she asked of him. Even after she had left, if she phoned our house to ask him to fix her car, or even the car belonging to her new man, he would still willingly oblige. I couldn't believe he'd do that but those kind acts show just how much he cared for her.

I'm sure he would have taken her back at any time if only she had wanted to. However, after a few years he met a lovely lady called Irena who he has since married. Dad had another son, Barry, and put the past to rest. Today, I don't have even one photograph of me as a kid with either of my parents, which is a shame.

The sad thing is, things never worked out well for my mother. Her relationship with her new bloke lasted only three or four years. She wasn't promiscuous but she also had two or three other failed relationships with different people, including the well-known former New Cross, Poole and England speedway star Bert Roger.

My first links with speedway probably came from a visit, aged 12, to New Cross and being around Bert and his equally well-known brother, Cyril. They were friends of the family, especially Bert, who was particularly friendly with my mother! I didn't know that there was anything going on between them at the time and their relationship only came to light as far as I was concerned when father and I were talking earlier this year. I think he had an idea that she was seeing Bert but preferred to turn a blind eye because he thought so much of her.

As most unhappy children do when their parents split up, I absorbed myself in other things. Well, one thing – motor bikes were my world. Father had built me a BSA-Bantam trials bike that we kept at my friend, Brian Maclean's place, which backed onto woods about four miles from where we lived. As soon as I came home from school, I'd rush over there and ride to my heart's content. It was the perfect release, an escape from a lonely home, a new focus in life and I soon found that I was quite a good rider.

It was actually my best mate, Alan Johnson's father, who taught me how to ride a bike when I was about 11. Fred Johnson took us both over to the woods and showed us how to ride properly on the bike he bought for Alan.

I was hooked and wanted to race competitively as soon as possible. Two years too soon, as it happened! The minimum age limit to compete on grasstrack was 16 but I made my debut as a 14-year-old, riding a Greeves scrambler bike that my father had built for me in the Maidstone Aces meeting at Headcorn. In those days you didn't need a licence, you just rode, so I simply told the authorities organising the meeting at Stockbury, Kent, that I was 16-years-old. I was quite tall for my age and because I didn't fall off or look out of my depth racing against older riders, I passed for a youngish 16.

So, you see, I was taking a few liberties with authority and bending the rules right from the very start of my racing career. There would be a lot more bigger scrapes to come…

2

GRASS ROOTS

Norman Hunter making sure I know just who's No.1 at Hackney in 1963.

SIMMO

AFTER leaving school at 15 with no qualifications, my first job was as an apprentice electrician on the boats at the Royal Naval Dockyard in Chatham, earning £2, four shillings and nine pence a week. Quite a lot of teenagers from our school also went to work there. I never minded the job or the seven-mile cycle ride to the docks but I had my heart set on becoming a professional motorcycle racer.

I first came to people's attention in Kent after riding in trials meetings for a couple of years. The Sittingbourne club put on a novices' event which I won, then followed it just a week later by winning the experts' class, an achievement that was unheard of at the time.

Riding a motorbike has never been a problem to me, it's always come naturally. I was lucky to be born with this ability, although I probably would have been more successful in one particular sphere of motorcycle sport if only I'd concentrated on one form of racing. Whether it was trials, grasstrack or speedway, I just wanted to ride them all.

On the road, I dashed around on the scooter I inherited from my mother, so I effectively became a Mod – even though I really wanted to be a rocker! I had the traditional parka with fur trim and the tall mirrors on the handlebars. I was into Elvis Presley and would slap on the Brylcream – I didn't really like the Beatles or Rolling Stones, who were of course all the rage at the time.

I was a successful grasstrack rider long before I turned to speedway at the relatively late age of 17. My father built my first proper grasstrack machine – a 250cc JAP. He used to look after the bikes of Fred Jarvis, who sponsored the biggest stars of that era in Don Godden and Reg Luckhurst and, later on, Fred also supported me. His two sons then took over the bikes and the shame of it for Fred is that his youngest, Glen, was paralysed after being hit by another rider and breaking his neck.

I then rode bikes provided by another grasstrack legend, Alf Hagon, who was approaching retirement after a very successful career. After Alf broke his ankle in a crash at Sittingbourne in 1963, he sponsored me on his machines and they certainly helped me to dominate more and more meetings. Kent, and the South-Eastern Centre, was a hotbed of grasstrack racing talent and the competition strong. At the end of the year, when Alf was fit again and wanted to resume racing, we bought the bikes off him and he built three new ones for himself.

Like many southern-based grasstrack riders of that era, I took my first speedway rides at the Rye House training track at Hoddesdon, in the winter of 1962-63, on a JAP borrowed from grass veteran Sid Jarvis.

By that stage I was winning almost everything on the grass, so speedway was a natural progression – not that it provided instant financial rewards. On the grass, where I had three bikes, a 250, 350 and 500cc, I had been used to earning as much as £60 at every successful Sunday grasstrack event. As well as individual meetings, they also put on match races between Luckhurst, Godden and myself who, after Hagon retired, were recognised as the sport's big three. Although I have to admit, I left most of the cost of maintaining the three bikes to my father and kept the majority of my winnings for myself.

The bike looks good, but those turned-up jeans . . .

One of my earliest major successes was in the first-ever televised grass meeting at Lower Halstow, near Iwade in 1963. Reggie Luckhurst was better than me at the time and was obviously going to win the final but the promoter gave him 25 quid to put on a show for the crowd and the Southern Television cameras. He asked Reg to take the lead and then deliberately knock off his plug lead, before re-passing the other riders to win the race.

He tried to do just that but fumbled a bit trying to get his plug lead back on and, in the meantime, I'd pissed off and won the race! Reg got his 25 quid but he didn't get the glory. He never lets me forget that and still talks about it today.

I did OK on my first speedway rides at Rye House until the frame on Sid's bike broke but I still must have done enough to catch the eye of Ernie Hancock, the manager at Rye House, who recommended me to Hackney promoter Mike Parker. He had brought speedway back to east London for the first time since 1939 and was building a new, young team to compete in the Provincial League (PL), or second division as it was.

My big problem, though, was that I was a grasstrack rider trying to ride speedway. On the grass, you don't skid into the corners, you're two-wheeling around, so the shale sport didn't come easily to me at first.

I signed for Hackney Hawks and my first-ever race was in the second half of their match at New Cross, early in the 1963 season. My bike was an ancient long-five JAP engine from the late 40s in a Huck Finn frame that I had bought from Reggie Luckhurst for about 50 quid. I don't recall the other three riders in my debut race but I do remember that I managed to win it. It was my one and only ride at New Cross, the south London track that sadly closed for good in August of that year due to poor attendances.

I didn't find it easy to break into the Hackney team, though. Their line-up at the start of the season was made up of the veteran Wal Morton, who was in his early

50s, captain Norman Hunter, Titch Read, Peter Sampson, Tommy Sweetman and Johnnie Poyser. I'm told the record books show that on the opening night of April 10 at Waterden Road, where racing had resumed after a 25-year break, I finished third behind Geoff Penniket and young Trevor Hedge in the second half Reserves' Scurry heat, before Eddie Reeves beat me in the final.

The history books also show that I made my Hawks debut as a replacement for the injured Read, in a heavy Southern League defeat at Exeter. I didn't score from three rides, while Len Silver scored a maximum for the Falcons. My first-ever official point was in the next home match, against Poole, after my race partner Hedgie fell.

Parker changed the team around, bringing in Colin McKee, Jimmy Heard and Ronnie Rolfe. I struck up a good friendship with Colin, a young lad from New Zealand, and we'd travel together to a lot of away meetings, even if I wasn't in the side. Jimmy was a really nice person and, having met him again recently at the Hackney reunion in 2005, I'm pleased to say he hasn't changed a bit.

Trevor Hedge is another who hasn't changed in all the years I've known him and we're still good mates today. Hedgie got on well with my father, who acted as both my mechanic and chauffeur, and I can remember Trevor being particularly helpful if I had a problem with my bike.

By the summer of '63 I had started to get going and the highlight of my first season came in August, when Hunter and I won a best pairs meeting at Hackney. I must have earned a bit of recognition by then because I can see from looking at press cuttings that they had suddenly dropped the 'd' they had inserted before the final 's' of my surname!

Mike Parker, a good promoter with a long memory, welcoming me to Hackney, 1963.

Grass roots

Norm was outstanding, our only superstar, and he liked to let us know that he was the No.1. He had the sort of attitude, 'I'm Norman Hunter – I'm the number one here', and that was how it was. That was fine by me. I was only a kid and didn't know any different, but I certainly knew he was our top man! I suppose I adopted the same air of superiority when I later became a No.1 myself. Norman didn't offer you choice of gate positions and, when I became a No.1, neither did I offer it to my partner. Second strings or reserves got what they were given but picking the best gate was the perk of being the top man in the team.

I found it harder when I moved up from the reserve berth into the team, although I have always liked being out in the first race. I was partnered with Norman and I've got to say that if I got out in front, he was good at covering me from the opposition pairing. Norman wanted to win but he wouldn't go by me until the last corner and we had the 5-1 heat advantage in the bag.

At first, I couldn't understand why he had to go past me and selfishly take the three points himself but his approach to team-riding obviously rubbed off on me a lot, because I did the same when I became a star rider. I'd team-ride my partner round at King's Lynn or Poole but I still wanted to be first across the finish line by half a wheel. Norman always rode the inside line, so it's probably from my time partnered with him at Hackney that I learned to ride the outside line.

There was no such thing as a 'signing-on' fee for me in those days. I started my speedway career earning just £1 per start and £1 per point, which wasn't exactly comparable to the 60 quid I could earn grasstracking on a good Sunday.

> **"Mike never did stop the money I owed him out of my pay packet but, years later, when I'd become an established star at Poole, and he was in his latter promoting days at Wolverhampton, I discovered that my pay cheque from Monmore Green was £50 short"**

As a promoter, Mike Parker had the reputation of being tough and uncompromising and he wasn't always popular among his peers, but I found him fine to deal with. I blew my engine in my first meeting and a set of crank cases then were around 50 quid. Mike offered to lend me the money to get my motor repaired, so I accepted. It was understood that he'd recover the money when I started to earn some money.

Mike never did stop the money I owed him out of my pay packet but, years later, when I'd become an established star at Poole, and he was in his latter promoting days at Wolverhampton, I discovered that my pay cheque from Monmore Green was £50 short. Mike had recovered his money some 20 years after lending it to me! He also put a note in with the cheque, saying: '£50 deducted for crank cases loaned at Hackney, 1963'. Which I thought was brilliant!

Parker helped to push me along in those early days. After a race, even though he wasn't our team manager, I can remember him telling me what I was doing wrong. I could recognise my own faults, mainly the difficulty I had in sliding the bike into the corners, which was alien to me having come from a grasstrack background. I have always maintained that it is far easier to go straight into speedway and learn the basics, rather than switching from grass to shale.

Looking for the grasstrack opposition.   Thankfully the helmets soon flattened those ears.

A good speedway rider will also be a good grasstrack rider but it's much harder to do it the other way round, although perhaps not as much today. Many of the grasstracks now are just big speedway tracks and they ride very similarly. But in my early grasstrack days, the tracks were mostly long straights and tight corners, and we had to use our brakes to get round the turns. A lot of the tracks had right-hand bends, too.

> "It was all about putting on a show for the public and, as I was fairly good, I'd actually stop by the pits gate after about 12 or 13 laps to refuel . . . before going on to win! Most riders would put a bigger fuel tank on their bike but I liked to show off!"

At two of the tracks, Lydden and Barham, the finals were contested over 20 laps. It was all about putting on a show for the public and, as I was fairly good, I'd actually stop by the pits gate after about 12 or 13 laps to refuel . . . before going on to win! Most riders would put a bigger fuel tank on their bike but I liked to show off!

Hackney was a really good race track but we didn't gel all that well as a team. For example, Tich Read was a loner who only really conversed with his fellow East Anglian Trevor Hedge, who had been signed on loan from Norwich. After Wal Morton left, we had a very young and inexperienced side but it was really no surprise that we finished fourth from bottom of the Provincial League (PL).

I wanted to stay at Hackney and continue to learn at second division level but I didn't really have a choice. Speedway as a whole was in turmoil, with outspoken PL chairman Parker the prime rebel in the breakaway from the more senior National League. As the 14 PL tracks were operating outside the Speedway Control Board's jurisdiction, it meant that any riders who continued to ride in the second

Grass roots

With Reggie Luckhurst, a grasstrack mentor, 1963.   Personality of the Year award winner, 1965.

division were effectively suspended and banned from holding an Auto Cycle Union (ACU) licence.

To someone like me, who was earning so well and enjoying great success on an ACU grasstrack licence, I really had no option but to move up into the top flight of speedway – even though I knew I wasn't ready for it then.

Parker couldn't possibly match what I was earning from grasstrack and, to be fair to him, I wasn't good enough at that stage to expect a better deal from Hackney anyway. I was a novice and lucky to be in the team.

But I didn't take leaving Hackney lightly and left it as long as I could, hoping the two warring leagues would sort out their differences, before finally accepting that I would have to leave them and join one of the seven National League clubs the following season. In fact, I had a bit of trouble with the ACU and had to re-apply for my racing licence after I appeared in a meeting at Rayleigh, one of the 14 blacklisted PL tracks, early on in the 1964 season.

As it turned out, the huge rift between PL and NL track bosses dragged on all year and it was a shame I had to leave Hackney. I didn't have far to go to continue my speedway education, though, as Norman Hunter and myself joined the Hawks' east London neighbours West Ham, who had reopened in '64 after an absence of eight years. I wasn't ready for the step up in racing standard, however, and I virtually found myself back to square one, fighting for a team place again.

3

TREBLE CHAMPIONS

I SPENT four years with West Ham and the best season by far was 1965, when we became the first team to win the unique treble of British League championship, Knockout Cup and London Cup. It must have been some achievement, because I've never been part of a league championship-winning team again, either before or since those happy days down Custom House way.

After all the problems between the two leagues that overshadowed the previous season, my first in the famous Hammers racejacket, it all came right for us in the year of amalgamation when the Provincial and National League merged to form the new British League (BL). From the riders' point of view, it was the best thing to ever happen – it meant we had so many more meetings, from Exeter to Edinburgh.

Our three heat leaders in the Hammers' treble-winning side were Ken McKinlay, Sverre Harrfeldt and Norman Hunter, who were all superb, while I received a lot of credit for my efforts as a leading second string. My partnership with my former Hackney team-mate Hunter was rated one of the strongest in the league.

It was a far cry from my first season at the Docklands track, when I struggled for half a season to get into the side and rode only 14 NL matches before ending my first year in the top flight with a broken ankle and the team stuck at the bottom of the table.

I didn't break my ankle riding speedway. The accident happened while I was riding a road bike to Sheerness, where I'd go along with some of the grasstrack boys to a nightclub on a Saturday. I was riding through the back roads – somewhere between Upchurch and Lower Halstow – on my way there one night, when a car suddenly turned right in front of me. As all good speedway riders do, I laid my bike down immediately to try and minimise the impact but I slid off and my left ankle was crushed between the bike and the back wheel of the car.

Tommy Price, the former World Champion and our team manager at West Ham, was very upset and laid into me for getting injured in such a silly way.

It was my old grasstrack rival, Alf Hagon, who recommended me to Tommy. He was very loud and pushy with me, although we got on well. Maybe he saw something in me and felt that I needed a kick up the backside if I was to reach the next level, I don't know. I'd been a bit down when I first went there – I wasn't ready to race against World Champion Barry Briggs and all the other big names, although the size of the big 418-yard circuit was more suited to my grasstrack riding style compared to the Hackney track. Perhaps another year at Waterden Road would have been better for me in terms of adopting a more suitable speedway style.

Tommy tried to persuade me to give up the grass but it always came down to money – I was hardly on much more at West Ham than the pittance I'd earned at Hackney in my first year – and I couldn't afford to concentrate solely on speedway

SIMMO

Team boss Tommy Price wasn't happy when I broke my ankle on a road bike. Looking at those ears again, it still doesn't appear that the helmet has done its job.

Treble champions

at that stage of my career. It was Reg Luckhurst who eventually convinced me to quit the grass, but that wasn't until 1969.

In my first season of National League racing I would just watch the top riders like Briggo and try to learn how I could go faster. The star riders didn't speak to me – I was a nobody – so I just had to watch and learn from them as best I could. I was determined to persevere at speedway, though.

My grasstrack equipment was always immaculate, while my speedway stuff was as good as I could get it given the little money I was earning, so I was surprised to find that Briggo's gear was the biggest load of crap I'd ever seen! There were wires and tape everywhere, holding bits and pieces together on his bike. It looked awful and made me wonder just how could he be that good.

If he'd had better machinery, something as good as Ivan Mauger had, or as good as the bike Ove Fundin rode, then I believe Briggo would have won more world titles than any of them. He won the individual World Championship four times even though his equipment was absolute rubbish. Fundin's spare was nothing special but his No.1 bike was very quick.

The atmosphere when West Ham first reopened was electric and it was brilliant to be rubbing shoulders with the top names. We were attracting crowds of between 12,000 and 15,000 in the opening weeks of 1964, due in no small way to Dave Lanning's hard work on the PR side. Dave was a larger than life character who had good contacts in the media and showbiz world and he could always be relied upon to conjure up a story or six about the riders – even though half the tales that appeared about us in *Speedway Star* and the programme were exaggerated for effect. Not that I was complaining. We got a lot of good publicity and with that came adulation, which I enjoyed. There were plenty of pretty, young women throwing themselves at the riders, although in my second season with the Hammers I had a steady girlfriend in Judy Wooster, who I'd known since school. Don Smith, who joined us in 1966, was the one who had the biggest groupie following.

The No.1 in the Hammers team in my first year there was Bjorn Knutson, very much a loner who I never really got to know. He won most of his races in style but he kept himself to himself. Ray Cresp was a good engine tuner and his stuff was ever so fast, which made him better than Alf, who had the same struggle I did in trying to adapt to

Loner Bjorn Knutson and the strong-willed Tommy Price, with Dave Lanning.

SIMMO

speedway. He was an out-and-out grasstracker who would come down the straight and hit every brake he could to get round the corners! But his equipment allowed him to do that well.

Reg Luckhurst was signed with Knutson from Southampton after they had closed at the end of 1963. The difference between Reg and Alf was that Reggie was a speedway rider competing on grass. He combined the two track sports well, although he built all his own equipment and was forever experimenting with it. In some ways, Reg was another Briggo and his equipment seemed to let him down a lot.

Reg Trott had a funny routine. Whether he won his races or finished last, he always did a lap of honour while waving to the crowd! He could finish half a lap behind the other three, but he'd always perform his post-race ritual. He was ever so quiet, but a fine person to have in the team and he came up with some valuable points in our title-winning season.

Ken McKinlay took over from Knutson as our No.1 and captain in 1965 and he was brilliant. I was paired with Ken, who was one of the first established names to actually let me choose gate positions. I couldn't believe it when he first offered me the choice – it was unheard of in those days for the senior rider in a pairing to defer to a team-mate of lesser ability.

I should know. When I was at Poole and rode with the Polish rider Andrzej Tkocz, I never gave him first pick of gates. I always liked the inside at Wimborne Road, where it was tight around the first turn and a big advantage to be next to the white line. One day Andrzej came up to me and asked: "Must I always have gate three?"

Ken McKinlay out-traps another fast starter, Colin Pratt, in this clash with London rivals Hackney.

Treble champions

I replied: "No, you can have four when I have two!"

That's how it was, although later in my career, at Poole and at Wimbledon, if I thought I could get out of the outside gate and we needed the points badly, I would take the less advantageous starting position. But what always got me was when I'd give my partner the better start position and then he'd waste it – I never saw the point in that.

'Hurri-Ken' and former England football captain Billy Wright brew up, although the canny Scot preferred his drink a little stronger.

A good engineer whose bikes were always immaculate, Ken did like a scotch and would be in the main bar at Custom House after every meeting until they chucked him out. Then he'd usually round the night off with a Chinese meal somewhere local. However, his drinking never affected his riding – I'm told he didn't drop a point at West Ham until June 1 in our championship year – although he could probably have been even better if he hadn't liked a drink as much as he did. But Ken was a very good rider and ever so fair – I don't remember him ever moving anyone off their racing line. He just rode his own race and I can't ever remember him falling off.

'Hurri-Ken' was also an expert trapper. I'd spent two years just learning to race, because I couldn't make a start to save my life. The ones I did make were down to pure luck. But Ken helped me a lot in setting up my bike and getting the clutch right. He didn't teach me to become a better gater – I still maintain to this day that you can never teach anyone how to make starts. You can show them *how* to do it but whether they can put what you are trying to teach them into practice, is another thing altogether. I spent Christ knows how many hours with Hackney's Barry Thomas, a renowned poor gater who scored the vast majority of his points from the back. He did everything right – Thommo could drop the clutch as quick as anyone – but it just didn't work when it came to a race situation. And despite all my efforts, it never did. Barry never worked out the best way to use the throttle and find the grip that would take him forward quicker than the others.

"Tactically, there was none better than the canny Scot. Because he always rode the inside line, he could slow a race down brilliantly to help his partner. Me and Reg Trott benefited more than anyone from our captain's track craft"

Ken showed me what to do but, most importantly, he taught me *why* I had to do certain things to make better starts. Before receiving his help, I had always changed my position on the seat depending on whether the track was wet and slippery, or grippy. If it was wet, I used to sit right up the back of the saddle, to try and get more grip on the start-line. But he told me not to alter my position on the bike under any circumstances, but to always do the same thing every time I went to the start.

He explained to me that I had to vary the amount of throttle I used at the gate, and that there were times when I should physically back it off going to the first corner, rather than hold the throttle flat out. If the wheels are spinning, you should shut the throttle off, but that's such a hard thing to do from a psychological point of view. When there are three others racing you to the first turn, it's not natural to want to shut off, is it?

"I went over to Briggo and called him a 'dirty bastard' among other things, but I don't think my words really registered with him. After all, I was just a snotty 18-year-old mouthing off after a very hard race, one that a rider of Barry's stature would have experienced a thousand times and more"

Luck also came into it and I was fortunate in that I could get a bike to grip at the start – the combination of the right hand controlling the throttle and sensing the 'feel' of the engine is important. A lot of it is feel – that, and setting up the clutch to suit the engine. I've always said that I wasn't one of the best gaters in the world – yes, I'd often fly out ahead of people – but I'd say that 50 per cent of the time I wasn't in front of the others at the start, but I was by the time we reached the corner. That was all about getting the bike to work between the start line and the corner, more than it was in purely dropping the clutch and making the start.

I don't think height and weight come into it much. Briggo was fairly big and heavy for a rider, while Fundin was very light, yet they both made consistently good starts. The best thing that happened to me was when they changed the rules to stop riders rolling at the start. I just couldn't cheat at the gate and neither could Ken McKinlay.

Tactically, there was none better than the canny Scot. Because he always rode the inside line, he could slow a race down brilliantly to help his partner. Me and Reg Trott benefited more than anyone from our captain's track craft.

Mind you, I wasn't in Ken's league when it came to drinking. I'd always go up to the bar after meetings at West Ham for a drink with the boys but while they became 'merry', I became ill! After a few attempts at drinking beer and spirits – I tried the lot – I decided it was making me too ill to enjoy it. Whether I drank either beer or spirits, I quickly felt sick – I never experienced the 'merry' stage in between, the bit

Treble champions

that most people enjoy most, so I thought there was no sense in me drinking alcohol at all. I just stuck to lemonade and, nowadays, I'll only have an orange juice and lemonade if I'm out socialising, or maybe a shandy, but mainly I just enjoy a glass of wine with my dinner.

I didn't get my chance in the West Ham team until after Bobby Dugard was forced – against his wishes – to move to Wimbledon by the dreaded rider control committee and I don't think Bob has ever really forgiven me for taking his place.

Oxford's Eddie Reeves and Bob Dugard light up. I replaced Bobby in the West Ham team and I don't think he's ever quite forgiven me.

We used to race against each other in the second half, while Bob was still in the team at reserve, but I beat him two or three weeks running and I'm pretty sure he has never forgiven me for it. He never said anything about our rivalry for a team spot and I could understand his disappointment when he was dropped from the side. But to this day, I still think he bears a little grudge against me for taking his place in the West Ham team 42 years ago! Maybe I'm wrong, but that's how I read it.

As I said, moving up into the top flight was like starting all over again – and I had to learn the hard way. The standard was much higher in the NL than it had been in the Provincial League with Hackney and, naturally, the opposition was tougher in every respect too.

An incident that confirmed that I was now mixing it with the big boys came the night Poole's New Zealand international Bill Andrew put me over the fence at West Ham, as I tried to pass him on the outside at the end of the home straight. There was no need for what he did to me.

I also had a big ding-dong battle in my first year at West Ham with Briggo. I was only a young kid and towards the end of the year I'd got going a lot better. I came round the outside of him down the straight but as he moved out towards the fence to block my move, I shut off the throttle. I guess I still had the incident with Bill Andrew in my mind.

I never crashed but I thought he'd left me no alternative but to shut off, or else I would have more than likely ended up back on the dog track, where Andrew had put me weeks earlier. Evidently, on that occasion, I'd only just missed hitting the starting gate that had ultimately claimed the life of Swindon's Teo Teodorowicz in the same season.

When we came back into the pits after the race, I went over to Briggo and called him a 'dirty bastard' among other things, but I don't think my words really registered with him. After all, I was just a snotty 18-year-old mouthing off after a very hard race, one that a rider of Barry's stature would have experienced a thousand times and more. Briggo didn't get flustered, he just said to me: "If you'd have had the balls, there was room. There wasn't much room but I would never stuff you in." And he just turned and walked away, leaving me speechless. It was a lesson learned from a superstar. He was saying, 'I won't stuff you through the fence, but I'll run you close enough to make you think I will!'.

I'd already been over the fence once that season – Andrew was renowned as a ruthless rider – so I didn't want to take another chance when I came up on the outside of Briggo, but I'm pretty sure he wouldn't have done what Andrew did to me. The crash caused by Andrew really shook me up – until then, I didn't think that sort of thing happened.

Fundin was another rider who wouldn't give you an inch – ever – although not that I was ever good enough to get close enough to him anyway. In my Provincial League days Ivor Brown was another who stood out as a very tough customer. Fundin caused Brown to crash very badly in the Internationale at Wimbledon that almost finished the Cradley Heath star's career.

Apart from another good lesson learned, that dust up with Briggo also showed that I was going well enough to even be in a position to make a move on someone as great as him, so that was another turning point for me.

Cup heroics

When people refer to my days with West Ham, they inevitably recall that epic KO Cup, third round replay we won 49-47 at Plough Lane in August 1965. It certainly brought me a lot of satisfaction at the time and was probably the night I truly 'arrived' as a speedway rider.

We went into the London derby cup clash without Hunter, who had married his bride, Jan, earlier that day, and Harrfeldt, who damaged his eye at Hackney the previous night and had to watch from the pits, while the Dons were minus my old Hackney team-mate Trevor Hedge. McKinlay and Dave Lanning, who had attended the wedding reception at Wembley, tried without success to persuade Hunter to ride on his wedding night. What chance did we have against the team who seemed destined for the league title?

Such was the pessimism among our supporters that a number of Hammers fans left the stadium even before the first heat after hearing that Harrfeldt wouldn't be riding. Tony Clarke, who was as raw as they came, was promoted into the team in Harrfeldt's No.3 racejacket. Geoff Hughes was hanging around in the pits and found himself roped in to make up the numbers.

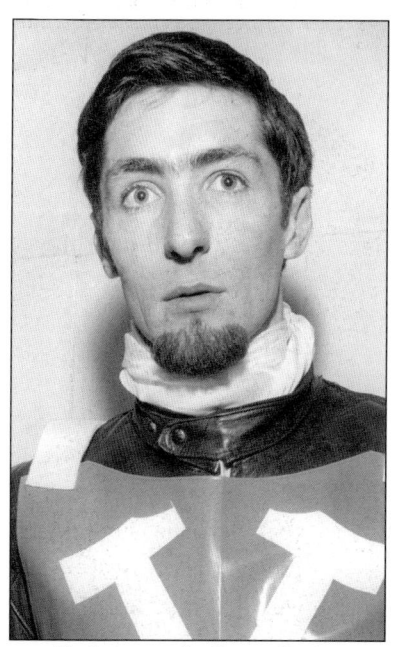

The honeymooning Norman Hunter.

Treble champions

No-one gave us a chance.

But the depleted West Ham team rose to the occasion. My press cuttings confirm that I dropped my only point in five rides to Reg Luckhurst, who had left West Ham for Wimbledon that year, in heat five. But I managed to bounce back to beat Reg and Olle Nygren twice apiece, including victory from the back over Luckhurst in the decisive, final heat 16, in which McKinlay completed our match-winning 4-2.

I got most of the plaudits for my 14 points but it really was a superb team effort, with Reg Trott and Brian Leonard also rising to the occasion with match-winning scores.

To cap a great night, I went on to beat Wimbledon No.1 Nygren in the Silver Sash match-race. Before the race, Reggie Luckhurst – who was riding for Wimbledon – came up to me and said that the way I was riding, I was quite capable of beating Olle. But he warned me: "If he traps on you, don't try and pass him".

Nygren had a reputation as a dirty bastard and he'd run you through the fence as soon as look at you. Briggo was ruthless but, in my opinion, Nygren was plain dirty. There's an important difference. You would be happy to ride side-by-side with someone as scrupulously fair as, say. Martin Ashby every time, but there were others you just couldn't afford to take that chance with. You soon got to know who you shouldn't attempt to ride around and Nygren, the hard-riding Swede, was certainly one.

Before I left the pits, Reggie added: "If Nygren out-gates you, just sit on his tail and when he gets tired on the last lap, as he tends to do, go wide and be ready to nip under him coming out of the corner". I did exactly that, passing Olle on the last turn to win the Silver Sash – thanks largely to his team-mate Reggie's advice! He'd known me very well since I was a kid starting out on the grass, and also knew my dad well, too, so we went back a long way.

I don't know why we beat Wimbledon that night but everything just clicked for me

Wimbledon's Reg Luckhurst and Olle Nygren. It was Reg who told me how to beat the wily, old Swede.

and the team. A lot of speedway is down to what happens in your first ride – it can make or break your whole night – and on that particular occasion I hardly put a foot wrong. Plough Lane was anyway a favourite track of mine.

That momentous victory at Wimbledon proved to be the turning point of our season – we went on to win all 15 of our remaining official matches, including victory again Exeter in the KO Cup final and beat the Dons again to lift the London Cup.

We lifted the KO Cup trophy with a six points win at Exeter, although we were relieved to leave the place in one piece after the Falcons' wild man, Chris Blewitt, caused both McKinlay and Harrfeldt to crash and ended up in hospital himself with a broken collarbone. Blewitt was a nutter, both on and off the track, and he proved it again by the way he knocked off our top two riders in the second leg of the cup final. Blewitt just had no respect for other riders, especially round Exeter, where the steel fence and steeply banked, narrow and dimly lit track frightened a lot of visiting riders. You had to ride right up near the fence to do well. It must have taken me about six hours to reach Exeter along the poxy A30 in those days, so there was more than enough time for the fear to build up inside me.

The stories about Exeter were legendary and enough to put you off wanting to ride there. I must admit, the place intimidated me too. I didn't meet many riders who did look forward to going there, right through my career. Even when I rode for King's Lynn, Terry Betts would say, 'Oh no, it's Exeter next week'. But to be fair, Exeter's safety record is probably as good as any other track's – there have been more riders killed at West Ham and King's Lynn than lost their life at the County Ground before it was closed and knocked down at the end of the 2005 season.

I didn't enjoy riding at Exeter until I joined Poole 10 years later, when we had so many local derbies with the Falcons that I had to get my head around the hang-up I had about the County Ground. After that, it was never a problem to me again.

Exeter's other hard man was Chris Julian but while he also had a screw loose when he rode around the big, fast County Ground track, you could not wish to meet a nicer person before or after the meeting. Talk about Jekyll and Hyde, he was unbelievable.

I know that McKinlay didn't like going to Exeter either and would ride well within himself

Sverre Harrfeldt and Ken McKinlay were targeted by Chris Blewitt.

Treble champions

The treble winning Hammers show off our silverware collection from 1965. Left to right: Reg Trott, Ken McKinlay, Norman Hunter, Dave Lanning, Brian Leonard, myself, Sverre Harrfeldt and Ted Ede.

at the Devon track, and come away in one piece. The place didn't concern Sverre Harrfeldt, though, he rode the same way wherever. Sverre would just stick his back wheel on the fence and didn't give a shit.

I got on ever so well with Sverre and last saw him about three or four years ago, when I rode in a veterans' longtrack event in Norway. He's now a multi-millionaire from selling luxury yachts.

Watching Sverre ride would always give me and the rest of the boys a buzz, because he never stopped until the flag came out. He did all his own tuning and had very quick engines. He was second to Briggo in the 1966 World Final, and there was no doubting his ability, but the way he rode, there was always a chance that he would get hurt. Sverre was never the same rider after breaking his thigh in the 1968 European Final in Poland.

"You had to be mad to even attempt to ride around Sverre but I got away with it that night"

He was a risk-taker who loved the outside line. I don't know what possessed me, but one night in the second half at West Ham I went round the outside and was level with him going round the first corner. I don't know how it happened but my bike lifted and the front wheel went over his back mudguard, then down on the other side of his bike, enabling me to somehow pass him on the inside. It wasn't a calculated move, it was just pure luck, but that was the first time I beat him. You had to be mad to even attempt to ride around Sverre but I got away with it that night.

My average at the end of 1965 had more than doubled from the previous season, to almost seven points a match, but none of the riders received a championship winners' medal for becoming the first-ever BL winners, and treble champions at that. A shame, because I never rode for a league-winning team again.

SIMMO

Dave Wills – a tragic waste

The only black mark on an otherwise brilliant '65 season was the tragic loss of our young Aussie, Dave Wills, who died at Queen Mary's Hospital, Stratford in June, the morning after crashing during a second half novice match between West Ham and Hackney.

Dave was a protégé of former Hammers' hero, Jack Young, who also hailed from Adelaide, and was a nice bloke. We weren't big buddies but we'd become friends. He was 26, by himself and probably finding it hard, just as I did. I could appreciate what he was going through to try and make the breakthrough and it was such a shame that he died in the way he did. It shouldn't have happened.

Dave had led when he fell and was struck by young Hawks' rider Barry Lee. He had so much time to miss the fallen rider – I watched the race and can remember that when Dave fell, Barry was at least one, if not even two riders, behind him. He was so far back that he didn't even need to lay his bike down – he could have avoided Dave by just riding round or to the inside of him.

But Barry came down the straight and rode straight at Dave – he didn't take any evasive action and just hit him. You never know how different people will respond until they are in those situations but it was completely avoidable and a terrible waste.

Speaking to Barry about it years ago, he said that he just completely froze when he saw Dave lying there on the pits bend and didn't know why he piled into him. He was grief-stricken and unable to explain his part in the tragedy.

Barry stopped riding speedway after Dave's death but I'm happy to say that he got over the incident and went on to have a very good career as a stock car champion and car driver, still competing on four wheels today.

Dave Wills was ever so quiet, you wouldn't know he was there most of the time. We will, of course, never know if he would have progressed to stardom but it was a terrible way to go.

What happened to Dave and Teo Teodorowicz at West Ham, and other riders who have lost their lives in the sport, never made me question my own involvement. Their deaths came in the first few years of my racing career and while I would never say I just forgot about what happened to them, I certainly put it to the back of my mind. You have to be like that as a rider.

I'd always said from Day One that if ever I thought speedway was too dangerous, I'd pack up. But that aspect never came into it and if it wasn't for my age, I would still be riding speedway now.

Dave Wills – a terrible way to go.

4 TO RUSSIA WITH BLOOD

AFTER the excitement and tremendous success of 1965, I felt that I stagnated over the next two seasons at West Ham. The main problem was that I began to experiment with different engines – the Czech ESO had emerged as a new rival to the established English JAP – and my form and points return suffered accordingly.

Sverre Harrfeldt took over from Ken McKinlay as the Hammers' No.1 but Norman Hunter continued to retain the third heat leader berth and I didn't progress higher than fourth in the team averages in either 1966 or '67, when Brian Leonard was pushing me all the way.

I bought my first ESO from newcomer Don Smith, who was the first at West Ham to have the new engine. Although Barry Briggs, who had been the first British-based rider to try one in 1965, was the Czech factory's main UK distributor, Don was the London-based agent for the modern motor that was fast catching everyone's attention. I think it cost me around three or four hundred pounds to buy that ESO from Don, thanks to money I borrowed from the West Ham management

In my eagerness to test the engine before using it for the first time in a meeting, I arranged to use it in a private practice at Custom House. Not that the behind closed doors session was much of a secret – due to the schedule for preparing the track for the meeting that Tuesday night, I had to blast around at seven o'clock in the morning! I think the revving ESO could be heard way beyond Prince Regent Lane and the Albert Dock. There were so many complaints about the noise from local residents that the coppers were called and came round to the stadium to bring a halt to my riding. It was my first encounter with the law but certainly not the last.

The ESO was brilliant, so much faster than the JAP, but it took a while to get used to. It steered easier and revved differently, although I couldn't make starts on it and had to score most of my points from the back. I still lacked experience to get the best from it but to prove that the new bike was much better than the JAP I'd ridden previously, Ken McKinlay would jump on it if he had a problem with his own machine and would win races easily. I think Norman Hunter wanted one, too, but decided not to switch from his JAP because Ken tuned his engines and very much favoured the trusty, old English engine that had monopolised racing in the 50s and early 60s. They both lived at Leicester and would travel down to London together, so Norman probably didn't want to do anything to unsettle their mutually successful arrangement. Harrfeldt didn't need an ESO – his JAPs were always very fast.

Don Smith was the ultimate speedway playboy, chatting up all the girls in the bar after meetings. I last met 'D.R.' – and don't ask me why we all called him that but we did – five years ago in Scotland and he still hadn't changed. From what Don used to tell people, and going by what was written about him, you would have

SIMMO

'D.R.'......"Hey Malc....if we were in front - we would'nt get covered in all this crap!".......

SIMMO......."And if YOU got out of the bleedin' way.... I might be able to!"........

WITH COMPLIMENTS - DON SMITH

Above: a laminated picture and message that Don Smith kindly sent me a few years ago. D.R. never lost his good sense of humour.

Left: When Don and I met up for the last time before he died, at the Scottish Six-Day Trials held at Fort William in year 2000.
Don will be sorely missed, but can the groupie angels finally clip his wings?

thought he'd been a world-beater at West Ham. But the reality was, he rode in only about 20 matches for the Hammers over a season-and-a-bit and didn't average more than three points!

He was a brilliant trials rider, however, and a very clever innovator when it came to engineering. He was one of the first to have a bike rack fitted to the back of his car and he also invented the folding footrest in the early 70s. I was very saddened to hear that he died of cancer in 2005.

Don came in briefly as a replacement for Ted Ede, who was a fine man. Like that other steady plodder, Stan Stevens, Ted really loved his speedway and still does today.

Another new arrival was Brian Leonard, a nice, quiet lad who was very popular with the girls, but he only ever seemed to ride speedway for the fun of it. I think his dad ran a big business, so Brian had enough money not to have to worry about scoring too many points. He'd make the rest of us envious by turning up for meetings in a gleaming Jag – he always had a fancy car and liked to look the part.

The only major change to the team in 1966 from the treble-winning side of the previous year was that Tony Clarke moved on to Oxford. He was wild on the track and did some equally crazy things off it. He was fine with me, and would always lend his bike to a team-mate in need, but he was regarded as a typical wide boy, a ducker and diver. Just how much so was obvious years later, when Clarkie was sent to prison for his involvement in the theft of bikes and other equipment belonging to the Russians at the 1972 Wembley World Final.

The swinging sixties were a time for experimentation but one experience I didn't wish to repeat was my first dabble at ice racing. At the start of 1966 the ACU invited two British riders to compete against the mighty Russians, Swedes and Czechs who were masters at this very dangerous form of speedway. Like fools, Don Godden and myself took up the challenge, the first Brits to ever race on ice, and we went to the Soviet Union to compete in the World Championships.

We'd never seen an ice bike before, let alone sat on one, but all of a sudden we were both thrust into the semi-finals of the World Championship at a place called Novosibirsk, in deepest Siberia. It involved us in a four-hour flight from Moscow and, apparently, we were the first two 'free' Englishmen to travel that far south of Moscow behind the communist Iron Curtain.

We were about an hour into the flight from the capital city when the cabin crew appeared and drew all the blinds across the windows of the plane. We weren't allowed to look out of the windows for about an hour-and-a-half before the crew returned to withdraw the blinds, so God knows what we'd flown over – probably some secret Russian military intelligence bases!

Don and I were certainly not on a spying mission but we were still escorted everywhere by KGB officers and weren't allowed to go anywhere by ourselves. It was something like 38 degrees below zero! The new overcoat I'd bought myself especially for the trip was about as much use as a flimsy t-shirt in those temperatures, so I was grateful for the bear-skin coats our hosts gave us to keep warm.

SIMMO

The scary stuff started before the meeting had even began, when I spotted a bloke walking around the pits with both his hands bandaged up. Our interpreter explained that the gentleman was the pits marshal whose job it was to start the bikes by spinning their back wheels, and that his hands had been ripped to shreds by the spikes on the tyres. Those damn spikes!

At this point I should explain that the fundamental difference between an ice racing bike and a normal speedway machine is that both tyres are fitted with around 100 steel spikes, just over an inch in length. I thought that the story about how the man had sustained his hand injuries was a wind-up designed to put the fear of God into us. Either way, it pretty much did.

As I soon discovered, as well as providing the necessary grip on the slippery track surface, those metal spikes are bloody lethal and can certainly inflict serious damage!

The meeting was staged over two days, with our combined scores added together. I did well to record 10 points in the first meeting and think I had eight from four rides until a close encounter with a Mongolian rider in my last ride. He charged up the inside of me and went straight over the back of my trailing left leg. I felt my foot getting hot and when I looked down, I saw that even though I was wearing so many layers – jeans and long-johns beneath my leathers – his spikes had still shredded everything. The Mongol was banned from the rest of the meeting but that was no consolation to me.

As the blood oozed from my leg, I made up my mind there and then that I'd had enough of ice racing. The ridiculous thing was, we were only getting paid one pound a point and a pound per start, plus the cost of our flights and other basic expenses.

The 1966 Hammers. Back row, left to right: Don Smith, Sverre Harrfeldt, Dave Lanning, Brian Leonard and Norman Hunter. Front: Reg Trott, Ken McKinlay, mascot Trevor Rushbrook and myself.

To Russia with blood

"As the blood oozed from my leg, I made up my mind there and then that I'd had enough of ice racing. The ridiculous thing was, we were only getting paid one pound a point and a pound per start, plus the cost of our flights and other basic expenses"

Although I vowed in Russia never to risk ice racing again, I was eventually pressurised into giving it another try, this time with the former Canterbury and Hackney rider Graham Miles for company, in February 1971. Andy Ross and Eric Boocock were originally nominated as Britain's only two World Ice Racing Championship representatives but they had the good sense to withdraw, so me and Graham went instead. We were paid £250 plus expenses, which was good money, for three meetings in Sweden. But our problems on this trip began soon after leaving the ferry in Sweden, as we were heading for the frozen far north . . . without special ice tyres fitted to our cars.

Sverre receiving an award from the grandfather of speedway, Johnnie Hoskins.

Our naivety in being so ill-equipped to take to the treacherous, icy roads became obvious when Graham's Mercedes skidded into a stationary vehicle that was waiting to turn in front of him. I was following a short distance behind, skidded and just managed to avoid the other two cars as I spun around 360 degrees on what was sheet black ice – although I hadn't realised just how icy the road surface was until I had to hit the brakes hard! We had to abandon Graham's Merc near the scene of the pile-up and just about managed to squeeze his bikes into my car before continuing our hazardous journey to the track.

The omens were not good and my enthusiasm for this latest adventure completely drained from me during practice at Ostersund. Before we'd even had a chance to unload our bikes, I watched in horror as a rider crashed into the

53

fence, closely followed by his bike . . . followed by the ice turning a distinct shade of blood red! The incident with the mad Mongolian on my previous ice trip to Russia came flooding back to me and I just didn't want to be there.

It's Sod's Law that when you don't want to make the start, you do – and I probably made 15 decent starts over the course of those three meetings in Sweden. But that scary feeling never left me and I can honestly say that while I might have been first to leave the start line, I contrived to be last going into the first turn every time! I didn't mind chasing the others but I didn't want to find myself in front at the first corner.

An old programme in my collection confirms that Oxford's Swedish speedway star Hasse Holmqvist won that meeting but I didn't score a point and Graham managed just one. No, ice racing definitely wasn't for me.

From ice to frosty farewell at Custom House

My relationship with West Ham had also become a bit frosty by 1967. Although the team had improved on a disappointing 1966 season – we climbed from seventh to third position in the final table, had led the league until the halfway stage and also reached the KO Cup final again – I wasn't happy and had a big fall-out with Dave Lanning.

I wanted more from the club but they wouldn't give me what I thought I was worth. I asked for a new bike, or maybe even an engine, but there was nothing happening. Previously our PRO, Dave had taken over from Tommy Price as team manager in 1966 but he also had to answer to the board of directors who ran the club, including the Coventry supremo Charles Ochiltree who also had a financial stake in the West Ham set-up.

It wasn't that I had one bike set up especially for my big home track and needed another engine for smaller away tracks. I had a theory, and I think it's still correct today, that if a rider has one bike set up to go fast, then it can be successful on any size track. If you need to slow the bike down, then use your right hand to do so. Throttle control is what it's all about as far as I'm concerned and I could never see

I'm at the back here, but even the normally fast-starting 'Hurri-Ken' was beaten to the first turn at Hackney by the home pairing of Roy Trigg and Les McGillivray.

To Russia with blood

1967 and the dyed blond look for me (far left). The rest of the Hammers are: Brian Leonard, Ken McKinlay (on bike), Norman Hunter, Sverre Harrfeldt, Tony Clarke and Stan Stevens.

Right: One of the happiest moments of my last season with West Ham – receiving the Silver Sash match-race title from Polish star and then World No.3 Antoni Woryna. I managed to beat three Swedes – Gunnar Malmqvist, Olle Nygren and Tommy Bergqvist – before losing the sash to Briggo, who held it at the end of the 1967 season.

the sense in taking two bikes to a meeting if you could only use one of them due to the size or requirements of that particular track. But if your bikes are all set up to go as fast as you can, at least you have the chance to slow them down if necessary.

Another factor in my need for better financial terms, and to make the kind of progress most people had expected from me, was that I had married Sandra Wood on May 14, 1966. We'd met at a friend's party at Rochester airport the previous winter when we were introduced by a mutual friend, Brenda Jarvis, who sadly died last year. Even though I didn't think it was love at first sight, our relationship began

SIMMO

I wish I'd never taken up smoking. The 40-a-day habit from my youth has caught up with me today.

We had two famous former riders as team manager at West Ham. After World Champion Tommy Price came Phil Bishop (left), who was tragically among those killed in the Lokeren road crash of 1970.

that night. I was still living at Rainham, at my parents' old house, and because it was winter and no grasstrack meetings to earn from, we didn't get out much socially. It was after I returned from that ice trip to Russia that I decided I'd had enough of what was a fairly lonely existence – mum had left long ago and dad was out working most of the time – so I asked Sandra to marry me. We set the date to coincide with her birthday, although I suppose my priority was still riding motorbikes. We didn't exactly go from the wedding to an exotic honeymoon location – the next day I was competing in a grasstrack meeting! I can't say I wasn't happy to get married – but did I tie the knot for the right reasons? Only time would tell…

Having got nowhere in my efforts to significantly improve my financial deal or my equipment, and concerned at my lack of progress in the past two seasons, I asked to be put on the transfer list at the end of the '67 campaign. Little did I know when I took that action that King's Lynn promoter Maurice Littlechild, his best friend Fred Carr and Fred's young daughter, June, had already been to watch me at Custom House before the end of that season. I don't know whether it was fate that intervened but June Carr would become my partner and wife to be almost three decades later!

To Russia with blood

The boys gave me the bumps the night I announced I was getting married.

I had a strong partnership at West Ham with Norman Hunter, and we're seen here together on our way to a 5-1 at the home of old rivals Wimbledon.

It most definitely wasn't love at first sight on June's part, though. She tells me now that while she rated me highly as a rider, she thought I was a *prima donna* with my bleached blond hair!

Apparently, Maurice had watched me several times and had made up his mind to get me some weeks before he reached a deal with West Ham to sign me soon after the end of the season. King's Lynn had opened on an open licence in 1965 before entering the British League for the first time the following year. I liked Lynn's Saddlebow Road circuit – like West Ham, it was a real racer's track – and while I think there was some interest from Hackney in re-signing me, I was very happy to be joining the Stars from Norfolk.

5

Leading Exeter's Bob Kilby around King's Lynn – a lovely place to ride.

THE INSIDE STORY

SIMMO

THE start of my King's Lynn career could hardly have gone any better – right from the first team practice session attended by around 3,000 supporters. How many Elite League tracks would like a crowd that size for a major meeting today!

It was at this pre-season practice that I first tested the ESO – fitted into a Howard Cole frame – that the Swedish star Gote Nordin had ridden to victory in the coveted Wills Internationale at Wimbledon the previous year, the same bike my new club adopted as its track spare. In those days, most tracks had a spare bike available to any team member who had problems with his own machinery but I liked this one so much that I swapped it with the club for mine.

This was the best bike I'd ridden to that point and I was scoring lots of points everywhere I went. At Wimbledon, where I'd been a KO Cup sensation for West Ham three years earlier, I scored 17 in the Cup. I romped to four consecutive maximums and broke the Saddlebow Road track record as the Stars beat Belle Vue in a thriller.

My average of 9.40 made me the top King's Lynn rider, ahead of the big crowd favourite Terry Betts, and the 16th highest ranked performer in the whole of the British League, which was considerable improvement on being no better than No.4 with the Hammers.

Bettsy had become an instant star among the Stars, firmly established as the club's blue-eyed boy since the track joined the BL two years earlier, but I had been consistently outscoring him as spring turned to summer. While Terry and I had scored the same points as each other in two league matches, I had out-scored him by 12 of the other 16 matches in which we had both appeared together.

Called up for the Great Britain team to face world champions Sweden, and with my move to King's Lynn having gone far better than I could have ever have dreamed possible, I was definitely on a roll.

I was also very happy to be riding for Maurice Littlechild, a lovely man from Waltham Abbey, Essex, who built his empire from thriving transport and horticulture businesses and, besides other things, buying and selling manure!

A little shit is how I could describe Maurice's partner, Cyril Crane, who was nowhere near as pleasant to deal with. They worked well as a partnership, though, and obviously deserve credit for transforming an empty field into one of the finest – and fairest – racetracks in the land.

As you'll gather, I didn't like Crane and we never got on, so I always

"I failed my driving test once and hadn't bothered to re-take it. I just thought I was a better driver than the people already on the road – including the examiner who failed me!"

The inside story

preferred to deal with Maurice as much as possible. I trusted him from day one and if Maurice agreed to a deal, he always stuck to it. I think he bought me a bike and paid a signing-on fee of £1,000 to help set me on my way at King's Lynn.

Talking of money, I had also taken a fancy to the young girl working in the office who made up the riders' pay packets after each meeting. Yes, I can admit now that my relationship with June started as an affair roughly a year after I signed for King's Lynn – much to the concern of Maurice, who knew June's dad very well and was dead set against us getting together. He tried so hard to put June off me, at one time he even told her that I was gay! Maurice also warned her that I was bad news where women were concerned but, thankfully, she took no notice of him!

June and I had both married different people in 1966 but hindsight has shown that it had been two years too soon in both cases. If we'd met earlier, I'm sure our lives would have turned out differently and for the better – and I'll explain more fully how our relationship developed later in the book.

I certainly wish the year of 1968 had turned out very differently for me. After weeks of being on top form for my new club, my season ended very abruptly in mid-summer, after I'd completed only 18 league matches in the Stars' gold and green racejacket. I couldn't even take my place in the British semi-final, the first time I had gone that far in the World Championship.

1968 – just before it all turned sour.

It wasn't a bad injury that halted my tremendous progress – it was much more serious than that.

I was on my way to prison . . . for six months.

The problem stemmed from the fact that I failed my driving test once, when I was 17, and hadn't bothered to re-take it. I just thought I was a better driver than the people already on the road – including the examiner who failed me! I thought 'stuff it', I'll just continue to drive anyway.

61

SIMMO

You can see why I fell for June Carr very soon after we met at King's Lynn. She was Miss Speedway beauty queen in 1968 and, after posing on the table for Alf Weedon (above), is pictured (below) with Stars' promoters Maurice and Violet Littlechild (far right) and other local dignitaries in the Mayor of King's Lynn's parlour.
Actually, June still has that mini dress – although she occasionally wears it now as a t-shirt!

The inside story

Up until '68, I had probably been caught, suspended and fined four times for driving with nothing more than my original provisional licence. One ban was meant to last a year but I just ignored it and continued to drive myself around regardless. I'd routinely attend court, receive my ban, pay the fine and then get back in the car and drive it out of the car park! I had total contempt for the law and, basically, didn't give a shit.

Everything came to a head the day my missus, Sandra, was stopped by the police while driving my Ford Zodiac. The Old Bill's attention was drawn to the tax disc displayed in the windscreen. The tax disc for my trials bike was legal, so I thought I'd get away with using that whenever I drove my car, too – well, they looked identical and the motor bike licence was registered in my name and all above board.

Sandra knew I'd put the bike tax disc in the car and when she was stopped that day by the police, not surprisingly, she wasn't prepared to take the blame for it. The coppers said afterwards that I would have been better off if I'd stuck a beer mat in the slot where the licence should have been, instead of inserting a fraudulent licence. To have displayed nothing at all in the front windscreen would have been better still.

Apart from the very serious issue of her driving without insurance and tax, I was charged with fraud for trying to pass off a motorcycle tax disc in a car and had to attend a hearing at Medway Magistrates Court, where I was supported by the Lynn co-promoters, Maurice Littlechild and Cyril Crane, plus Barry Briggs, who were my character witnesses.

In hindsight, it would have been a lot better all round if Sandra had taken the blame and said that she knew about it, which she did. As a first offence, she would probably have got nothing worse than a fine.

As I said, I was bang in form at the time my case came to court, although my prolific scoring form on track for King's Lynn and the Great Britain international call-up went against me at the hearing. In his summing up, the judge made the point that as I was in the public eye so much, he had decided to make an example of me. I probably would have been treated more leniently by another judge, on another day, but this particular one was determined to make me pay and impose the biggest punishment possible for the crime I'd committed. Maybe the judge who sentenced me simply got out of bed the wrong side that morning, or had had a row with his missus before setting off for work. Whatever, he sent me down for six months.

In my sheer arrogance, it had never even crossed my mind that I would be sent to jail. Maurice had kindly arranged for a proper barrister to represent me and even this legal expert didn't consider the possibility that I might be given a custodial sentence.

I had gone there thinking that I'd probably get away with a big fine and a further year's driving ban. I was so cocky and confident I'd get off lightly that before the trial, I didn't even mention my court appearance to Sandra, who was expecting our first child at the time. Nor did I mention it to my father. The first they knew of my sentence was when I made the obligatory one phone call from the basement of the court to tell Sandra the shocking news. She cried when I told her that I would be

SIMMO

going away for six months – and hearing her cry down the phone only made me shed even more tears.

The verdict and imprisonment certainly brought me down a peg or two. Maurice Littlechild, who had done all he could to protect and provide the best possible representation for me, was as devastated as I was at my guilty verdict and the hefty sentence. He'd lost his most in-form rider, his No.1 at the time, and I was about to lose my freedom. Maurice organised an appeal on my behalf and didn't spare any expense in trying to save me from prison but, ultimately, it was all in vain.

I was immediately taken from the court by police van, with its blacked out windows, to the low security Canterbury Prison. I've never really spoken about this very unhappy episode before but, the truth is, I was frightened out of my life. From the strip-search on arrival, I found everything about life behind bars degrading. It wasn't nice having to use a bucket as a toilet in the cell, in full view of other inmates, and not being able to empty it out until the next morning. We were allowed to take a shower only once a week. We were up by six o'clock every morning and an hour later they brought round a razor blade for us to shave with. Half an hour later, the warden would return to collect the blade – we prisoners weren't to be trusted with it. Stripped of my dignity, I found it humiliating all the way down the line.

I was thrown into a cell with two other blokes, although I can't recall their names and didn't have a clue who they were. They were a couple of thieves and regular criminals but I was lucky in that they were fine with me – one of them even taught me how to play chess! I didn't know or hear of any major problems between the prisoners at Canterbury, which was really a holding prison where only small-time criminals were sent.

> **"From the strip-search on arrival, I found everything about life behind bars degrading. It wasn't nice having to use a bucket as a toilet in the cell, in full view of other inmates, and not being able to empty it out until the next morning"**

The day after I arrived at Canterbury, Sandra was allowed to visit me for an hour and in that very short space of time we had to try and work out how she would cope without my income from racing while I served my time. That was much easier said than done, because for the first three months we could only communicate with each other through a glass screen. Even so, we were only allowed visitors once a month.

As if being locked up wasn't awful enough in itself, the fact that I could hear the bikes – and, if the wind was blowing in the right direction, even the tannoy announcements – from the nearby Canterbury Speedway, just rubbed further salt into my wounds. Canterbury had been one of the tracks that opened in 1968 as part of the new British League Second Division but the noise of the engines from the Crusaders' home track made life even more unbearable for me. One considerate prison officer was a Canterbury fan and would bring in a marked-up programme to show me the morning after their Saturday night home meetings. It was a nice thought on his part but what with the sound of the bikes and being denied the chance to race myself, I asked him not to bother after a while. Losing my freedom had got to me that much.

The inside story

I couldn't get my head around being locked up virtually all day – I just wouldn't accept it. While I was naturally worried about Sandra and how she might be managing on the outside, I was also very concerned about how I would cope on the inside. We didn't have any financial savings put aside to see us through a bad time like this and the speedway journalist, Peter Oakes, summed me up brilliantly when he said: "If Simmo earned one hundred pounds, he'd spend one hundred and one!" He was dead right and, with no money saved for a rainy day, Sandra had to live off social security benefits while I was banged up.

All things considered, I was allocated quite a good job in prison, working with one of the electricians, and although I stuck at it, it never became fully acceptable to me. I'd been earning decent money at King's Lynn but the simple things in life, like having a smoke, were suddenly taken away from me. Prison jobs paid peanuts and it was difficult to earn enough on the inside to be able to afford even half an ounce of Old Holborn tobacco.

Feeling as low as I've ever been, I admit that I did, briefly, have suicidal thoughts although they quickly went away. I did, though, wonder how I would cope, physically, especially after my appeal was turned down and my depression deepened.

It was after spending eight weeks at HMP Canterbury, and having lost my appeal, that I was transferred to the open prison at Sheerness, on the Isle of Sheppey, in Kent. An open prison meant only one thing to me . . . a great opportunity to escape. From the moment I first applied to be moved to an open prison, I had only one thought on my mind.

Although I'd gone from a tiny cell I'd shared with two other blokes at Canterbury to a dormitory with around 20 others at Sheerness, the open prison routine was still very much regimented. I found the criminals at this more rural outpost more hardened, although I don't remember much about them other than there seemed to be more Londoners among them.

I spent my first days there in a haze, walking around the place like a zombie, and after the setback of losing my appeal I didn't want to stay there a minute longer than necessary. I desperately wanted to escape what was, to me, a living hell.

The inside story

After being in there for a week, that's just what I did.

It wasn't pre-planned, and I hadn't even thought it through properly, but it was dead easy to walk out of the place. After all, there was only a gateway to the prison, with little offices either side of the main entrance, and no perimeter fencing to keep us in. One morning, after breakfast, I sneaked unnoticed out of the back door and just walked and walked and walked . . . until I was in the middle of nowhere, trudging across open fields and heading for freedom. Or so I hoped.

I eventually reached the nearest road but made it only as far as the edge of the built up area of town when, as luck would have it, I spotted a police car coming towards me. I immediately dodged into the first garden I could see to try and hide but, dressed in my grey prison uniform, I wasn't exactly hard to spot. The police quickly arrested me and escorted me back to prison.

As blitz-outs go, this wasn't exactly Steve McQueen's famously spectacular motorcycle stunt from *The Great Escape* movie! It was madness really. If I'd thought through my escape plan properly, I would have somehow arranged for a friend to be waiting for me on the outside, with a getaway car. How did I expect to get off the island on foot, dressed in prison gear?

"I had to wear overalls that had bright yellow patches sewn on, which signified to everyone that I'd been as an escapee. I suppose it might have given me a bit more credibility among my fellow prisoners, or, on the other hand, it possibly marked me down as an idiot who got caught!"

Don't ask me why but I had it in the back of mind to try and make it all the way up to King's Lynn, to the Maid's Head pub in the town run by a nice couple, Colin and Mary Atkinson, who were big speedway fans. It was a favourite haunt for us riders after every home meeting but quite why I wanted to go there while on the run, I don't know. It's not as if I could have walked into the pits the following Saturday, as if nothing had happened, and gone out to race for the Stars again!

The fact is, I hadn't thought things through at all, I just left Sheerness Prison on impulse. I had been locked up for a couple of months by then and I couldn't handle it – it was as simple as that.

I think Steve McQueen's on-screen character, the baseball-bouncing Virgil Hiltz, coped with his punishment in the infamous 'cooler' of that German prisoner of war camp a bit better than the 24 hours solitary confinement that awaited me upon my return to HMP Sheerness. That was the lowest point of all and the time when the hopelessness of my dire situation finally hit me.

After a day spent in solitary with my morale at its lowest ebb, they transferred me back to Canterbury jail, where I still recall my old electrician colleague telling me what a bloody idiot I'd been for trying to escape. Having proved myself untrustworthy, I wasn't allowed to resume work with my electrician friend and, instead, had to make do with the mundanity of stitching mailbags. Cigarettes were also out of bounds to me for two weeks as part of my period on what was known as 'limited privileges'.

I did gain some kudos, though, from my original cell-mates, who I immediately rejoined. I went up in their estimation quite a lot following my escape efforts at Sheerness. In their eyes, I'd gone from being a bit of a cry baby, who was always upset and feeling sorry for himself, to a proper prison rebel! During work duties, I had to wear overalls that had bright yellow patches sewn on, which signified to everyone that I'd been an escapee. I suppose it might have given me a bit more credibility among my fellow prisoners, or, on the other hand, it possibly marked me down as an idiot who got caught!

To measure the passing of their sentence, some prisoners would draw six vertical lines on the wall of their cell, with a seventh horizontal one crossed through the middle to mark the passing of another week. But I was advised not to do that, because it just made your sentence seem to drag even longer than it did already. Another tip I was given by one or two of the more experienced inmates was not to write my initials on the wall. They reckoned it was a bad omen and that if you did it, you'd be sure to find yourself back in that same cell at some time in the future.

My attitude to prison life changed for the better when I went back to Canterbury and I finally accepted that I had to knuckle down and do my time without feeling sorry for myself. After a while I got a much better job in the shower room, dishing out towels to my fellow inmates, which was brilliant because it meant I could shower myself each day and wear clean clothes all the time. I also got the pick of the best shirts with the smartest collars that weren't frayed like many of them were.

And by sorting out better clothing for some of the more hardened lags who thought they were the bollocks, they'd reward me with half an ounce of tobacco, or, if it was someone from the cook-house, perhaps some spoonfuls of sugar. Tooth paste and nicer quality soap were other little luxuries that gratefully came my way as time passed.

What my escape farce did, though, was to extend my sentence. If I'd behaved myself, I would have been out after four months but I lost most of my remission and a local magistrate extended my sentence by an extra six weeks and six days, so I virtually ended up serving the full six months' term.

While I was inside, my daughter Lisa was born on September 19, 1968. I found out about the birth when Sandra phoned the prison and her message was passed on to me. I was naturally upset that I couldn't be on the outside to see my wife and new-born baby, although I must confess that I wouldn't have attended the actual birth – I don't 'do' babies!

1969 and a nervous return to the track.

The full-face crash helmet makes its first appearance on me in 1970, seen here leading Coventry's Rick France.

Starting over

If I hadn't made that ludicrous escape attempt, with time off for good behaviour I could possibly have ridden again before the end of the 1968 season. As it was, my release came in mid-November. There was a social gathering at King's Lynn stadium very soon afterwards and I remember approaching the event with great trepidation. I knew I had to go and front it out but I was very apprehensive about the reception I'd get from everybody there and wondered if I would be welcomed back to the track when the new 1969 season started the following March.

I'd obviously let everyone down – the promoters, the team and the supporters, as well as myself – for getting sent to prison for such stupid offences and I didn't know how the people of King's Lynn would react to seeing me there again.

But I was so delighted, and very relieved, when they cheered me into the room because I'd hadn't expected anything like the wonderful reception I got. The only person who had even the slightest dig at me and mentioned my prison sentence on that night – or at any time since then – was Cyril Crane, who muttered something about: "If you can't do the time, don't do the crime."

I don't know if my near six months spent in prison changed me at all as a person, but at least it made me take a driving test! I left it a year or so before trying my luck by re-applying for my licence, and was surprised to be told that there were only three months of my driving ban remaining. I thought my suspension had much longer to run but I wasn't going to argue.

I took – and passed – my driving test on Monday, July 14, 1970, a date that will forever be remembered in speedway circles as the day of the Lokeren road crash that killed five members of the West Ham speedway

> "I'd obviously let everyone down – the promoters, the team and the supporters, as well as myself – for getting sent to prison for such stupid offences and I didn't know how the people of King's Lynn would react to seeing me there again"

party who were returning from a meeting in Holland in the early hours of the morning. I had passed my test later that day and was just starting my first legal drive by car when I turned on the radio to hear the awful news. Hammers' famous manager Phil Bishop and riders Pete Bradshaw, Gary Everett, Malcolm Carmichael and Martyn Piddock had all lost their lives when their minibus crashed on the motorway in Belgium. Colin Pratt and my old West Ham team-mate, Stan Stevens, were among those who survived the wreckage, although Pratty's neck injuries were so serious that he never raced again.

I had known all of those involved in speedway's biggest ever disaster and I just couldn't believe it – I was so shocked and completely stunned, at first I thought I'd misheard the radio report.

Pete Bradshaw was actually living with us at the time. A young rider trying to make his way in the sport, he had recently returned from Melbourne, Australia for his second season in England – Maurice Littlechild had sent June and I to collect him from the airport – and, ironically, Pete had switched between the same tracks as I had in 1968, although in reverse. Pete had started at Lynn in 1969 and joined West Ham the following year but I'd hardly had time to get to know him before Lokeren, which cast a huge black cloud over the whole sport.

My former lodger Pete Bradshaw in Hammers' colours shortly before that fatal road crash in Belgium.

The inside story

Howard Cole in his familiar white shirt and the skipper Terry Betts. We had some fun with Coley's flowing scarf when referee Lew Stripp was in town. In the background of this picture is Poole's Ted Laessing, who became one of my main sponsors – through his Maximum Racing business – when I joined the Pirates.

King's Lynn Stars, 1971. Back row, left to right: Ian Turner, Clive Featherby, Barry Crowson, Bob Humphreys and team manager Alan Littlechild. Front: Howard Cole, Terry Betts and myself. This picture was taken before a match at Poole.

6

FOND FAREWELL TO OUR SHINING STAR

Maurice Littlechild (far left) lines up with his co-promoter Cyril Crane and the Stars of 1970. The rest are: Alan Bellham, myself, Allan Brown and Howard Cole. On bike: Terry Betts and David Crane. Sadly, Maurice only lived for another couple of years.

SIMMO

FROM being King's Lynn No.1 midway through the previous season, I couldn't regain those high standards at the start of 1969 and realised then what six months in prison had taken out of me.

More than anything else, my period inside had knocked my confidence for six. I don't know why but it took me from the heights I'd scaled in 1968 until 1971 to recapture the same level of consistently good form.

Following my release from Canterbury Prison, I certainly wasn't as brash and cocky as I'd been before I was sentenced. I was also concerned that I'd lost some of my riding ability. Apart from inflicting new World Champion Ivan Mauger's first league defeat in 45 races when Belle Vue visited Saddlebow Road in May 1969, I failed to reach the British semi-final of the World Championship and rode poorly for most of that year.

My form deteriorated even further in 1970 when I slipped to third in the Stars' averages – behind Terry Betts and the improving Howard Cole – as my CMA dipped below eight points a match for the first time since I signed from West Ham.

Here's a story that possibly sums up what a disappointing year 1970 was for me. I went to Germany for my first-ever foreign grasstrack meeting, at the Klein-Krotzenburg track, and managed to win it. In addition to the prize money on offer, the organising club also presented me with a very large trophy in the shape of a golden pheasant, although it looked more like a chicken to me!

I brought the trophy home and just plonked it on our sideboard, where it stood for years. In the winter, I used to repair cars to earn a few extra bob and I was at home one day when someone whose car I'd fixed came round to pay his bill. While we were chatting away, he noticed my 'golden chicken' and seemed to take a keen interest in it. He then asked me what I thought it was worth and I told him I didn't have a clue. "Probably nothing," I said.

My local customer went on to say that he had a friend who could value it for me, so he took the trophy away with him and I really didn't think any more about it. As the years passed, I never saw the man again – we're talking about the mid-70s by now and, as I say, it didn't really bother me that I'd probably never see my chicken again.

Anyway, in the year 2000, the people at Klein-Krotzenburg got in touch and invited me and other past winners of their annual meeting back for a special millennium ceremony. They couldn't believe I was still riding but it was nice to turn back the clock and return to a place where I'd been successful 30 years earlier.

During the celebratory day, June spoke to the lady who helped run the meeting and casually mentioned to her that we'd had our old trophy stolen, before asking her how much she thought it would be worth. June also enquired about the possibility

Fond farewell to our shining star

of purchasing a smaller replica of the one I'd been presented with in 1970. But the German woman couldn't help us, explaining that even a small replica of the original Goldenen Fasan trophy would cost . . . wait for it . . . EIGHT THOUSAND POUNDS!

When June then asked why it would be so expensive, the woman replied: "Because the trophy is made of pure gold!"

Now I realised why the man, who stumbled upon the old pheasant in my house that day by chance, never returned to get his car repaired by me again! God knows what that original trophy I won back in 1970 would be worth today.

For the first time in my career, I began the 1971 season with a brand new (ESO) engine and it soon proved its worth. I scored 13 points in a challenge match against West Ham at Custom House and returned to my former track several weeks later to win my first individual title in speedway – the Hammerama trophy – after dropping my only point to Wembley's Bert Harkins. Three weeks later, I appeared at West Ham yet again, this time as a guest for Sheffield, and led them to a 40-38 victory. I loved the wide, open spaces of the Hammers' track, as many riders did, and it was such a shame that '71 was the last full season that speedway was staged at the famous, old east London stadium before it had to make way for housing redevelopment.

By amassing a century of points more than I had in 1970, I regained the No.2 spot in the Lynn averages from Howard Cole, who missed a month of the campaign with

1971 – and a brand new ESO engine for the first time.

Me and Barry Crowson put Wimbledon's Graeme Stapleton under pressure at Plough Lane.

a kidney problem following a bad crash at Leicester. Apart from his beard, Howard stood out for wearing his trademark white football jersey over his leathers and long scarf that trailed behind him. One night at Lynn, over-fussy referee Lew Stripp told Coley that he had to shorten his scarf the next time he rode with it, because it was dangerous and could interfere with other riders.

For a laugh, and to show just what we thought of Stripp's pettiness, a few of us decided to have a little game with him, by sharing Coley's white scarf between a few of the team in the second half of the meeting. Bettsy went out wearing it for his race, with the scarf extended even longer, and was fined for his actions. Then I lengthened the scarf even more for my next ride and got fined too.

> **"Bettsy went out wearing it for his race, with the scarf extended even longer, and was fined for his actions. Then I lengthened the scarf even more for my next ride and got fined too. We had the last laugh on Stripp, though"**

We had the last laugh on Stripp, though. He used to get to and from meetings by motorbike so, when his back was turned, Bettsy changed the plug leads on the engine and when the time came to go home, Lew couldn't get the thing started. He called out the AA, but even they couldn't get his bike to fire, so he had to spend the night in King's Lynn before someone fixed the problem. Lew blamed me for that prank for years but it was all Bettsy's doing.

I'd hoped to round off a much improved 1971 with a strong performance in our traditional end-of-season Pride of the East classic but had to miss King's Lynn's big finale after suffering an adverse reaction to the smallpox and malaria injections I'd received for my imminent first visit to Australia.

The British Lions touring party consisted of: George Hunter, Chris Pusey, Tony Lomas (the only other new boy), Nigel Boocock, Bert Harkins, Jim McMillan and myself. There was controversy in the first Test at Sydney over Aussie John Langfield's use of the old 22-inch back wheel and allegations that the home riders were using nitro methane, which had been banned by the FIM from international racing earlier in the year. The following week, the Aussies falsely accused us of

Fond farewell to our shining star

Arriving in Australia on my first British Lions tour with Tony Lomas and Chris Pusey.
The rain wasn't the only rude awakening we had.

I particularly enjoyed my visits to Perth, but it was that man Mauger (again) who stood on top of the rostrum.

The three Scots in the 1971-72 Lions squad – Jimmy McMillan, my life-safer George Hunter and Bert Harkins.

using the illegal fuel additive.

The Lions won the third Test at Brisbane, where rolling starts were replaced by traditional UK-style standing starts at the near circular Exhibition track. Pusey scored the lot, while Jimmy Mac injured his eye when a stone from the heavy surface pierced his goggles. It was some feat for us to win at Brisbane, where we'd lost the second Test, because it was John Titman's home track and it seemed most of his family worked there in one capacity or another and had the place sewn up between them.

I hit the headlines with a 15-point maximum for the Lions in our triangular match against the hosts and Sweden at the Sydney Showground, recognised world-wide as one of the hardest, most dangerous tracks to ride. I talked earlier in the book about the perils of Exeter's old County Ground track but the Sydney Royale was every bit as fearsome as Exeter – it was bigger and faster with a high brick wall for a so-called 'safety' fence.

> "Thankfully, after what seemed like an age, Glasgow's George Hunter must have noticed my panic movements – he dived straight in and probably saved me from drowning!"

It wasn't an oval shape – it was more like three corners – but I obviously got the hang of the place and did well there until my next visit. On this occasion, we were on the pre-meeting parade while somebody back in the pits sabotaged my bikes by loosening the oil pump. The pump completely fell off during my first race, causing the engine to seize. I never found out who the culprit was and there was nothing we could do about.

Even so, that minor setback didn't stop the Lions from clinching a 4-3 series victory with a 77-31 thrashing of Australia in the seventh, and final, Test in Perth. I particularly liked all three tracks we rode at in Western Australia, as well as the local people and the place itself.

Described as a 'second-rate team' on arrival in Australia, we had recovered from a 3-1 deficit to regain the Ashes and silence our critics.

Fond farewell to our shining star

To be fair, John Langfield, who was at the centre of that first Test storm, deserves praise for helping me to settle quickly in Oz, after Coventry's Tony Lomas and I had been left to fend for ourselves when we first touched down in Sydney. While most of the others in our party knew local people from previous visits and had pre-arranged to stay with them, Tony and myself found ourselves isolated from the rest and lodging with total strangers. It was better once we'd had a word with Nigel Boocock, our tour organiser and captain, who arranged for the pair of us to move to Langy's place, where Pusey was already resident.

Tour leader Nigel Boocock.

'Puse' was the team joker and while Tony and I lived in the house, the Belle Vue star slept in a caravan at the bottom of the garden. He had cause to regret that decision one night, when he was getting ready to go out on the town, opened the caravan door dressed in all his best gear . . . and was drenched by the water bucket that Langy had placed strategically above his head! Pusey was going to kill everybody in sight that evening and it took him about a week to calm down after being the victim of a typical Langy prank.

Off the track, there were the usual high jinks but the riders behaved themselves and we all got on well together. There was one very scary moment for me in Perth, though, when we met up for a barbecue. The people who hosted the party had a large swimming pool and I took the opportunity to continue learning to swim. I was doing OK going from the deep end to the shallow end until I tried it for a third time and got into trouble. I dived in but instead of swimming forward towards the shallow end as before, I just got stuck in deep water and suddenly found myself in great difficulty.

As I came up for air and tried to attract attention by waving frantically at the others who were sat around the side of the pool, I guess they must have thought I was just messing around. But, thankfully, after what seemed like an age, Glasgow's George Hunter must have noticed my panic movements – he dived straight in and probably saved me from drowning!

Financially, that first trip was a disappointment. With the Swedes also touring Australia at the same time, the Brits averaged only one meeting a week and I returned home convinced that more money could be made from going to Oz as a freelancer, rather than as a member of the official touring team.

Being 12,000 miles from home, I did get a bit homesick. Sandra joined me out there just before Christmas, so at least we were able to see the sights, but it was a pity that our three-year-old daughter, Lisa, had to remain at home with Sandra's parents in Rochester.

79

The Littlechild legacy

While I was on tour Down Under, Maurice Littlechild had been taken into hospital for a major stomach operation, although he had typically insisted on returning to work in time for the start of the 1972 season.

As well as his Norfolk Speedways partnership with Cyril Crane at King's Lynn, Maury was also a director of Allied Presentations, whose group of tracks included the rapidly emerging Crewe. Maury had pioneered speedway at Earle Street, the biggest and fastest track in Britain, from 1969 and the Kings were on the verge of great success at Second Division level.

Despite my successful winter in Oz, I didn't start the '72 campaign as well as I'd hoped after regaining something like my old form in 1971, although King's Lynn enjoyed their best-ever start to a season.

We actually topped the British League table in July, having lost only two of our first 18 matches, but the buzz of excitement turned to sadness when Maurice suffered a relapse of his cancer condition. The ambitious co-founder of King's Lynn Speedway, and one of the most well-liked and respected promoters in the country, died of pancreatic cancer at Waltham Abbey War Memorial Hospital, aged 52.

Maurice loved his speedway, ever since he witnessed the first-ever meeting as a wide-eyed eight-year-old, at High Beech in 1928. I had only known him since he signed me for King's Lynn 40 years later but his enthusiasm for the sport never left him until his dying day.

Maurice's funeral was a very special occasion and said much for his reputation and the affection so many people had for him. It needed a police escort to guide the cortegé through beautiful Epping Forest to the tiny Parish Church at High Beech, and then on to Maury's last resting place at leafy Upshire. Five Lynn riders – Terry Betts, Howard Cole, Barry Crowson, Bob Humphreys and myself – acted as pall-bearers while 500-plus mourners packed into the church.

It was a sad, though grand, occasion and also the scene of one of those tragi-comedy moments I'll never forget. Maury's send-off had gone smoothly until we almost dropped the coffin as we carried his body from Upshire church.

At 5ft 11 ins, I was about four-to-six inches taller than anybody else in the team – and with Ian 'Tiddler' Turner standing only about 5ft 4ins in his platform shoes, there was a definite imbalance among the pall-bearers as we gingerly walked from the church entrance, down a slope and towards the grave area. I was at the front, bearing most of the weight of the coffin, while Turner – who was in the middle – was so small that there was actually a gap showing between the bottom of the coffin and his shoulder. He wasn't taking any of the weight!

I think Bettsy was at the front with me and as we started to descend the grass bank, we both slipped slightly on the greasy surface and God knows how we managed to keep our balance and stay on

> "I had only known Maurice since he signed me for King's Lynn but his enthusiasm for the sport never left him until his dying day. Maurice's funeral was a very special occasion and said much for his reputation and the affection so many people had for him"

Fond farewell to our shining star

our feet without dropping poor, old Maury.

As Bettsy and I reached the bottom of the slippery slope and found flat land again, we looked across at each other and couldn't help but break the sombre mood by laughing at what had just happened. We were cracking up with laughter but we both knew we'd come so close to a catastrophe.

It wasn't the first time Ian Turner's stature caused a funny scene. On the way back from Scotland, where we'd been riding the previous night, all of the King's Lynn team met up at Linda and Ken Whitmore's house at Long Sutton, not far from Saddlebow Road. Linda and Ken have been very good friends of mine for many years and still occasionally stay with June and me. Anyway, on this particular day, Bettsy had collected our team leathers from the manufacturer and we were all gathered on Linda and Ken's front lawn, trying on our nice, new gear. Trouble was, they were individually packed – and all the riders' names had got mixed up. It was comical to see me trying to squeeze into Bettsy's leathers and Barry Crowson's pair coming up so short because they were meant for 'Tiddler' Turner!

Maurice Littlechild certainly left both the Lynn and Crewe teams in very good shape. We had to settle for third place in the table after being overhauled by championship hat-trick winners Belle Vue and Reading. But Crewe, spearheaded by the outstanding Aussie Phil Crump, won the Division Two KO Cup after beating Peterborough in the final and then completed the coveted double by winning the league. To complete a momentous year for the Cheshire outfit, Crumpie added the Second Division Riders' Championship to the Earle Street trophy cabinet. Yes, Maurice would have been mighty proud of his Kings . . . . and at the way things were shaping up at King's Lynn.

We certainly had our fair share of characters, including Maurice's son, Alan

Ian Turner – very spectacular on a speedway bike but not very effective as a pall-bearer.

Leading England and Leicester captain Ray Wilson, 1973.

Littlechild, who got more involved with the riders after his father passed away and remained Stars' team manager for many years.

Al was a nice guy – I loved him as a bloke – but he could be a bit of a prat, too, and I think he thought he would end up inheriting the world. When he took over, he promised everyone in the team that we would be provided with new bikes once he took over his mother Violet's shares in the promoting company. It was pure bullshit but I think Al believed it really would happen.

He could take a joke, though. He used to drive an old Mercedes 90 Diesel that used to go well, but only once it got up a head of speed, especially approaching a hill. To help pass the time and have a little fun on the long, boring journeys to places like Glasgow and Sheffield, Bettsy and I would position ourselves in front of Al's Merc, then deliberately slow up so that he'd lose all momentum, before pissing off into the distance and leaving him struggling at the foot of the incline! That was the kind of silly, little thing you did in those days. The team would travel in convoy to the farthest away meetings but that wouldn't happen now, would it?

Another silly prank we'd play on Alan would be to arrange for him to receive a 5am wake-up call in his hotel room, but he never twigged that it was his riders who were the practical jokers.

Alan was too free and easy to have filled his father's shoes, although Maurice was obviously a very tough act for anybody to have followed. If Al had taken over as promoter, we would all have been on top money, that's for sure. He'd have just given it to us – he was very generous like that.

One character from my earlier days at Lynn was Allan Brown, who arrived from

Fond farewell to our shining star

The 1974 team with Alan Littlechild. Eddie Reeves, Bob Humphreys and Barry Crowson are at the back, with Ray Bales, myself, Bettsy and Ian Turner at the front. Perhaps Bob, Ray and Ian couldn't fit into their team leathers.

New Zealand and came to live with me at Sittingbourne for a while, although he seemed to spend more time in his car than he did at our place. He was absolutely loopy but very good fun to be with.

One escapade that comes to mind was when we were driving, in separate cars, to a meeting up north. Allan's cars were always breaking down and that day was no different. We were speeding along the A1, at Christ knows how fast, when the engine in his Zodiac started to over-heat. His simple answer to that problem was to chuck half a gallon of methanol into the radiator!

Anyway, he couldn't have closed the bonnet properly, because a few miles up the road his bonnet suddenly flew over the top of my car and disappeared into a nearby field! We stopped to search for it but it wasn't to be seen anywhere, so he just drove off minus his bonnet! Allan didn't let things like that worry him, he was just a harem-scarem character, but he really could have been a better rider than he was.

Speedway riders must spend half their lives on the road, just getting to and from meetings, and I've had some good laughs along the way. One Whit Monday afternoon, Terry Betts and myself were driving at high speed through the Fens towards Wimbledon, where we were riding in their big Internationale meeting that same evening. Terry was going so fast along this otherwise tranquil country road that the side of his car brushed a little, old man off his cycle and he tumbled into a bush!

The old boy had only just picked himself and his bike up when Barry Crowson, who was following next behind Bettsy, did the same thing – and sent the poor cyclist flying.

I was third in the King's Lynn convoy and, yes, you've guessed it, I too edged him back into the brambles. As I flew past and looked in my rear view mirror, the look on the fella's face was priceless, as he peered out from the bushes, wondering anxiously if there were any more lunatics from Lynn to follow!

On another occasion, Bettsy damaged the gearbox on his car when he hit a stray milk crate on the M1 while we were returning from Sheffield one bleak, wet night. I had to tow him back to Essex but, because his car wouldn't start and the lights were very dim it turned out to be such a hairy journey for Terry that he said there were times when the trailer came off the ground and he couldn't see a thing in front of him.

We would regularly put up Aussie riders at our house when they first came to England and another who joined us was Bob Humphreys, a friendly bloke who loved working on his engines. He'd always be tinkering with one thing or another and if he'd only concentrated more on his racing, he could have gone a lot further in the sport. (If you're reading this, Bob, please get in touch – I'd love to hear from you again).

Clive Featherby was another in the mould of Exeter's Chris Julian – ever so softly spoken, a nice, mild-mannered bloke . . . but once he put his crash helmet on he became a man possessed and, in my view, a bit dirty. He made a footrest from an old car starting handle, two or three inches wider than anyone else's. It enabled him to drive hard underneath his opponent and just lift their left leg off the track as he went past. Unbelievable!

Howard, Terry and I always got on very well as a heat leader trio but Howard was always the underdog of the three of us and didn't get as much recognition as

Clive Featherby (left), who had the widest foot rest ever known, and (right) the tinkerer, Bob Humphreys.

Fond farewell to our shining star

he deserved. He never really hit the big heights over a sustained period in the BL although he was England's only qualifier for the 1969 World Final at Wembley and a good rider in his own right.

> **"Women loved Barry and, of course, he loved them in return. We shared the same sponsor – King Helmets – and appeared together on their stand at the Motorcycle Show held at Alexander Palace in north London. I spent most of the day alone on the stand, while Barry kept disappearing to attend to one female admirer after another"**

The Sheene machine

Barry Sheene, the twice 500cc World Motorcycling Champion and major pop-style pin-up of the 70s, would have been a great character for speedway but he was in love with road racing and brilliant at it. I once spent a day with him at King's Lynn, when he wanted to have a try at speedway, and he did very well considering he was a road racer.

I would like to have tried road racing myself but couldn't afford to, although I was delighted to accept Barry's reciprocal offer to spend a day riding at Brands Hatch in 1975. But I never did get my day out with one of motorcycling's all-time greats – just weeks before we were due to meet up again, he suffered his horrendous 175mph crash at Daytona 200 that shattered almost every bone in his body and left him held together with metal screws and bolts.

Women loved Barry and, of course, he loved them in return. We shared the same sponsor – King Helmets – and appeared together on their stand at the Motorcycle Show held at Alexander Palace in north London. I spent most of the day alone on the stand, while Barry kept disappearing to attend to one female admirer after another. He would jam the lift doors open until he'd done the deed and no-one could quite work out why the lift wasn't operating between floors!

The stupid thing about it was that despite two really bad crashes in his career, at Daytona and later, in 1982, at Silverstone, he died of cancer. I believe Barry never chose to have the prescribed therapy he needed when he was diagnosed with throat and stomach cancer, although who knows if the traditional chemotherapy or radiotherapy treatment would have worked any better for him than the homeopathic cures he sought down Mexico way. He lost his six month battle against the disease and died, where he went to live in Australia, in May 2003, aged 52.

The motorcycling world missed Barry Sheene as much as speedway – and King's Lynn and Crewe in particular – missed another charismatic character, Maurice Littlechild.

7

BETTSY... AND WHY I HAD TO LEAVE

A taste of the big time – my Wembley debut for England v Sweden in the final of the 1973 Daily Mirror International tournament. Me and Terry Betts are on our way to a heat win over Tommy Jansson. It wasn't often that I stole the limelight from Bettsy – but this is where I began to . . .

87

SIMMO

THERE is absolutely no question about it . . . there is only one Mister King's Lynn Speedway – and that has to my great friend, Terry Betts, whose contribution to the west Norfolk club is unsurpassed.

No-one has scored more points for King's Lynn, nor given them greater service over such a long period than Terry, who was a hero there from the moment he arrived in 1966 and still the main man when he left Saddlebow Road for a final season with Reading in 1979.

Universally popular with riders and supporters alike, you won't find anyone who has a bad word to say about Bettsy – one of the nicest guys the sport has ever known and a very loyal servant to both club and country.

Terry and I enjoyed many great times together for both club and country in the first half of the 70s and it's only right that he has a chapter of his own in my book. We still meet up occasionally, at social gatherings and reunions, and talk fairly regularly on the phone.

You can't fault him as a person, he's a lovely bloke. He would help me if I needed it and give me anything – and vice-versa. We lent each other our speedway bikes if either of us had a mechanical problem but I also bought a couple of cars from Bettsy. He took the mickey out of me big-time after my new Ford Capri got pebbledashed in shale while parked up on the first bend banking at Coatbridge, where the riders used to leave their cars during the meeting.

As a rider, you make

1968 – the first of seven seasons together at King's Lynn.

Bettsy...and why I had to leave

hundreds of acquaintances in speedway, but very few real friends. He is one of the few I am proud to call a friend and that's how we were throughout our time together at Lynn. We were friends rather than simply team-mates.

There were often times when we carried the King's Lynn team together, especially away from home, but we also enjoyed racing against each other in second half finals. On many occasions, in the case of an easy home win, these furious tussles would be the best race of the night. Did I want to beat him badly? Too right I did. I had to prove that I was better than him and he wanted to do the same to me. Even though the second halves in those days were split, with all four riders sharing the prize money on offer, Terry and I still went hell for leather to beat each other.

King's Lynn No.1 personality, 1971.

Towards the end of the '73 season, Bettsy pushed it too far and broke his arm when he crashed badly at Lynn. In trying to pass me on the outside, he somehow got his handlebars and arm caught on the top of the fence and then ran into a lamp standard. That's how much we both wanted to put one over on each other.

A lot of riders used to abuse the split final agreement, by pulling onto the centre green at the first corner, feigning engine problems or just not bothering to make a decent race of it. But whenever Terry and I were in opposition, we would go flat out to win, while still racing fair and square. I'd run him wide, but I'd never stuff him into the fence, and vice-versa. We had complete mutual respect at all times.

All riders get nervous before a meeting but we'd coped with it in different ways. I would sit quietly in the pits but Bettsy would try to disguise his nerves by cracking jokes – even though I could see from his eyes, which always turned red, that he was just as nervous as me. You had to be nervous to be good.

I always liked to arrive at the stadium very early, at around six o'clock, to leave myself enough time for a cuppa and a chat, as I did in the canteen at King's Lynn before most meetings. If I was late, it would make me uptight. Terry was the opposite, though, and preferred to get there for about seven o'clock, just 45 minutes before the first race. You knew he'd be there, but you knew he'd be later than the rest of us.

On the day of a meeting, I'd have a light breakfast and not eat again until after the meeting. Someone once told me early in my career that if you were badly hurt in a crash and the hospital needed to operate, it wasn't always possible if there was food inside you.

For all that we were, and still are, great mates, Terry was the main reason why I left King's Lynn at the end of the 1974 season. We never fell out, or even had a cross word with each other, but I knew that I had to get away from him – and King's Lynn – if I was ever to gain the recognition I thought I deserved.

> **"For all that we were, and still are, great mates, Terry was the main reason why I left King's Lynn at the end of the 1974 season. We never fell out, or even had a cross word with each other, but I knew that I had to get away from him – and King's Lynn – if I was ever to gain the recognition I thought I deserved"**

It was obvious to me that no matter how successful I became, for as long as I remained at Saddlebow Road I would never become a No.1 rider in my own right. Terry was very firmly established as the big crowd favourite at Lynn and no matter how many points I scored, he would always attract more individual and open meeting bookings than me. In those days, every track had at least one major open meeting a season, but they liked to book all the respective number ones first and that meant I missed out on a lot of bookings. Bettsy was also a very popular choice as a guest rider, so I was missing out on a lot of extra opportunities by being in his shadow.

In 1973, my sixth season with the Stars, I even topped the Lynn averages for the first time with a CMA of 10.26 a match, compared to Terry's 9.95. I rode in four more official matches and scored 63 extra points than him.

If only league matches were taken into account, my average climbed even higher, to 10.39. If you didn't include Halifax's Eric Boocock, who missed a lot of the season through injury, I had the highest final average of any English rider in the BL that year. In fact, I rode in more matches than any of the top six senior league riders of 1973, including the three who broke the 11-point barrier: Anders Michanek (11.55), Ivan Mauger (11.30) and Ole Olsen (11.10).

My achievement was all the more impressive because I'd scored the points I did while riding in the more demanding No.5 position in the team, which meant I always met the opposing No.1 rider at least twice in every match – and our second scheduled clash would be in the final heat. On the other hand, wearing our No.1 body colour, Terry only met his opposite number in the first race, unless he was brought in later as a tactical substitute.

Howard Cole had it included in his deal with the club that he would only ride at

Bettsy...and why I had to leave

Above: At least someone appreciated my form in 1973, although Bettsy doesn't look too pleased with the way the pre-meeting parade at the 1973 Daily Mirror International Tournament is going.
Later that season, we returned to Wembley and both played a part in Great Britain's first World Team Cup victory with an all-English squad. Not sure if the big wigs at the Control Board liked my new leather jacket, though.

When we retained the World Cup as England in 1974, Bettsy missed the final in Katowice after breaking his arm. At least I made sure he didn't miss out on the champers as well when we were invited back to the RAC club.

No.3, which meant he was partnered with one of our reserves for three of his four programmed rides in the old 13-heat formula, as it was then. I think Coley liked riding with a team-mate he knew he would beat 99 times out of 100, because three was the easiest position in the team. Mind you, he and I combined for our fair share of last-heat deciders over the years.

Terry wanted to wear the No.1 racejacket and although I vaguely recall once asking the management if I could switch from five to three, I didn't get anywhere with my request. After Coley left to join Cradley United in 1973, Ian Turner took over his position in the team, although he wasn't quite as effective as Howard had been.

In 1973 I was, at long last, Kings Lynn's top rider – or at least I was according to the record books. The point is, though, I never got the feeling that I was treated like a No.1 and I always had to play second fiddle to Bettsy in every sense. He even had better luck than me when it came to gaining a big sponsor.

After Maurice Littlechild died in July 1972, his half-share in King's Lynn was taken over by his widow, Violet, although she left all the financial negotiations with the riders to Cyril Crane. I never thought that I got what I was really worth from him and my efforts to improve my financial position suffered a major blow when I missed out on a big sponsor – all thanks to the toss of a coin.

Peter Thurlow, who ran the Abbeygate Group of Companies from Bury St Edmunds, and a friend of his both became interested in sponsoring a rider at Lynn, but couldn't decide between them who to sponsor out of Terry or me. They tossed

Bettsy...and why I had to leave

a coin to decide the choice and Terry got Peter's company while I was left with the other bloke, whose name escapes me.

The problem was, my sponsorship deal didn't even get off the ground before my intended backer's company went bust!

It was a very unfortunate toss to lose, because over the next few years Terry's support through Abbeygate was astronomical – Thurlow became probably the club's largest ever single benefactor, spending thousands helping numerous individual riders and the club as a whole.

Terry was already on a better financial deal at King's Lynn compared to me, which I accepted at the time because he was the No.1 rider, but the extra help a big sponsor would have provided could probably have kept me at the track beyond 1974.

After I'd topped the Stars' average at the end of '73, in which Terry and I had both hit the headlines and won World Team Cup winners' medals for Great Britain at Wembley, he regained the No.1 status at Saddlebow Road in 1974 . . . even though I actually scored 51 more points than him and netted nine full maximums compared to his three.

It was thanks to Bettsy's shoulder injury that I received a call up for the 1974 World Team Cup final in Poland, where I played a part in England's win with eight points. But my biggest moment of '74 was winning the prestigious Daily Express Spring Classic at Wimbledon with 13 points – one more than Dave Jessup and Ole Olsen. Apart from the £500 prize money, that victory meant a great deal to me because it was a world class line-up and to show just how strong a field it was, Anders Michanek (who would be World Champion later in the year), Peter Collins and Olsen all failed to score from their opening rides.

In my eyes, I was a Number One rider – and probably would have been at numerous other British League tracks at that time – but at King's Lynn, I would never be truly recognised as the top man.

The difference in how the King's Lynn management viewed Terry and myself was also reflected in our financial dealings with the club. I had always known that Terry earned more money than me during our time there together and, as I say, when he was the No.1 he was entitled to be on a better deal than the rest of us. But when I took over that mantle in 1973, I still didn't think that my deal was even on a par with his. I remember going in to see Craney about better terms at the start of the '74 season and he said to me: "Oh no, that's more than Bettsy's getting".

In my view, you can't top your team's averages and not be classed as the highest earner. It just didn't seem fair from where I was sitting.

Naturally, Terry never told me what he was earning – and neither would I have expected him to – but it hurt me some years later, after I'd left to join Poole, to discover that King's Lynn had also apparently been paying him a percentage of the gate receipts. It was a promoter from another track who passed that information on to me and I was very dismayed to hear it.

It wasn't Terry's fault he was paid more than me – he obviously asked for as much as he could get and good luck to him – but it was a bit much for me to discover later that he'd also benefited from the good crowds we attracted to Saddlebow Road in the early 70s. The Stars team had become relatively successful and more attractive, while speedway in general was enjoying a boom period, and it seemed to me that our home attendances were consistently around the 5,000 mark every Saturday at Lynn in those days. And it wasn't only Terry Betts they came to see.

Full marks to Bettsy for negotiating a cut of the gate money. He went to Lynn in 1966 not knowing whether they'd pull crowds of 500 or 15,000, so he probably accepted what the promotion first offered him and just said: 'I'll take a per centage of the attendance revenue, too', not having a clue how much that element of his deal would be worth in the future. What a brilliant decision by him that turned out to be.

My first major individual success – winning the Daily Express Spring Classic from Dave Jessup and Ole Olsen at Wimbledon in 1974. Even the green Kawasaki leathers didn't prove a jinx. But for all the acclaim I received after this well publicised win, I knew I still had to get away from Lynn.

Terry looked after his money very well, much better than I ever did, and I always say he squeaks when he walks! He never spent money on what he considered to be unnecessary items – his bikes looked rubbish compared to mine but they still went as quickly. My bikes looked 20 times better than his, but they also cost me a lot of money. That's how Terry was and his approach obviously didn't do him any harm.

I wished I'd taken as much care of my money. My problem was that I had a wife who spent it just as quickly and as easily as I did. If I'd been with June then, I would probably have retired from speedway when I did and been able to live off my on-track earnings, instead of having to continue working like I do now. June is brilliant with money but I never have been.

My ex-wife Sandra was a lot like me in that whenever we had money, she'd spend it. I'd buy anything that was going, wasting cash on trivial things for my bikes. For instance, if I spotted a little chip in one of my mudguards, I'd throw them both out and get a new set. I had to have the best looking bike . . . or the best looking leather jacket. I didn't need it, but that's how I was and I could have done with someone like June then to have curbed my extravagance.

I didn't invest any money in property either. I dread to think what the large, detached houses we used to live in, in nice Kent towns like Strood and Shorne, would be worth today if I'd owned them. They would probably be valued at around three-quarters of a million now.

Whenever I did think about buying a house, it was always difficult for me to obtain a mortgage. As a speedway rider, you are very much a high risk client and the mortgage companies were never keen to take you on. And the homes we could

Bettsy...and why I had to leave

afford weren't big enough for Sandra's liking, so we just continued to rent one place after another.

Sandra didn't work, and I never asked her to, so I was always the sole breadwinner. That was fine in the summer but it left us a bit short in the closed season, especially the way we used to spend money like it was going out of fashion.

It meant that come the start of each season, when I sat down with my promoter to thrash out a new deal, I was virtually skint and not in a good negotiating position. I couldn't afford to call anyone's bluff and sit it out hoping they would come back and offer me more – I usually had to accept the first thing they offered. It became a known fact in speedway circles that Simmo would always do a deal for the money on offer, because I always did.

I was always stupid where money was concerned, even though I was probably one of the highest paid riders in the sport during my peak years in the mid-70s. One of my favourite sayings is, 'I came into speedway with nothing and I left it with absolutely nothing!' June and I now own our house at West Kingsdown but I do still look back on my past financial mismanagement with a lot of regrets.

The subject of money, and a No.1 rider's true worth, reared its head again in a very enlightening discussion between England stars during my first season with Poole, in 1975. The England squad was on its way to a meeting abroad when the riders were all gathered together on the boat, trying to kill time. There was Ray Wilson (Leicester), Martin Ashby (Swindon), John Louis (Ipswich), Peter Collins (Belle Vue), Terry and myself all sat around drinking and chatting casually when, suddenly, the subject of riders' deals entered the conversation.

I think we were discussing what a certain move might be worth to so and so, or how much of a signing-on fee we should ask from our promoter at the start of the season. One of us suggested it would make more sense all round if we all knew what each other was earning from our respective tracks at the time, so that we'd be sure that we were receiving what we considered we were worth. In turn, we'd also then know how much – or little – we were valued by our clubs.

Anyway, we went round the table, each of us revealing our current deal in turn.

Well, Martin Ashby nearly died! It turned out he was getting about only six grand a year for signing-on at Swindon – little more than half the £11,000 up front deal I had at Poole and John Louis was on at Ipswich. Ray Wilson was getting a bit less than us, I think,

Martin Ashby wasn't laughing when money became the topic of conversation among England stars.

95

while PC was the highest earner, on £12,000. The signing on fee we received would be in addition to the standard start and points money and would normally be paid in two or three installments.

'Crash' was visibly upset by the revelation that he was being paid so much less by Swindon than his fellow No.1s were getting at other tracks, but I've always said that these differences in pay are down to the riders themselves. If only they would all get together and confer on what they are getting, instead of keeping their so-called 'super deals' to themselves, they would all enjoy one big pay day. All number one riders should earn the same money – let's face it, Martin Ashby is every bit Mister Swindon as Bettsy is Mister King's Lynn. When Briggo left the Robins at the end of 1972, 'Crash' carried the side single-handedly on many occasions and he deserved to be rewarded better than he was by the Wiltshire club.

Going back to the conversation on the boat, the only one who wouldn't put his cards on the table that day was Terry Betts. Maybe he didn't want to hurt my feelings any more, even though I was No.1 at Poole by then and very happy with my lot. When it came to his turn to spill the beans, Bettsy just started laughing and wouldn't show his hand.

"I'd better not!" he said, which I took to assume that he was earning more than any of us!

> **"The only one who wouldn't put his cards on the table that day was Terry Betts. Maybe he didn't want to hurt my feelings any more, even though I was No.1 at Poole by then and very happy with my lot"**

King's Lynn splashed out to sign Dave Jessup from Reading in 1979 – but they had no need to let Bettsy go. Watching DJ sign his new contract are, left to right, Alan Littlechild, Martin Rogers, Violet Littlechild, Cyril Crane and Peter Thurlow, whose Abbeygate company sponsored Dave. Pity I missed out on their backing years earlier.

Bettsy...and why I had to leave

My move to Poole only enhanced the on-track rivalry between Bettsy and myself, although I'd say that we became even better friends. When we lined up against each other in heat one of a Poole versus King's Lynn match, I was more desperate than ever to beat him. And the best thing about it was, he hated riding at Poole! He broke his arm there before the '74 World Final and never did like the Wimborne Road track.

Ironically, my first meeting back at Lynn as a Poole rider in 1975 was for Terry's richly deserved testimonial, an individual event which saw us finish as joint top scorers. I'd always previously loved to beat Bettsy but this was *his* day and there was no way I was going to finish anywhere other than second in that run-off with him.

Terry had another four good years with the Stars after I moved on, two of them as No.1 before he was overtaken by the rapidly emerging Michael Lee. I still say that the worst thing King's Lynn ever did was let Terry go to Reading in 1979. They paid a lot of money – £15,000 – for Dave Jessup but they could have brought DJ from Reading *and* kept Bettsy, who still had a lot to offer. Unfortunately, Terry's heart was never going to be in it with Reading and he retired after just one season with the Racers.

Lee and Jessup achieved more than Terry did on the international and World Championship scene, finishing one and two in the 1980 World Final, but no-one has ever been able to replace Bettsy in the hearts of the Lynn public.

Terry Betts was King's Lynn . . . and he still is to this day.

I left King's Kynn for the first time at the end of the 1974 season but a piece of my heart has always remained there. In March 2005 I was delighted to attend a 40th anniversary reunion of former Stars riders and, naturally, the best part of the evening (above) was meeting up with Bettsy again. It was lovely, just like old times again..

8

THE NEW BLUE-EYED BOY

A bird's eye view of me and Ipswich's John Louis, the man I succeeded as England captain, racing at Poole in 1977. We were both Weslake works-sponsored riders and wore identical leathers.

THE Poole promotion I signed for in 1975 were great people to ride for. I always dealt directly with Charles Knott when it came to my financial deal, although he'd routinely refer money matters to the more senior figure of Charles Foot, the first elected BSPA President, for him to approve before it would all be signed and sealed.

I don't know exactly how much Poole paid King's Lynn for me but my new promoters did make the point during our opening negotiations that I'd have to accept a little less than I was asking for, because they'd had to fork out a sizeable sum to bring me there. I think I received about £8,000 – a lot of money at the time – which they paid in three or four installments over the course of the year. That was about £5,000 more than I'd been getting at King's Lynn the year before – and I wouldn't have got much more if I stayed there in '75. At Poole, you couldn't go in and ask for your money before it became due but, on the other hand, the payment was never late in coming.

I didn't have a problem with the Poole management or the entire Knott family – as well as Charles, his brothers Jack and Jimmy were also co-directors, following the death of Charles senior – from day one. They were some of the nicest people I'd met. The only time I fell out with them over anything was right at the very end of their time in charge at The Stadium, which I'll come to later.

Once I'd made up my mind to leave King's Lynn for the reasons explained in the previous chapter, I set my heart on going to Poole and wasn't interested in any other club. I usually had good meetings at Poole and, in fact, I made my first move to join them during the 1974 season when I first made it known to the Poole promoters that I'd be very keen to join the Pirates. I had a quiet world with Charles Knott at Poole one night and then, when the Pirates visited Lynn later that season, I gave their team manager Tony Lewis a gentle nudge to remind him of my wish to move south. Having sown the seeds for my move, I was delighted when the transfer went through smoothly in the following close season.

While the Poole promotion never put me under any pressure to achieve great things, I put myself under extra pressure. For the first time in my career, I'd signed as a No.1 rider and, as the team I'd joined didn't have a recognised outstanding top man, I knew I had to get my average back up to at least the 10-points-a-match mark. They hadn't had a dominant 10-point man since the British League was formed in 1965, so they were obviously expecting me to produce the goods.

It didn't start well and I struggled for the first month or so, probably trying too hard to impress and live up to my own expectations. But I soon learned the quickest way round the track. Pete Smith was the long-established skipper and that was fine by me – I didn't ask for nor expect to be given the captaincy. My new team-mates

The new blue-eyed boy

The Pirates of 1975, my first year at Poole. Back row, left to right: Charles Knott jnr, Eric Broadbelt, Colin Gooddy, Neil Cameron, Pete Smith, Tony Lewis. Front: Neil Middleditch, myself and Christer Sjosten.

were all very welcoming and I immediately felt at home.

Everything was good about Poole – still is, in my opinion, now that Matt Ford is at the helm – and I was obviously delighted to finish my first season there as an undisputed No.1 with a CMA of 10.41, and 15 full and one paid maximum to my name. Almost overnight, I had moved up into the superstar class. I thrived on the adulation from the local people and didn't mind the fact that I was often virtually carrying the team single-handedly, especially away from home.

The Poole supporters took me to their hearts and I loved the attention – the sight of all those blue-and-white 'Super Simmo' sun visors on car windscreens as the traffic made its way to The Stadium on Wednesday nights gave my ego a big boost. The fans always appreciated the best efforts of the away riders too. If you had a really good race and were beaten by an opponent, they stood up and clapped, because they'd been treated to a good race.

Not that we gave the Pirates fans anything to cheer about when it came to winning trophies. Apart from the 1969 BL title, no other major honours found their way to Poole and we didn't win anything of note in my six seasons with the club. The team for 1976, when we finished 10th in the table, hadn't changed from my first season in the skull-and-crossbones racejacket, when we ended up as low as 15th. Ninth place – in my last season there in 1980 – was the highest we managed to finish in the BL during all my time on the south coast.

The promoters didn't seem all that bothered whether we challenged for the league championships and cups, as long as we weren't at the bottom of the table and they were drawing big crowds, which they always did. Attendances of around 5,000 were the norm.

SIMMO

I must admit, as much as I would've liked to have been part of another championship-chasing team again, it didn't unduly bother me that we never progressed beyond being a mid-table outfit. I was more interested in personal glory – a selfish attitude, but it's true.

I'm not saying I wouldn't help my team-mates with the loan of my bikes when needed, and I'd certainly try and team-ride my partner home to a 5-1 where possible, but I never became obsessed about winning league titles and cups.

I still won my share of individual trophies along the way, though. Poole's plum meeting of the year was their annual Blue Riband, which I won in each of my first four seasons as Pirates' top rider. I was proud to be the first home rider to win it – in front of a 7,000 crowd. The winner usually received a good quality television, or some other electrical goods worth decent money, and after I'd won it for the third time, Charles Knott said to me: "Just tell me what prize you want us to get for you!" I told him I didn't need another telly, thanks all the same!

Charles – I always called him by his proper name, never 'Charlie' – was good with the riders and would just let us get on with it. Occasionally, to try and spice up the pre-meeting parade lap a bit, we'd suggest different things to him. For instance, one week we'd go out on to the track in pairs, and another time the home riders would form the shape of an arrowhead. He appreciated those simple, little ideas. With its family feel and the multi-coloured 'fairy' lights lining the stadium, there was always a great atmosphere about the place.

The 1977 team, just days before Kevin Holden was killed. Back row, left to right: Richard May, Colin Gooddy, Christer Sjosten, Pete Smith and myself. Front: Eric Broadbelt, Neil Middleditch, Kevin and the mascot.

The new blue-eyed boy

I suppose our team manager, Tony Lewis, typified the laid-back approach at Poole. A super bloke, and a useful rider himself in the 60s, but he didn't have the get up and go in him to be a successful team manager. He wasn't strong enough with the riders. There were times, when we were racing away, I'd score more points than the rest of the team put together. To be honest, I quite liked being the outstanding one and the acclaim that went with it, but there were times when some of the others should have been hauled over the coals for their poor performances, but nothing was ever said by Tony. We never had a dressing room chat to try and get a bit extra out of the boys and the promoters wouldn't interfere either.

Jack Knott would be up in the announcer's box on race nights, reading out the results and winning race times with a calm authority . . . and clearly enjoying his favourite tipple! Sometimes he'd have a few scotches too many and you'd hear him slurring a bit but it was all part of Poole Speedway's charm. The third brother, Jim, was just as nice as the others and while he didn't seem to do much on race nights, he was always present to lend moral support.

Charles Foot left Charles Knott to run the track and it was, for me, a super set-up, I really loved the place. I could talk to Charles Knott about anything and, after a while, he became like a father figure to me. I knew when it was time to discuss my financial deal for the following season, because he'd always phone me in the first week of January and, in a quiet, well spoken voice, say: "Can you please pop down for a couple of hours?". But it was never a couple of hours. I'd walk into his office, tell him how much I wanted and then he'd go and make his usual courtesy call to Charles Foot. He'd return a couple of minutes later and say: "That's OK." And that was it – all done in quarter-of-an hour. He never played hardball with me over terms – I think they increased my signing-on fee to 10 grand in 1976 – and I'd come out of our meetings thinking that I'd undersold myself!

It wasn't always fun at Poole, though. I'd seen Dave Wills killed at West Ham and was riding at Poole the night, in April 1977 against Reading in the KO Cup, when team-mate Kevin Holden lost his life in an accident at Wimborne Road. It was such a dreadful shame and his fall so innocuous. Kevin didn't crash badly, he just slid into the kickboard at the end of the straight while trying to go round Bob Humphreys. Anybody else, at any other time, would have just got up and dusted himself down but Kevin didn't move and was gone before the ambulance even arrived on the scene.

A post-mortem showed that he had ruptured his aorta – the main artery that leads to the heart – and that may explain why he simply just slid into the fence without turning at the end of the home straight. Maybe he actually died before he reached the safety fence? Married with two kids, Kevin had recently joined us from Exeter and while I soon found him to be a nice lad who had shown plenty of promise in the few meetings we'd ridden in together, I didn't have the chance to get to know him properly before fate intervened.

With its long straights and tight corners, the fast Poole track didn't please everyone – Terry Betts for one – but it never, ever concerned me. The old-shaped track was very tight going into the corners – especially the third and fourth turns, where you could easily run into the fence – and it took some getting used to.

During my time there, the wire mesh fencing on the bends was later replaced by solid, wooden boards but I see pro's and cons in both set-ups. There's always the risk of getting your footrest caught in the wire fencing but, then again, you can bounce, or glance back off, the boards and sometimes even continue to race without falling. With a solid fence it depends so much on how you hit it. Take King's Lynn, which has always been regarded as one of the finest and fairest tracks in the country – and yet look how many riders have been killed there compared to many other tracks.

Wire mesh or solid boards, it never really worried me either way. The only time I ever got into any real trouble on the Poole track was when other riders put me in it. Halifax came down one night in 1978 and every time I went to go round Craig Pendlebury he would run me right up to the fence.

I got so annoyed that I forced Pendlebury into the pit gate as we made our way back in after the race. He got off his bike, looking all agitated, and all I remember is my team-mate, Kelvin Mullarkey, diving between us and really laying into Pendlebury. I think Neil Middleditch had to restrain Kelvin while I just walked away and left them all to it!

Middlo had his first full season with Poole in '75, while doubling up with second division Eastbourne in the National League. He has given the club great service over a very long period, as both rider and now team manager, and Poole Speedway is in his blood, especially as his father Ken was such a big favourite there in the 50s and 60s. Neil, like Mullarkey and Martin Yeates, were stars in the NL and benefited from top flight experience with us.

It was tough attending the funeral of Christer Sjosten, seen here leading Hackney's Zenon Plech.

The new blue-eyed boy

Eric Broadbelt and myself representing Poole in the 1976 BL Best Pairs Championship at Ipswich.

The fence at Poole – and most other places – was like a magnet to our Czech, Vaclav Verner, who could be so wild that no-one in the team wanted to ride with him. And I believe he'd calmed down a lot since his Exeter days! I was just glad that I was a consistently better trapper than him!

Kevin Holden wasn't the only team-mate we lost through tragic circumstances. I got on ever so well with Christer Sjosten, a talented and spectacular little rider, and it was very sad for me to be Poole's representative at his funeral in Sweden after he'd been killed in a crash at Brisbane at the end of 1979. We were all saddened by his loss but probably none more so than his elder brother, the more famous Belle Vue and Swedish star Soren Sjosten. Soren used to drink a lot but I think the death of his younger brother only hastened his own demise.

Eric Broadbelt, who had been Poole's top rider the year before I arrived and gave me most solid support in my first two seasons at Wimborne Road was . . . well, Eric. He was a fruitcake! He had a number of bad crashes and I wondered at times, like the night he struck a lamp standard going down the straight at Poole – how he got up from them, let alone go on and fulfil a long career. Eric could have been a good eight-point rider but he seemed forever recovering from one injury after another. He was spectacular, lovely to watch – but Christ, he would be hanging off the fence a lot of the time.

Colin Gooddy, who was ever such a nice bloke, reminded me of Ken McKinlay – an old hand, who remained faithful to his JAP and liked to get up to the bar as soon as the meeting had finished! 'Joe' – as everyone knew him – was not so much a cheat as a great anticipator at the start, and he would usually be first away.

Proving that I did team-ride at Poole – this time with Pete Smith (also below) on my outside.

"He never showed any resentment towards me after becoming Poole's new No.1 and, accordingly, I didn't really want to take his job as captain"

In fact, whenever we met in the second half, I'd always watch his clutch hand – rather than the tapes – in trying to make a fast start. I knew that if I watched his hand, I had a chance of passing him going into the first corner, whereas if I watched the tapes, he'd leave me standing. It was good to be partnered with Joe though, and we won a best pairs meeting at Poole in '75.

I also got on fine with Pete Smith, who had a lot of engine troubles when I first joined Poole and even went into temporary retirement, which meant I took over the captaincy. He never showed any resentment towards me after becoming Poole's new No.1 and, accordingly, I didn't really want to take his job as captain. I wouldn't have called Pete a motivator but, then again, in my first two years at Poole, he probably spent much of that time trying to solve what seemed like continuous mechanical problems. When you are bogged down with your own problems, it's difficult to think about others. He had been with Poole since 1962, led

The new blue-eyed boy

Rumours of a rift between me and Ron Preston (above and below) were way off the mark.

them to that one and only BL title seven years later and was awarded a richly deserved testimonial in 1976.

Richard May was a loner and liked to spend time by himself, so I found it difficult to get to know him. The same could be said of our first American, Mike Curoso, who was an unusual character. He and his wife were a bit, well, hippyish, and into strange foods and other alternative stuff. Mike was fine but it wasn't easy to get to know him.

It's always been claimed that I never got on with our second American signing, Ron Preston, who joined us the year after Curoso, in 1979, but I don't know how or why that rumour started. Perhaps people thought that I'd resent the threat of him challenging for my No.1 spot but I never thought he would – not at that time anyway. He'd beat me occasionally in second half races but I consistently came out on top.

The rumours of a rift between us sparked from the night that our home track was a bit iffy and, completely by accident, Preston fell while we were racing each other in the second half. We'd gone into the corner together, on a really slippery surface,

107

SIMMO

The Pirates of 1978, Left to right: Martin Yeates, Andrzej Tkocz, Neil Middleditch, myself, Tony Lewis, Colin Gooddy, Mike Curoso and Christer Sjosten.

and I slid towards the fence, he hit it . . . and I didn't.

From that day on, some people suggested that I couldn't handle him trying to take over my No.1 mantle at Poole but that never entered my mind. I never considered him as a threat, I welcomed his arrival and especially the fact that he gave me stronger support than anybody else had done at Poole. We never showed any ill feeling towards each other, we got on fine, and it was just other people who put two and two together and came up with five. What happened that night on an icy track surface was purely a racing accident and soon forgotten by both Ron and myself. The Poole track had a chalk base and it became awfully slimy when it was wet.

A personal highlight of a wonderful first season as a Pirate would have been the home and away maximums I scored against King's Lynn, when I was obviously determined to prove a point – the 39-39 draw at Saddlebow Road was particularly satisfying.

While new teenage sensation Michael Lee was effectively my replacement at Lynn from the start of '75, another new signing for the Stars that season was the controversial character, Garry Middleton. I could tell you some stories about this crazy Aussie character, but I'll keep it clean...

One day we were travelling together in his car to an open meeting in Germany, when he suddenly whipped out an impressively large trophy. I thought it was something he'd won at a recent meeting – until I realised he'd had it especially engraved with his name on it proclaimed as the winner . . . 'winner' of the meeting we were on our way to! Garry couldn't see the harm in what he'd done and just glibly said: "If I don't win the meeting, no-one at home will be any the wiser once they see my trophy!"

Loud and lairy, he was never shy of self-promotion and acquired the nickname

The new blue-eyed boy

'Cass' for shooting his mouth off in the style of Muhammad Ali. He would do just about anything to try and further his career.

On another occasion, I heard that Garry and Barry Briggs had been racing against each other in a continental meeting somewhere or other and Briggo asked Garry if he would take his bike back home in his van. I think Briggo had arranged to fly off to another meeting and would only be driving a short distance to the nearest airport and then heading for another destination, leaving Middleton alone to drive on ahead with their machinery.

Anyway, Garry had gone some way down the autobahn when curiosity got the better of him and he pulled over at a service area . . . to take Briggo's engine apart! Barry had just beaten him in the meeting, so 'Cass' was determined to find out the secret of the legendary Kiwi's success. He had Barry's engine in bits in the back of his van and was examining everything in fine detail when, suddenly, Briggo drove up behind him and caught him red-handed! I'm not sure what Briggo said or did but it's a story that sums up Garry Middleton.

I'm sure he wouldn't have discovered anything 'special' at all about Briggo's engine – he just couldn't accept the simple and obvious explanation that Barry was a better rider than him.

Another time, Middleton had to be shown out of Cradley Heath Speedway under police escort, after he'd pulled a gun on the home rider Roy Trigg in the pits. I don't know whether the gun was loaded but it sure had Triggy worried and the police were called.

Mauger turning point

A key turning point for me in my development as a top rider came from spending some time with Ivan Mauger while visiting Australia. I'd never spent much time with Ivan before then – he lived up near Manchester and I was down here in Kent, so we only ever really met up at meetings when we were invariably racing against each other.

But I got to know him a bit better when we were both riding in Perth during the English winter of 1974-75. We'd chat occasionally during meetings and when we met up at one or two functions. We didn't discuss my riding technique, it was all about my attitude and how that needed to change if I was ever going to fulfil my potential on the world stage.

Gate one has always been a big advantage at Poole.

109

Ivan talks about himself so much that it is bound to rub off on you, providing you listen and take in what he's saying.

I had always thought that I was good on preparation but Ivan pointed out that I needed to spend more time on minor preparation – on things like setting up the clutch. He gave me some very useful pointers there. For instance, in those days, clutches used to come encased in a cage with a bearing, but Ivan would throw that out and insert a complete set of bearings, which made his clutch run more smoothly.

He took all of the oil seals out of the countershafts and the wheels, so that they, too, ran that much more smoothly. He never used grease – only oil. They were just little things really but they all added up to give him that extra edge over the rest of us. And because he could trap so well, that extra mile or two per hour meant he would just pull away from the chasing pack.

It was an eye-opener being so close to Ivan for a couple of months. He told me to focus a lot more on my mental attitude to racing, making the point that if I really wanted to be the best, I had to *think* very positively. He told me that the biggest problem with English riders was that we lived at home and therefore didn't have to put ourselves out. He said that we had it too easy and just didn't put enough into becoming the best. He was right. And I still say now, even after those enlightening conversations with Ivan, that I still didn't put enough into my speedway – I could have done a lot more.

> "I still say now, even after those enlightening conversations with Ivan, that I still didn't put enough into my speedway – I could have done a lot more"

Not equipment-wise, because I think I spent more money than anybody making sure I had the best equipment

Ask Ivan to show you his medals and he's always had more than anyone – as me and Peter Collins found out.

The new blue-eyed boy

and that I kept it looking great. The only aspect of my machinery that Ivan criticised was my handlebars, which were the Ole Olsen's patented bars made by Renthal. But I think he said that more for commercial reasons – Ivan had his own style of Renthal handlebars in competition to Olsen's! There was only a slight difference between the two – Ivan's were flatter – but because I was as tall as Ole, I found his bars more comfortable than Ivan's.

I should've put more of myself into it, been more single-minded. To become the speedway World Champion you have to have tunnel vision and although I did put a lot into trying to be the best, it still wasn't enough. I'm not saying bikes weren't my life – they were. But I should have ridden a lot more often than I did. I should have taken the trouble to get bookings on the continental grasstracks, instead of sitting on my arse at home. I'd be in the garage tinkering with my bikes when I should have been out somewhere riding them.

I used to moan and groan about not having as many sponsors as I thought I deserved, which was nowhere near as much as Ivan used to get. But, as he again pointed out, we English riders didn't used to put ourselves out as much as he did. John Davis was probably the English exception to that rule. He'd get just as much sponsorship as Ivan but he was only half the rider Ivan was. John – and Simon Wigg after him – used to get in front of big sponsors and tell them all how good they were. They actually believed they were as good as they claimed to be, but I could never do that. I was never a bullshitter and would let my riding do the talking for me, but that didn't do much to help me attract top sponsors. I could have got a lot more if I'd put myself out more and not been the lazy so and so I was.

They say you're never too old to learn and even in my first season at Poole, I was still learning plenty myself. I was right up close behind Coventry legend Nigel Boocock on the back straight at Brandon one night and there was no doubt that I was going to pass him. But just as I was lining up to go by him on the inside, Nigel's left hand went out and up a little bit – nothing dramatic, but enough to make me think, 'shit, his engine's stopped'. It meant I had to shut off or go wide, so I drifted out to go round him . . . only to see him disappear into the distance.

When we got back in the pits, I said: "What was the problem there, then Booey? Did your motor cut out?"

In his Yorkshire accent, he replied: "No, rider . . . I was just telling you I was turning left!"

"You bastard!" I laughed, managing to see the funny side of it.

Booey always called everyone 'rider' – he didn't seem to know anyone's name!

But it was a trick I learned and I got Bruce Cribb with it once at Cradley. I could hear him coming up behind me – you could hear Cribby easily because he was always on the gas and his motors revved so hard – and I just did going into the corner, what Booey had done to me at Coventry previously. The next thing, as I went round the corner, I could see Cribby going across the centre green, having taken evasive action to avoid me!

I'd already laid the foundations for the trick move by telling him in the pits beforehand how I'd been having trouble with my engines when using Duckhams

Oil, and that I'd be switching back to castor oil. I warned him: "If I put my hand up during the race, you know my engine's about to seize."

It's true what they say, though, about never being too old to learn. When Barry Briggs came out of retirement again and signed for Hull Vikings in 1976, I told him he was being a prat for coming back, that he was too old and wouldn't be able to hack it. Poole went to Hull and I beat Briggo twice – and to rub it in, I taunted him as we went down the straight at The Boulevard by waving him on.

The following week, Hull were riding at Poole . . . and Briggo beat me in heat one! I felt ever so humiliated, brought back down to earth with a bang. Another lesson learned. Still, we got over it and are still good friends today.

It was in my first season with Poole that the four-valve revolution began. Newport's Australian star Phil Crump, who had briefly been a team-mate of mine at King's Lynn, set the ball rolling with his Neil Street Jawa conversion and then the English Weslake appeared and took over from the old two-valve Jawa. I would soon enjoy a lot of success on the Weslake but I should have switched to them earlier than I did.

I made a big mistake before my first World Final in 1975. My Jawas had been going really well in the build up to the big night at Wembley, until I hit a problem with my magneto during practice on the Thursday. Ron Valentine – who designed the Weslake and who I'd known for years because he used to tune my 250 grasstrack engines – visited me at home that night. He'd heard I'd had a few problems at practice and suggested I should change to the Weslake for the World Final itself, two days later.

> **"I would soon enjoy a lot of success on the Weslake but I should have switched to them earlier than I did... I made a big mistake before my first World Final in 1975"**

I had never even ridden a Weslake

Talking to Ivan Mauger improved my psychological approach and one of the positives to come out of my move to Poole was finally conquering a phobia about Exeter. Here I am leading Falcons' Steve Reinke.

The new blue-eyed boy

before and with the biggest meeting of the year less than 48 hours away, I was very reluctant to take such a drastic step on the eve of my World Final debut. Ron tried to convince me that what he was offering was simply quicker than my Jawa. He had three engines

The Weslake gave me a smooth, fast ride.

with him that he said I was welcome to borrow for use at Wembley.

I pointed out that I hadn't had a chance to even use the engine before, let alone set it up to suit my needs and to make good starts – there were very few of the new motors around at the time. In the end I said I'd only take the Weslakes off him if he gave them to me, but he only wanted to loan them, so I said 'no' and told him he should have approached me two weeks earlier.

If I'd been unhappy with my Jawas I would have accepted his offer, but it was still a mistake to turn him down. I should have tried the Weslake at Wembley, where I scored 10 points on my Jawa, because it was definitely better, but I decided to stick with the Czech engines for the rest of that season. I think John Louis, who did well to finish third behind Ole Olsen and Anders Michanek, and Ray Wilson were the only two riders who rode them at that World Final.

I used a firm near me in Ashford, called Piper, to take care of my cylinder heads and provide cams. I kept what they did for me a closely guarded secret, because other top riders were sniffing around wanting to know what I had that made my engines go so well. The most inquisitive among them was Ivan Mauger and although I could never quite be sure, I think he somehow managed to prise where I got my cams from my mechanic and manager, Ken Beckett. All I know is, Ivan then started to get his cams from the same supplier as me!

You don't want to let on to other riders some of the trade secrets, if you can help it, especially when it comes to mechanical things. But, Ivan being Ivan, he was very persistent and I guess he must have worn Ken down – even if Ken didn't intentionally reveal our source. Ivan could see that I had something going really good and, understandably, he wanted the best for himself. To be fair, though, Ivan helped me to change the course of my career.

It had been a brilliant first season for me at Poole and after reaching my first individual World Final, as well as appearing in England's World Team Cup-winning side at Norden, Germany, I couldn't wait for 1976.

It turned out to be the best – and worst – year of my career.

9

TURNING UP THE HEAT
1976-77

Katowice, where I rode in front of more than 100,000 fans at the 1976 World Final, was always one of my favourite tracks. But, looking back, I'm gutted to have finished runner-up to Peter Collins that day.

SIMMO

THE long, hot summer of '76 holds many great memories for so many people in British speedway but the one who must cherish that year most of all is Peter Collins. I recall it as my most successful season but to this day I feel it should have ended with me winning the World Championship instead of the Belle Vue youngster PC.

I rode very well in the World Final at Katowice – as well as I possibly could under the circumstances – but I couldn't stop PC passing me in our race and going on to win the title. I'd got the better of Peter most times we met throughout that season – both before and after the final in Poland – but he did it on the day that really mattered.

Most people will say that I should feel proud to have finished second in the World – and I suppose I am. It was, after all, my greatest achievement in the sport. But who really remembers the rider who finishes second? I know I was good enough to win that World Final and I still blame the Weslake Engineering factory for the fact that I didn't. If that sounds very ungrateful from a rider who enjoyed a tremendous works sponsorship deal from the English engine manufacturer (in association with Gulf Oil), then let me explain the background and what really happened in the build-up to the final . . .

The 1976 season, my second with Poole, went brilliantly right from the start. After declining the eleventh hour offer from Weslake to switch from Jawa to their new four-valve engine for the 1975 World Final at Wembley, I was delighted to secure a full works sponsorship deal with the fledgling Rye (Sussex)-based company headed by Michael Daniels. My England colleagues John Louis and Peter Collins also had new backing from Weslake, although PC's agreement saw him receive all his engines and parts via the northern-based tuner Dave Nourish, who prepared Peter's motors for him. I always preferred to look after my own engines.

I'd never been considered much of a wet track rider, so I was pleased to win the first big individual meeting of the season, the Internationale at Wimbledon, an annual Whit Bank Holiday Monday showpiece event that still attracted a world class field back then. The meeting was delayed while the Plough Lane track staff tried to fix the damage inflicted by the rain and, on a track full of sawdust to soak up the surface water, I came out on top, ahead of youngsters Chris Morton and Michael Lee.

Although England suffered a shock defeat by Australia and were eliminated from the World Team Cup at the UK round stage (see next chapter), Louis and myself won the World Pairs semi-final at Miskolc, Hungary and then the final, at Eskilstuna, Sweden.

My form earned me a second crack at the Golden Helmet, which needed two new

Turning up the heat

British semi-final winner at Leicester, ahead of Ipswich's John Louis and Swindon's Bob Kilby.

challengers after the holder, Tommy Jansson, had been tragically killed during the Swedish Final in Stockholm. I'd been beaten over two legs by Swindon's Martin Ashby in the first month of the season but I was flying by mid-summer and was given another chance to defeat the brothers, Dave and Chris Morton, in successive months. I only lost my grip on the match-race title when the BSPA stripped me of it after failing to go to Newport to take on the local hero, Phil Crump, in September. I told them I was in bed suffering the 'flu, but I had no intention of travelling to south Wales to ride on what was then the most dangerous track in Britain.

In the individual World Championship, I hardly put a wheel out of place. After scoring a maximum in my British qualifying round at King's Lynn, I finished ahead of Bob Kilby and John Louis (the only man to beat me) to win the British semi-final at Leicester and then went forward to Coventry and won the British Final with another maximum 15. The meeting at Brandon, where only the top five riders qualified for the Inter-Continental Final, was probably the toughest all season in England but everything went right for me on the night and it provides some of my most treasured memories.

I unveiled a flashy, all-white set of leathers for the occasion but I can't say I went to Coventry full of confidence or even thinking I would win the coveted British Championship. The scramble for places to the next round meant it was always a nervy, cut-throat meeting – one machine failure, tape exclusion or fall could spell elimination. I did get nervous before the big meetings, which probably stemmed from a lack of self-confidence. It was around this time that I started seeing a hypnotist, who would help me focus more clearly on what I needed to do and give me some inner-belief. Lining up against the likes of Mauger, Olsen or Peter Collins in a straight one-to-one battle never bothered me, I always believed I could beat them hands down. But for some reason, I don't know why, I used to get nervous and uptight if I found myself facing *three* top riders together in the same race.

I first visited a hypnotist while in Australia around 1974-75. I got to thinking that one town – Christchurch – in a little country like New Zealand had produced three multi-world champions in Ivan, Briggo and Ronnie Moore, so I wondered why that was and whether there was anything mystical in it? Perhaps there was a hidden force behind the legendary Kiwi trio who had mopped up 12 individual world titles between them? Then Ole Olsen came along, learnt under Ivan and he too started winning world titles. Anyway, I tried it and found that it helped me in that first year. I did begin to feel more confident and able to overcome my nerves. I went two or three times again later on in my career and even recommended a hypnotist to John Davis, after I signed him at King's Lynn in 1988. John used to suffer from the same mental block as me and I definitely think a lack of confidence was one of my downfalls at times. It's a fine line between confidence and arrogance and there were definitely times throughout my career when I became too uptight before big races.

Even after I'd beaten PC in my opening ride – heat three – of the 1976 British Final, I didn't start to believe I'd actually win the meeting, which was televised by the BBC. I got the better of Louis second time out, in heat five, and made it three wins out of three by leading home Chris Morton in heat 11. My toughest of the five rides that night was against Sheffield's Doug Wyer, who was the only other rider unbeaten on nine points when we met in heat 16. We raced elbow-to-elbow to the first corner and the advantage of starting from gate one paid off as I just eased Wyer aside around the first turn to move on to 12 points.

> **"To win the British Final was great but it wasn't all down to me . . . After collecting the trophy I handed the winner's cheque straight to Ken, as a gesture of my appreciation"**

I knew I needed to win my last race, heat 18, to clinch the British title, while second place would have at least guaranteed me a run-off for the title against any one of Wyer, PC and Chris Morton who all had 11 points going into heat 19. I led my last ride all the way from Dave Jessup, John Davis and Jimmy McMillan and was grateful that it wasn't my clutch that I thought I could smell burning as I completed the four laps and my biggest success in speedway. Mort, Wyer and PC all joined me on the rostrum at the end, along with Louis who won the last race to clinch the fifth, and last, qualifying berth for the ICF at Wembley. Jessup's second spot behind me in our last outing cost him a run-off with Louis for the last qualifying place.

To win the British Final with a maximum was great but it wasn't all down to me. My Weslakes were going beautifully and I also had my mechanic, Ken Beckett, to thank for his help in the pits. After collecting the impressively large trophy – actually, they'd spelt the title of the meeting incorrectly, the silverware being inscribed as the 'British Championsip' without the third 'h' – I handed the winner's cheque straight to Ken, as a gesture of my appreciation. It was something I did occasionally by way of thanks and after this notable victory it was clear to me that I'd need even more back-up and support from my friend.

Turning up the heat

HOW THE BRITISH CHAMPIONSHIP WAS WON... IN PICTURES

Looking relaxed on the British Final parade with Hackney's Dave Morton and Chris Pusey of Halifax.

I wanted to keep my nice, new white leathers as clean as possible, so good starts were more important than ever. Here I am leading heat three from Bob Kilby and Peter Collins, with Dave Morton the man down.

119

SIMMO

Taking control of heat 11 from the inside, with Chris Morton leading the chase and George Hunter and Chris Pusey behind.

Heat 16 – my toughest race – and I just manage to come out on top in this elbow-to-elbow duel on the inside with Doug Wyer, with Reg Wilson and Bettsy out wide on the first turn at Brandon.

Turning up the heat

Another view of heat 16, after I'd held off Dougie Wyer going into the first corner.

The clincher – beating old friend and rival Dave Jessup in heat 18 to complete my maximum. At one stage, I thought I could smell my clutch burning out but, fortunately, my Weslake held together for all four laps.

SIMMO

Home and dry . . . I'm British Champion, in front of a massive Coventry crowd.

The taste of success . . . John Louis, Chris Morton and Doug Wyer wait to see if I've left them any champers.

Turning up the heat

Celebrating in the Coventry pits with some of the fabulous Poole fans who made the long trip . . .

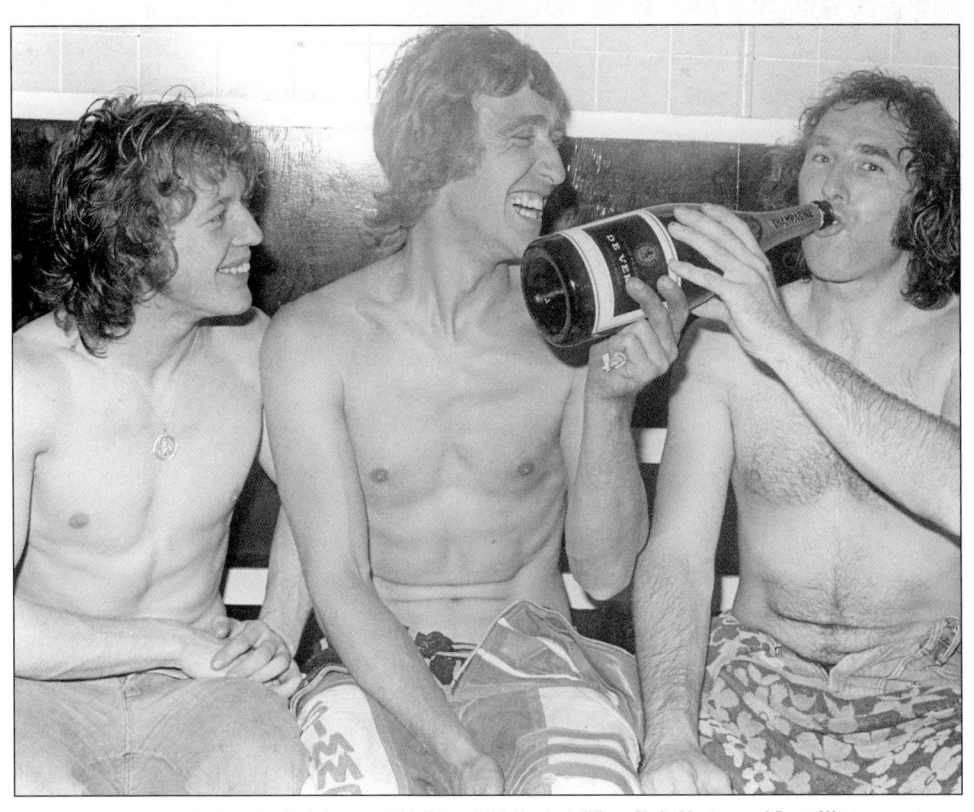

. . . and sharing the dressing room bubbly with fellow qualifiers Chris Morton and Doug Wyer.

Ken Beckett gets to work in the pits before the '76 British Final.

A London black cab driver with a typical Cockney wit and 'ladies man' smoothness about him, Ken and I met years earlier, during my racing days at West Ham. He followed me to King's Lynn in 1968 and was my regular spanner-man and chauffeur for years. We shared a lot of laughs over the years, as well as a few downs when meetings didn't go as well as we'd both hoped, but we remained firm friends until he and his wife Anne emigrated to Perth, Western Australia, in the early 80s. Ken and I had a little system going in the pits, where he had certain responsibilities – like turning on the ignition box – and I had mine, such as switching on the fuel taps. Occasionally I'd forget my job and when the bike stopped after a lap or so, I'd come back in the pits and go off at Ken! We never fell out, though. We stuck to our agreed pact that any cross words said between us during the meeting would be forgotten as soon as we left the stadium.

I would drive to most of my meetings in England, although Ken always drove home, because I'd usually be feeling tired by then. Ken, who lived just a few miles from me, liked country and western music and, as I was never too fussed what we had playing on the car stereo – ELO were probably my favourite band – this is what we usually listened to. I could appreciate Ken's choice in music – I was nearly always asleep anyway, so it didn't bother me – but not his occasional liking for foul-smelling cigars! They didn't half stink, though, and I hated him smoking them.

Becoming British Champion meant that the invites to individual, open meetings and guest bookings came flooding in, so I 'promoted' Ken to the new combined role of manager, mechanic and chauffeur and employed him full-time for around £200 a week. Having a prestige title meant I could charge a higher appearance fee and

Turning up the heat

Leading Bengt Jansson and Billy Sanders (above) at Wembley in the Inter-Continental Final and (below) ahead of Doug Wyer. It was another meeting I should have won but for a mechanical mishap.

having Ken around more helped to ease much of the day-to-day burden, allowing me to concentrate more on what I did on the track and in the workshop.

Ken would clean the bikes and then drive them to meetings abroad, while I'd usually be riding somewhere in England and then fly out the next day to meet up with him at the track. In those days, going to and from an Iron Curtain country like Poland could be anything but smooth and Ken was once arrested by border guards for taking Polish zlotys out of their country. Not that he made much of an effort to conceal the notes – the guard could easily spot them in the top pocket of Ken's shirt! They even banged Ken up in a nearby jail for the night but he was freed the next day and had learned his lesson.

That sweltering summer rolled on to Wembley, where temperatures and pulses soared even higher for the penultimate round of the World Championship. I would have won this meeting, too, but ended up with 11 points and fourth place after

SIMMO

going from first to last while leading PC in one ride. We couldn't work out what had happened to my engine – it was probably nothing more than a bit of dirt in the carburettor, because it was only a momentary stoppage, although enough to cost me the race win and the three points that would have made me Inter-Continental Champion. Peter led the eight qualifiers from Wembley to the World Final in Poland but I was still as confident as possible going into the big one at Katowice.

My relationship with Weslake had been great until just before the World Final. Although they did the big-ends on my engines, and supplied any parts I needed, I did all the basic maintenance, service and tuning of the motors myself. They didn't pay their sponsored riders any money – the sponsorship was in the form of engines and any parts that we needed. I suppose it was worth around 10 grand a season to me at that time, which was a lot of money.

Having said that, I felt that John Louis was favoured a little more than me by Weslake. He signed his factory deal before me and one instance stood out which led me to believe that John was getting slightly preferential treatment. Weslake brought out a new cam but no-one could get it going well. I offered to test it in second halves for them, to see if I could find the solution to their problem, and after three or four weeks of experimenting with the timings, and a lot of effort, I felt I'd got it going really well. But when I gave my feedback to Weslake, they told me that they were no longer concerned about developing that particular cam and would instead turn their attention to improving another one. That was fine by me – but then I found out later, through John himself, that they had given him the same cam to use that had previously been in my engine. John hadn't known that but I thought it was a bit sneaky of Weslake, who subsequently admitted to me they were looking to John for a second opinion.

> "I was immediately unhappy at the thought of handing over my motors, which I prided myself on maintaining, to a stranger at a factory who had no real knowledge of how I'd set them up specifically to my requirements"

But apart from that, and some other niggly little things, Weslake were great for me. Well, everything was fine until I received a call from the factory to say they needed all three of my engines back so that they could give them a complete overhaul before I went off to Poland. I was immediately unhappy at the thought of handing over my motors, which I prided myself on maintaining, to a stranger at a factory who had no real knowledge of how I'd set them up specifically to my requirements. I used to lighten some of the inner parts, which gave them slightly different characteristics to the bog standard motors Weslake sold to everyone. My form all season, highlighted by the Internationale and British Championship successes, proved just how well I'd got my engines going and the last thing I needed now, entering this crucial phase of the season, was for anyone to tamper with them unnecessarily.

In the end, I more or less had to go along with Weslake's wishes. After telling the chief engineer, Ron Valentine, that I didn't want to send back my engines, he put me on to the top man, Mike Daniels, who insisted that I did. Daniels basically issued me with an ultimatum: either return the engines for his blokes to prepare for me, or

Turning up the heat

My Weslakes were going great until the factory took them back to carry out an overhaul before the World Final.

I'd lose my works sponsorship. While they were happy for me to have tuned and maintained my engines all season, they wanted to make sure they wouldn't break down at the World Final.

I just couldn't afford to chuck away the best sponsorship deal of my life, so I co-operated with great reluctance. They went over everything at the factory and gave all three engines back to me to test at Poole in the week of the World Final.

And all three were absolute rubbish.

My worst fears had been realised. None of the three motors ran anything like as fast or as good as they had done before the guys at the factory laid their hands on them. I was furious. I phoned the Weslake factory from Poole and told them that I'd be driving all three engines straight to their door that same night with the instruction that they had to sort them out – fast. It was the early hours of the morning, and no-one was around when I drove in through the factory gates at Rye, so I just left the engines outside their back door with my handwritten note pinned to them that read: "These are the biggest load of crap I've ever ridden – FIX IT!"

Weslake chief Michael Daniels gave me an ultimatum.

To ensure that they would have to strip them right down, and not just gloss over a few parts, I grabbed handfuls of sand – which was lying on the dog track at Poole – and deliberately threw it into the inlet ports. It was the only way I could be sure that they took every bit of those engines apart and rebuilt them properly, as I'd had them running before they took them back off me.

127

The five Englishman who reached the 1976 World Final enjoyed great support from the thousands of British fans who made the long trip to Poland by air, sea, road and train.

Weslake had very little time to put them right, because I was leaving for Poland the next day. Of course, despite all their assurances, the engines I took to the World Final were still not as good as I'd had them running all season. Nothing like it. They sent me to Katowice with engines that were ultra reliable and were going to finish five races. But I had lightened certain parts in my engines and used different timings that I'd worked out for myself during the season, to make them go that extra bit faster. We did try playing around with them in the pits but there is only so much you can do to an engine in that situation – the real work is done beforehand in the workshop. We got them going a little bit better as the meeting progressed but never as good as they were.

I couldn't blame anyone but myself, though, for finishing second to Phil Crump in my opening ride, heat four. I had a nervous reaction on the start line and missed the gate something rotten. I was third for a long time, until I got underneath the Russian, Vladimir Gordeev, and pushed him wide.

It all came down to my clash with Peter Collins in heat seven. As I said, I'd beaten him consistently all year, I made the start on him in Poland, I was riding good and I was in front.

He was third or fourth at one stage in our race but, somehow, he managed to pass everyone and win that race. We know PC was a tremendously skilful and fast racer, of course, but he came by me down the home straight like I was standing still. PC passed me even though I didn't put a foot wrong.

Having said that, I did leave him a little too much room – thanks to mistaken

Turning up the heat

Chris Morton and me about to get wet on parade.

identity. The Pole in that race, Jerzy Rembas, had similar coloured leathers to the orange and blue gear PC was wearing that day and when I glimpsed him coming, I genuinely thought it was Rembas. I knew that he would only try and go round me, so I made my entry to the pits corner a little wider – say three foot – than I would normally, just to move him out wider. It was only a little gap but PC took full advantage and blasted past me on the inside going into the next turn. If I'd stayed on the same line I'd ridden for the previous three laps, the gap wouldn't have been there and he'd probably not have been able to get by. I made the classic mistake of not riding my own race but was too concerned at looking for my opponent – the fundamental fault that I told John Davis he should eliminate.

PC had made a very good turn around the third/fourth bend but I couldn't believe the gap I left him. I didn't think PC could pass me, I'd been riding the right line, but I didn't know he had that much more speed than me until he went past me in a flash. I knew in that moment that my engines were not quick enough. Dave Nourish always did such a good job for Peter. He was into speedway, knew the sport and what PC and other riders expected from their engines. On the other hand, Weslake's were simply into producing speedway engines to sell, not to tune. That was the major difference. But I believe my tuning ability put me on equal terms to Peter.

> **"PC had made a very good turn around the third/fourth bend but I couldn't believe the gap I left him. I didn't think PC could pass me, I'd been riding the right line, but I didn't know he had that much more speed than me until he went past me in a flash. I knew in that moment that my engines were not quick enough"**

129

I won my last three races in Katowice to finish on 13 points – one less than PC who could afford the luxury of finishing second to Ivan Mauger in heat 20. I've no doubt that had it come to the crunch, and Peter needed to win that final race, he wouldn't have had any worries about Ivan messing him up – they were, after all, good long-term friends and former Belle Vue team-mates.

My argument that I would have beaten PC in Poland had my engines been the same as they were before Weslake messed them up, was borne out at Poole a week after the World Final. I'd managed to put one motor back together as I'd had it before . . . and I beat him to win the Blue Riband.

I will always maintain that Weslake cost me the world title that year because the engines they supplied me with for the final were too slow. I don't want to take anything away from Peter Collins but he and I were equally good on the night . . . and, crucially, he had the fastest bikes.

What should have been a great end to an otherwise fantastic year for me came undone that day in front of 100,000 supporters in the vast concrete bowl of the Slaski Stadium. At the time, I was happy to have finished runner-up to Peter, who became only England's second World Champion and the first since double winner Peter Craven, who had triumphed in 1955 and 1962. I felt my 13 points was a bloody good achievement and if you look at the tape of me being interviewed by Dave Lanning afterwards, I couldn't conceal my delight.

It wasn't until I returned from Eastern Europe, and Ken Beckett and myself were talking about those poxy motors and how much they had cost me, that it sunk in that I could have won the 1976 World Championship. But the reality is, who remembers second?

The fact that PC was the new World Champion only rubbed it in for me – I'd much rather have finished second on the rostrum to Phil Crump, who

PC and me bring home the cut glass crystal from Poland. But I'd much rather have left there with the gold medal.

"It wasn't until I returned from Eastern Europe, and Ken Beckett and myself were talking about those poxy motors and how much they had cost me, that it sunk in that I could have won the 1976 World Championship. But the reality is, who remembers second?"

Turning up the heat

One of the many great races PC and I had over the years.

had to settle for the bronze medal. At least I would then have been the top Englishman in the world, but that honour – and the top sponsorship deals and other perks that followed – were Peter's to enjoy and exploit. When the promoters were handing out bookings for their top meetings, it was obviously so much better to say you were World Champion than it was to be the runner-up. For the sake of one meeting that season, I was second best in most people's eyes. But for 90 per cent of the year I was the best around.

It sounds very selfish, but the honest truth is I never took satisfaction from seeing an English rider finish above me in the World Final. Much as I liked Peter Collins, John Louis and Gordon Kennett – who were also World Final silver medalists in the 70s – as England team-mates and riders who I shared success with at World Team Cup and World Pairs level, and who I'd help out in my role as England captain, I didn't enjoy seeing them successful in individual World Finals and other major meetings. All that meant was that the glory and spotlight moved away from me and towards them.

That's where the Grand Prix series is so good and it would have suited me fine. I wish it had been around in my day, because I think I could have won two or three between 1975 and 1978, when I was in my early 30s and at my peak.

SIMMO

Pain in the grass

I had strong words with Weslake after what happened at the '76 World Final but I couldn't afford to lose their support. I would normally tell a sponsor who'd let me down like that to stick it but, for once, common sense prevailed and I bit the bullet. They conceded that they had buggered up my engines for the final and it was a lesson learned on both sides, albeit a very costly one on my part. So we buried the hatchet and turned our attention to another serious assault on the World Championship in 1977, the year of The Queen's Silver Jubilee.

I don't know, though, quite what Mike Daniels would have made of me if he'd heard about the accident I had soon after leaving the Weslake factory just prior to the 1977 season. I'd been down there to collect all my equipment for the season, enough to build three brand new bikes. I was driving back home, in a dream thinking about all this new stuff I had in the back, when I miscalculated a bend and went off the road.

I ended up down one of the many dykes there are in the Rye area, with the front wheel of the car submerged in water. I quickly got a lift back into Rye village, where I arranged for someone at the local garage to come out to my car with heavy lifting gear, to extricate my car before it disappeared any further under water. Thankfully, they managed to pull the car clear of the dyke but all I could think about while all this was happening was my car and three brand new Weslake speedway bikes disappearing under 10ft of water!

The 1977 started very well for me and I felt ready to go all the way in the World Championship this time. But you never know what's around the corner in this life and, just three days before the defence of my British Championship, I suffered the worst injury of my career.

A fine start to 1977 included victory in the World Pairs Final with Peter Collins at Belle Vue. We beat Anders Michanek and Bernie Persson of Sweden and the Germans, Egon Müller and Hans Wassermann.

Tributes

I'm kicking myself now for not chasing more lucrative bookings on the continent when I was in my prime but one invitation I very much regret accepting was to appear in a grasstrack meeting at Osnabruck, Germany on Sunday, July 10. The season had again started very well for me – in addition to taking over from John Louis as England captain, Peter Collins and myself retained the World Pairs Final at Belle Vue and I added victory in the Superama at Hackney to a maximum in the British quarter-final of the World Championship at King's Lynn.

I was looking forward to trying to become the first Englishman to win back-to-back British Championships but by the time I arrived at Coventry I knew there was no hope of that.

It all went horribly and spectacularly wrong for me on the third lap of my second race at Osnabruck when, at 100mph, I felt my handlebars tilt slightly downwards as I roared along the straight. I immediately sat up straight in the saddle and gave the bars a little tug upwards but that wasn't the problem. As I was about to very suddenly and painfully discover, the handlebars had not come loose at all. The centre bolt holding together the front forks sheared off, causing the front of my bike to collapse. I was thrown God knows how high in the air and must have bounced down the track at least half a dozen, maybe 10 times. And each time I bounced, I came down heavily on my left shoulder.

I'm told my bike broke up into so many pieces that the German track staff had to use a bucket to collect most of the debris from my crash. I could replace the bike, but what I couldn't do very quickly was repair my battered shoulder. I'd damaged the ligaments, broken my shoulder blade and my left arm was all but useless. I couldn't move it at all and when I asked the first aid medics if I'd be OK to ride in the British Final the following Wednesday, they just looked at each other and laughed. I'd probably be all right to ride again in six weeks, but not three days, they reckoned.

I saw Aussie Phil Crump on my way out of the track. Crumpie was following me when I crashed and he said that he never realised a grasstrack bike had so many parts to it!

I got home to Kent and underwent intensive physiotherapy in a desperate battle to be fit for the vital World Championship qualifier at Coventry. Not that the treatment did much good – my shoulder just became increasingly sore and painful and I arrived at the British Final still unable to move my left arm.

The build up to Coventry included winning the big Superama individual at Hackney.

133

SIMMO

Down and out . . . I dropped the clutch alongside Doug Wyer but the pain was too much and I couldn't hold on.

Turning up the heat

I somehow managed to convince the track doctor that I was fit enough to take my place among the 16 British Finalists – I just had to go for it, otherwise my World Championship dreams would've gone up in smoke again for another year. I've no doubt that other national speedway federations would have just seeded through their national champion if he'd suffered the kind of ill-timed injury that I had, but the BSPA and Speedway Control Board were never capable of taking such sensible decisions and I'm sure nothing has changed in that respect either.

Anyway, before my first race, Ken Beckett got together six or seven rubber bands that he'd cut up from an old tyre innertube and used them to strap my left hand to the handlebars. He left just enough room for me to wiggle two fingers needed to operate the clutch lever off the start.

My best hope of winning the World Championship – gone forever.

I arrived on gate four for my first ride, dropped the clutch and, because in reality I had only one useful arm, the bike looped and threw me off the back. I fell onto my already badly damaged left shoulder and the agony was horrendous. As I lay on the track, Barry Briggs and Ole Olsen rushed over to see if I was OK. Briggo tried to offer some hope when he said: "Simmo, if you win your next four rides, you can still qualify."

I looked up at him, and having been through so much pain and discomfort for the previous three-and-a-half days, just said: "You must be f****** mad. The last thing I want to do right now is get back on any f****** bike!"

Even today, I still have only limited

> **"I arrived on gate four for my first ride, dropped the clutch and, because in reality I had only one useful arm, the bike looped and threw me off the back. I fell onto my already badly damaged left shoulder and the agony was horrendous"**

135

SIMMO

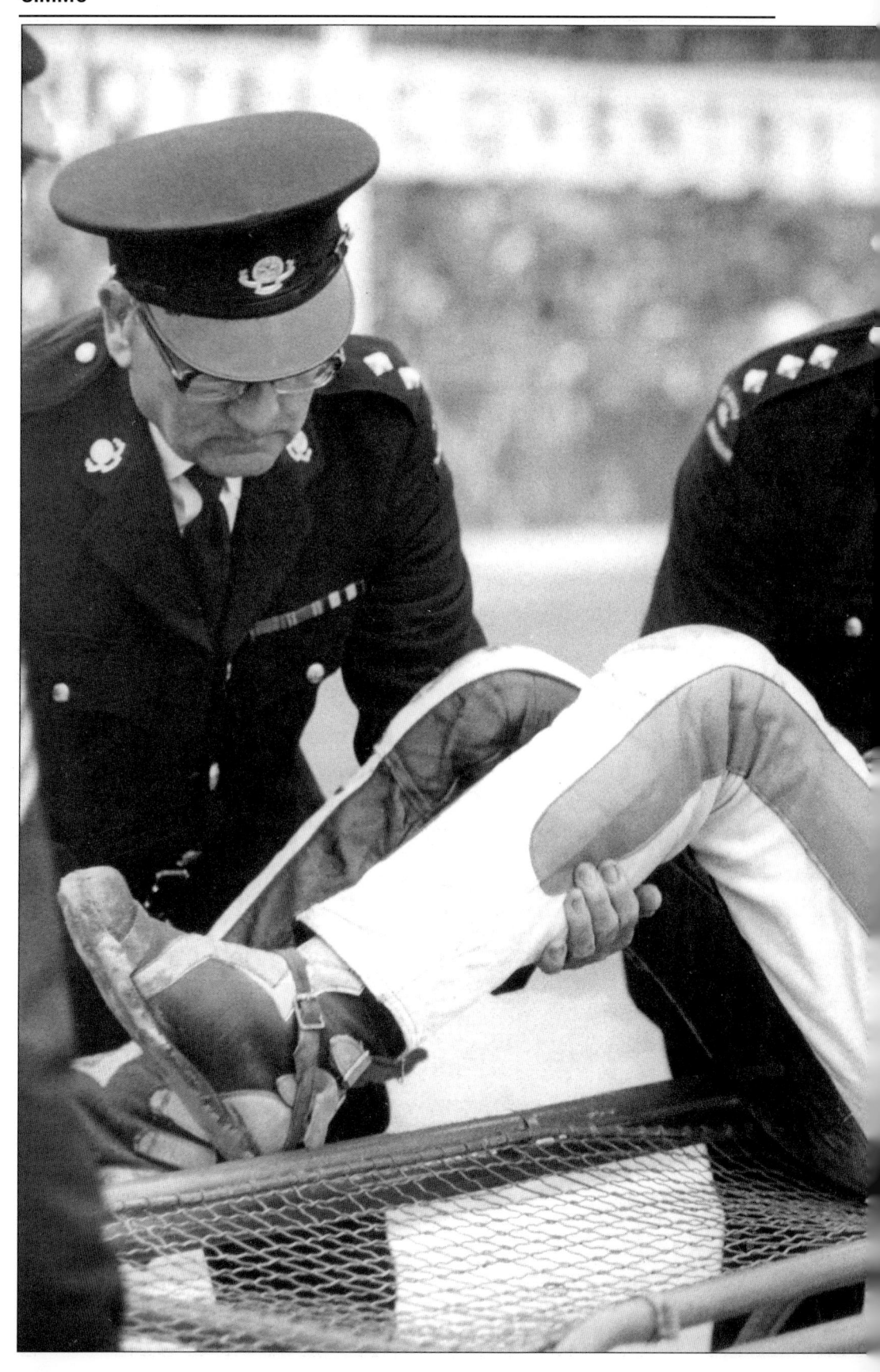

Turning up the heat

movement in my left shoulder and have had three operations on it in the past 30 years to keep it moving. I was riding better than ever when I broke my shoulder and who knows what I might have achieved if I'd qualified from that British Final in 1977. The meeting was won by the fast-emerging Michael Lee and it was him and Peter Collins who carried England's hopes in the World Final on a rainy night in Gothenburg. PC still curses the badly damaged leg that proved such a big handicap to him in the final but I look back at that dramatic crash in Osnabruck as costing me my best chance of winning the ultimate prize. Michael would go on to win the world title in 1980 but neither PC nor myself would challenge as strongly again after 1977.

In '77, I was riding well enough – and certainly better than in '76 – to convince myself that, for the first time, I really could win the World Championship. That crash in Germany knocked me for six and I'd say that I never ever did fully recover from it in a psychological sense. I wasn't used to crashing, especially in the spectacular way I did at Osnabruck that afternoon, and I think I permanently lost a good 40 per cent of movement in my left arm. I was always conscious of trying to over-protect it, to avoid damaging it again, and through that I lost a lot of confidence. The riding side wasn't a problem. It was in my head.

After taking three or four weeks off to recover, I rode again before the end of the '77 season but the arm was still troubling me. The problem was hit home to me in the dressing room at Poole one night, when I had to ask the track doctor, who was standing nearby, to help me on with my leathers. He couldn't believe the state my arm was in and arranged for me to go to go to Poole General hospital the next day for an operation. The joint had seized up.

My last appearance in the World Final was in 1978, when I scored 10 points and repeated the same score as I'd managed in my first final, also at Wembley, three years earlier. I recorded five second places but the damage this time had been done in the pits before the meeting, when my No.1 Weslake blew up while we were warming it up. It was just one of those unfortunate things that can happen very occasionally – a valve broke and went down into the engine, making it irreparable – and no-one was to blame. I'd prepared the engines myself for this World Final, but there was nothing I could do but get my second bike ready.

I wore the No.1 racejacket and really should have won the opening race from the inside gate, but Scott Autrey beat me and I came back into the pits and decided my bike wasn't good enough. It was a stupid reaction. Even though my second bike really was just as good as my preferred choice, the blow up in the pits had affected me badly from a psychological point of view and I couldn't get over it. That's when I needed someone alongside me in addition to Ken, a motivator who would have told me to forget about what happened, put it behind me and just get on with it. Someone who would lift my spirits and convince me that my second

> "I came back into the pits and decided my bike wasn't good enough. It was a stupid reaction. Even though my second bike really was just as good as my preferred choice, the blow up in the pits had affected me badly from a psychological point of view and I couldn't get over it"

Turning up the heat

Above: Ken was very good for me in many ways but he was not the sports psychologist I really needed to lift me in the Wembley pits in '78.

Right: Chasing Gordon Kennett in the second ride of my third, and final, individual World Final. Gordon went on to snatch second place in the meeting behind champion Ole Olsen, but I was never happy to see another Englishman grab the glory at my expense.

bike really was as good as my No.1. The top Dane, Nicki Pedersen, now uses a sports psychologist to help him in the pits but I had no-one like that around to help me. Other top England riders had good motivators in their corners of the pits – PC had his Belle Vue general manager Eric Boocock working with him, while John Louis had his Ipswich boss John Berry whispering in his ear, but there was no-one from Poole who could offer me any back-up.

I was 32-years-old and at the time I thought there would be another chance for me to win the World Final. But now I'm gutted to look back and think that I should have ridden in a lot more.

10

ENGLAND PRIDE

One of the proudest days of my career – leading Aussie John Boulger in the UK round of the World Team Cup at Reading on the day I was confirmed as the new captain of England.

141

SIMMO

RIDING for England always meant something very special to me and when team manager John Berry made me his captain in 1977, it was one of the proudest days of my life.

I hadn't expected to be given the captaincy – it was just before the World Team Cup UK qualifier at Reading, where Dave Jessup and myself both scored maximums as England easily beat the USA, Scotland and New Zealand. With Berry being the promoter at Ipswich, most people expected him to choose the Witches' No.1 John Louis as his captain. Even if Louis had been dropped, I still half-expected him to be around the pits as skipper, in the way that Ray Wilson helped out after he lost his place in the main World Team Cup squad a few years earlier.

Louis did, in fact, captain the team in the Test series against the Rest of the World in May of '77 but he wasn't in the WTC quartet selected at Reading the following month, when Berry turned to me for the first time in an official fixture (I'd led the side against Rest of World in a one-off match at Vojens, Denmark in July 1976).

I was honoured to be chosen to lead my country – it still means as much to me today as it did then – and I was also impressed that Berry would put his faith in a rebel like me. After all, it was the refusal of myself and Jessup to ride at the dangerous Bristol track that forced the cancellation of the sixth, and final, Test against The Rest. Although we slipped up and didn't reach the World Team Cup Final in 1976, the Aussies weren't then good enough to beat us in a six-man Test match and there was no-one else to even challenge England's dominance at that time. The Swedes, Poles, Russians and Czechs were all a spent force, while the Danes and Americans were still nobodies in world speedway terms.

The BSPA asked Barry Briggs and Ivan Mauger to put together a Rest of the World team to face us and it produced a lot of great racing between two evenly matched teams. Apart from the two legendary Kiwis, The Rest also called upon former World Champions in Ole Olsen and Anders Michanek, plus the best of the Aussies – Phil Crump, Billy Sanders and John Boulger – and other big names like Scott Autrey, Egon Müller, Edward Jancarz and Mitch Shirra.

Once the Test venues were announced, I was horrified to hear that Bristol had been chosen to stage the sixth match in the series. I spoke to all the other senior England riders in the squad and we all agreed that we didn't want to ride in the scheduled sixth Test at Bristol. But as often happens in these cases, the riders rarely stick together and in the end it was only DJ and myself who stuck our necks out and said we wouldn't go there. The rest backed down but I was adamant.

I'd been to Bristol with Poole and while I was reluctantly prepared to turn out there for my club in official league or cup fixtures, there was no way I would ride there in challenge matches, open or individual meetings, or even a Test match – not any meeting where I had a choice.

The track was just too dangerous. It had no base to it. Peter Thorogood used to go down there every week and try to prepare a speedway track that effectively doubled as the greyhound surface – it was stipulated by the people who ran the greyhounds that no shale could be added to the sand, because it would have cut the dogs' paws. If they had laid a proper track down at the start of the year and used the right materials to make it bind together, they could possibly have got away with it. But to try and prepare a track in that way on a weekly basis – lay the sand track, pack it down as hard as possible and then hope it makes for good speedway – was just asking the impossible. Peter was an experienced track man with a good reputation but the Bristol promoters were asking him to perform a miracle. The sandy texture was never going to work for speedway.

The first race at Bristol wasn't normally too terrible but after that it just got so deep and so rutted that it was like riding on the beach. It was awful. John Davis had gone through the fence there and it nearly ripped his arm off, so that certainly contributed to my way of thinking that the Eastville track was just too dangerous. I had certain principles and if I saw something was dangerous, I'd never be afraid to say so. If other riders didn't want to back me, then that was fine by me – it made no difference to how I felt. By riding at Bristol for Poole, I probably wouldn't have dropped any more than a point or two, which gave my complaints credibility – it wasn't like I was whingeing after scoring only a few points there.

The shape was fine, although it was ever so narrow coming off the corners. It was also very dark and badly lit, which created another problem because you couldn't actually see what was happening with the track as the meeting unfolded. Even on the start line, the track was so deep that you dropped the clutch and sat still – with your engine on the floor. The wheel would sink into the sand, and the second it hit the sand it just went straight down even further to the base. Your footrest would inevitably drag along the sand – it was bloody dangerous.

Promoter Wally Mawdsley (centre) opens Bristol Beach, or should that be Speedway? I hated the sandy surface.

Len Silver with Peter Collins and John Louis on the day Australia shocked England in the WTC at Ipswich.

In the end the BSPA cancelled the Test scheduled for Bristol and I was pleased that John Berry backed our protest 100 per cent. John knew the importance of a track that was at least half-decent. If only they could have done something better with the track there, because they always attracted very big crowds to Eastville and the atmosphere was usually great. The track had got slightly better by 1978 – the last year speedway was staged there – and John finally managed to convince me to ride for England against Australasia. I top-scored with 15 points in our first Test defeat but, apart from official duty for Poole, that was the last time I ever rode at Bristol.

Without doubt, Bristol was the worst speedway track I've ever ridden.

I hated Bristol as much as I loathed Newport, another track run by the Wally Mawdsley-John Richards promotion. The Somerton Park circuit was square in shape, the surface was awful – they didn't have the excuse Bristol did with their dog track – it was just a very dangerous place to ride. I was so determined to avoid the place that I even spoilt my own chances of winning the VW Grand Prix series by pulling out of a round at the South Wales track.

Top riders used to moan about Newport and say they didn't want to go there but, with the exception of a few of us who refused to risk our necks, most of them still went and rode there anyway. That's the trouble with speedway riders – they never stick together on the major issues like track safety. I'm not talking about asking the authorities to put in an air fence or anything too costly, just better and more thorough preparation. If everyone who hated Newport had stood up to be counted and didn't back down until improvements were carried out, then the promoters would've had to do something about track conditions. Newport didn't faze me, and I know I could've gone there and won that GP round but I was determined to

England pride

make a stand against what I – and many others – saw as consistently dangerous track conditions.

As I've mentioned earlier, Exeter was another west country venue that was unpopular with many visiting riders. But I wouldn't put the Exeter track in the same bracket as Bristol and Newport. The County Ground was a frame of mind thing, I used to get psyched out of going there by listening too much to other people. When I had to go there and do a job, like when I became Poole's No.1 and captain, I found that it wasn't as bad as a lot of people made out.

Former Exeter rider Len Silver, who I'd ridden against in my first season at Hackney in 1963 (Len's last as a rider), was the first England manager to pick me on a regular basis.

I never had any fall-outs with Len, he was a good team manager and you could never knock his enthusiasm – he leapt up and down and waved his arms about whenever he was with England just as he did at Hackney on a Friday or Rye House on a Sunday. I just got on better with John Berry, who took more personal interest in me than Len did.

John afforded me time and he made me captain when a lot of people probably wouldn't have done. I think he told me initially that I'd matured enough to be tried as captain. It did my self-confidence a lot of good and he obviously saw something in me that others hadn't – that I could motivate and offer hands-on help and be a team player. There's no more glory or any extra money, but you can help the team a lot. When the pressure was on, John obviously felt I could handle it that little bit better than the others.

If he'd made PC captain it might have detracted from his riding. The thing about riding for England, especially in World Team Cups, is that while you are part of the team, you are out there on track as an individual, competing against riders from three other nations, you just rode as hard as you could. Being captain, I never took my responsibilities lightly.

Even when I wasn't riding to my best, John still saw something in me that was worthwhile and I was proud to hang on to the captaincy for as long as I did. I don't think there were many who captained England over such a long period.

If we were racing abroad, John would get us together in the hotel to discuss things before going to the track and he always showed complete confidence in us. I didn't feel that he put us under any undue pressure, other than that he thought we were good enough to win. I've got to say that the team he had, and the amount of good riders he had to pick from, especially in the late 70s, took some of the pressure off him. He was a good team manager, who kept us all going with the right word here and there, but I've always said that a team manager is only as good as the people he has working for him. Take football. I could manage Chelsea today, given all the millions of pounds Jose Mourinho has had to spend. He can't fail to succeed in the Premiership.

But whether you're John Berry or Jose Mourinho, you cannot make a team win if they are simply not good enough in the first place. John could come across as a somewhat difficult person to get on with at times but I never once had a problem

Michael Lee looking better than he did when me and a few others had to hold him up after a night on the town.

with him. He said what he had to say and I respected him for it. We had some bloody good times together – he would be serious when the meeting was on and building up to it, but John would also join in the fun with his riders afterwards. He could let his hair down just like the rest of us.

One night, before a big meeting in Poland, Michael Lee got so pissed out of his head that we had to shield him from John's eyes while we were all staggering back from a nightclub. My manager and mechanic, Ken Beckett, PC and myself had Michael propped up between us, hoping John wouldn't notice the state his young star was in. If John had seen how drunk Michael was, he would have done his pieces. Obviously Michael recovered from his hangover and probably scored some good points the next day.

John was different where Michael was concerned. Whether he saw himself as a father figure to Michael, I don't know, but he'd shout at him and cajole him a bit more than he did the rest of us. If he thought I did something a little out of order, we'd just have a chat about it, whereas he seemed to come down harder on Michael, who was obviously younger than the rest of us and more easily led. He knew that certain riders had to be handled differently to others and it didn't matter to me that John has never been a rider himself – he knew what went on in speedway and learned fast. He knew what he was talking about, he knew the programme and the way meetings unfolded inside out and what was required from any given race. Berry was totally on the ball and I always took him at his word.

I think he appreciated the time, in Wroclaw for the 1977 World Team Cup Final, when I stood down because I wasn't fit enough and let the reserve, John Davis, take my rides. Much as I badly wanted to ride for my country that day, I thought too much of England to ride when I knew my damaged shoulder wasn't up to it. That's why John and I got on.

I never saw any favouritism between John Berry and John Louis, despite their obvious and long-standing Ipswich connection. In fact, I saw more favouritism between the Weslake factory and Louis. Berry was the same with all of us, in his own way.

But there was definitely a bit of a north-south divide within the England camp at times. John was accused by fans and sections of the press for leaning towards southern-based riders, as Len Silver had been before him, which was especially the case during the 70s. But once Eric Boocock and Ian Thomas took over as joint-managers and led England to the grand slam in 1980, the northern-based riders from Belle Vue and Halifax got more of a look-in. Based on ability, PC and Chris Morton had to get into any team – PC all the time and Mort at certain times – and that's more or less how it panned out.

I don't think that PC and Mort really understood Berry very well, though. John could be blunt and to the point and I don't think they accepted him as readily as the rest of us southern boys did. He'd also have a laugh and take the piss out of their Mancunian accents but they didn't seem to see the funny side of it. They should have just laughed along with him and got on with it.

I was disappointed that I didn't get the chance to meet and chat to John again when he came back to England recently to launch his book, *Confessions of a Speedway Promoter*. In fact, it was reading John's book about speedway in the 70s and 80s that got me thinking about writing my own story.

John Berry may not have been everybody's cup of tea but he was certainly the best team manager I ever rode under.

Honest PC, I'm not laughing at your accent. The north-south divide did exist, though.

Wembley Wonders

I suppose I really came to the fore at international level when England hosted, and won, the Daily Mirror International Tournament at Wembley in 1973. I don't have any recollection of making my England debut against USSR at West Ham in 1966 but no-one could forget their first appearance under those famous Twin Towers.

Strangely, Terry Betts and I rode as a pair and it was good for both us – we knew very well how each other rode – and probably a wise decision by manager Len Silver. The fact that we were England's joint-top scorers with 10 points in the final against Sweden says that it worked well on the night. We didn't get much chance to team-ride, though, scoring mainly 4-2s in a tight match that ended 39-all.

I'd always thought the Wembley track was much bigger than it actually was. Evidently, from speaking to people, it was similar in size and shape to Cradley Heath. You really had to ride around the inside – you could maybe get away with a big blast round the outside once, but not often. I liked it, because it allowed you to make mistakes. The surface wasn't particularly good, as it had to be laid and then dug up for each meeting, so it induced mistakes and that allowed for passing. You didn't have to be the quickest, you just had to be smart and try to be in the right place at the right time.

To win that Daily Mirror-sponsored series final was great for all the English riders involved. I don't know to this day whether Anders Michanek knocked off Peter Collins or not – that's between those two. I don't wish to take sides in this great debate but from what I saw, I don't think Mich did cause PC to fall. He came under

We rode under the name of Great Britain, but Ray Wilson, myself, Peter Collins, Terry Betts and unused reserve Dave Jessup were the first all-English winners of the World Team Cup at Wembley, 1973.

England pride

...And here we are again back at the RAC Club in Pall Mall at the end of 1973 to receive our World Cup winners' medals from the Control Board. PC was obviously due on the golf course a little later.

him ever so hard and I think PC thought he was going to be beaten and saw a way out by dropping it. If Mich had got by him, there's no way Peter would have re-passed him.

Len chose PC to represent England in the match race decider and that was fair enough, even though Bettsy and me had been our top scorers. Peter was going fastest at the end of the meeting and deserved his chance. And, looking back, I wouldn't have wanted to carry that kind of enormous pressure in that situation. Peter could anticipate the gate and if you look at the tape of that meeting, he made such a flier that Mich wasn't even in the same race at the start.

Even after beating the Swedes at Wembley that July, I still wasn't confident of being selected for the World Team Cup Final back at the Empire Stadium in September. Remember, in my mind, I was still only a No.2 to Bettsy at King's Lynn and I think a lot of people thought Len would choose Ipswich's John Louis for the WTC final. I wasn't aware that Len had upset John by pulling him out of the England v Rest of the World match that followed our clash with Sweden earlier in the season.

Again PC stole the show at Wembley in the WTC final. He had solid support from Bettsy, myself and our captain, Ray Wilson, with Dave Jessup unused at reserve. Although we rode as Great Britain with the Union Jack on our body colours, we were effectively England. It was the first time four Englishmen had ridden together in the team final. 'Willie' was a good captain, a hard rider who would motivate us and didn't just do his own thing. He was for the team and very patriotic. Ray must have been very proud to become the first Englishman to score a World Team Cup maximum in Poland in 1971.

149

SIMMO

In 1974, I established myself as an England regular as we brushed aside the fading Swedes (who were banned from competing in the British League that season) and Russians in the summer Test series. I was chosen again when we retained the World Team Cup at Katowice, Poland. Bettsy was ruled out by a broken collarbone but Louis came back into the line-up and we were just as strong. This meeting is best remembered for a great race won by Dave Jessup and also starring Sweden's Christer Lofqvist and Poland's Zenon Plech, all covered by the proverbial blanket and with places changing at every corner. What a superb race it was.

It was difficult to win in Poland, where you were taken afterwards to a typical banquet where you didn't know what you were eating – only that it was inedible! These boring ceremonies can drag on forever, so it was a case of getting pissed on the local schnapps – even though I very rarely drank alcohol. On one occasion, I remember crawling to bed and being ill, which was a pity because when I arrived back in my hotel room I discovered I had a black German girl and her Swedish friend for company! I couldn't take advantage of the opportunity that night but it's fair to say that there were usually a few loose girls hanging around on these overseas trips, especially in Poland, and it wasn't unknown for one or two members of our party to sample the local talent!

We completed a hat-trick of WTC wins at Norden, Germany in 1975, when we were perhaps not such hot favourites to win. PC was flying, Louis was still going very well too and I was enjoying a new lease of life after joining Poole that season. Martin Ashby was the newcomer to the team but he fitted in well and enjoyed probably the greatest meeting of his career. We couldn't believe how well he did and I was delighted for him. The stupid thing about it was, the Germans picked one engine from each team to test after the meeting and they chose Jessup's . . . who hadn't even ridden that day!

Another brilliant day for England. Jack Fearnley and Len Silver join riders Peter Collins, Dave Jessup, Martin Ashby, John Louis and myself after retaining the World Cup at Norden, Germany, 1975.

England pride

It was pure complacency that stopped us winning the World Cup four years on the trot. We went into the UK qualifying round at Ipswich fully expecting to win it and we were caught out on the day by a very good Australian team. PC got 11 points but Louis, Jessup and myself scored only eight points each and it wasn't enough. The Aussies got off to a good start, their tails were up and we couldn't claw back the deficit.

Everyone – from Len Silver to the riders – was too complacent going into that meeting at Foxhall Heath. We had been top of the tree for three years, and we were all still riding very well, but we underestimated the Aussies on the day and got a shock. Anyone would have expected Louis to have scored a maximum on his home track at Ipswich, with Jessup and me getting, say, 10 each. But we didn't and we paid the price. So did the BSPA, who suddenly found themselves in the nightmare financial situation of hosting the 1976 final at White City without the host team to draw a big crowd. Australia beat Sweden, Poland and Russia in London but we really should have been there going for another record.

"I had put club before country and took only my second bike to the pairs final – we could only take one each – and I kept my best bike back for Poole. Eskilstuna was a pretty big track, bigger than I'd expected it to be, but my No.2 bike wasn't quick enough. I thought I could get away with it but it was an important lesson learned"

Of course, it wasn't all doom and gloom for the English riders that year. PC won the individual world title in Katowice and John Louis and myself became only England's second World Pairs winners – after Ray Wilson and Bettsy had triumphed in 1972 – when we won the final at Eskilstuna, Sweden. John was the outstanding half of our pairing with 17 points, while I just did a job, though not a good one. I had put club before country and took only my second bike to the pairs final – we could only take one each – and I kept my best bike back for Poole. Eskilstuna was a pretty big track, bigger than I'd expected it to be, but my No.2 bike suffered some carburettor trouble and wasn't quick enough. I thought I could get away with it but it was an important lesson learned. In the future, I would always try to take at least two bikes to every international meeting, where possible, and certainly my No.1 bike at all times.

We didn't team-ride much in the meeting – there was usually an opponent between us in the races – although I thought John was more of an individual than a team player. I don't know much about what he did for Ipswich, but he didn't seem to want to team-ride with anyone when we rode for England. It appeared to me like he was out for a bit of glory and most of the time it didn't matter anyway.

Being beaten by the Aussies at Foxhall was a big shock to our system and we didn't make the same mistake in Poland the following year, when John Berry had succeeded Len, who took a lot of stick for our disappointing performance in front of a huge Ipswich crowd in '76. My shoulder was still feeling the effect of those two crashes in the summer – one in Germany and the other in my first ride at the British Final – and I found it really, really hard to ride at Wroclaw. I could have thought of the glory but I put England first and called Berry aside to tell him that I wasn't up to

SIMMO

Studying the programme at the 1977 World Pairs Final – but it was PC who chose the best gates in the second half.

it and that he'd be better off using our reserve, John Davis, instead. JD did well to score six valuable points and I think I did the right thing for the good of the team. We had a great team spirit, all working together to overcome a spate of bike problems that affected Michael Lee in particular. In the end, I think the bikes of PC and JD were the only two working properly but we pulled away from the Poles to win by 12 points. It was a tremendous all-round effort.

Although injuries wrecked both PC's and my hopes of winning the individual World Championship in '77, we combined well to retain the World Pairs title for England in the final at Belle Vue. Like John, Peter was a glory-hunter. Before the start of the meeting, Peter asked me if I minded him taking the outside gate position, which I was happy to agree to. But, as it happened, in the first half of the meeting I did well from the inside gates and won our first three heats. Peter had obviously looked at it and, on his own track in front of so many Belle Vue supporters, he obviously didn't wish to be seen to be playing second fiddle to me in the second half of the meeting. He wanted the best (inside) gates for himself and, fair enough, I was happy to give them up to him. We still won, with Peter scoring 15 points and myself 13, so he was happy to have ended the night as England's top scorer.

A very similar thing happened at Hackney in a Test match against Denmark. I was partnered with Chris Morton, who put forward the same suggestion as PC had about switching gate positions. After winning all my races from the inside gates in the first half of the meeting, I agreed to swap positions in the second half but it backfired on myself and England. I found it difficult to make decent starts off the outside, which happened to be poor on this particular night, and Mort being the sluggish starter that he was a lot of the time, didn't get off the inside gates too well either.

Our switch had a serious effect on the result of the meeting and if I'd been more of an individual, who put myself before the good of my country, I would've said 'no' to both PC and Mort – and all the other times I gave up the best gates to my England partner. England's overall team total always mattered more to me than my individual tally, but some riders chased the limelight and loved to see their name in the papers or on Teletext!

We fancied our chances of winning the World Team Cup trophy again in Germany the next year but on a gater's paradise of a track at Landshut, it was Denmark's turn to seize the moment. The Danes, led by Ole Olsen, had been brought up on tracks exactly like the powdery, white-coloured stuff we encountered in southern Germany. On this occasion, there was no lack of preparation on our part and we certainly didn't go into the meeting this time feeling complacent. We were as quick as the Danes throughout the race, but not off the start line. Olsen didn't have to gee

England pride

his boys up, because they were all trapping well – and that's all they needed to do. If we'd made better starts than them, we'd have won the meeting. Simple as that.

We'd never experienced a track that slick for a meeting of such importance. It was ridiculous really and there was an overreaction to the result in the press. The reporters present, who represented the national papers covering the sport in those days, immediately called for John Berry's resignation. But it wasn't his fault that the Danes swept aside ourselves, Poland and the Czechs. John picked the best team he had available – everyone who should have been in the team was in it that year – but we simply didn't get it together on the night.

We went to the track with a team of non-trappers. I could trap OK and Michael Lee too, but Michael didn't on the night and neither did Dave Jessup. PC and Gordon Kennett were never the best out of the start and on that track it was just impossible to come from the back.

Well, almost impossible. I managed to pass the fast-starting Hans Nielsen, the outstanding Danish rider, but that was the only pass I made all night and it only happened because I pushed him so hard into the corner that he went wide. It was the only point Nielsen dropped – otherwise, you just couldn't make up even a yard on people in front of you. And it got to the stage where there was not even any point in trying.

It was stupid that we should have to ride in a World Final on a track like that, with one line around the kerb and you didn't dare move off it. The genuine racers had no chance of passing anyone that night and it was just a shame that John took so much stick over the result, because it was his riders' fault that we finished runners-up to the Danes.

No, it's not ice, but the white stuff the Germans served up as a 'track' for the 1978 World Cup Final at Landshut. I was the only rider to beat Danish hero Hans Nielsen but it was a night to forget for England.

Another first for Ivan

The 1978 season saw me set a record for winning the World Pairs title for the third consecutive season and with a third different partner. After John Louis and Peter Collins, this time I had White City's Gordon Kennett alongside me in Katowice. We thought we went there well prepared – well I know I was – and this was the first year we weren't allowed to use cut tyres in international meetings. It was the FIM's latest way of trying to slow us down but, like a lot of the things they brought in, it didn't. Whether it was tyres, silencers or smaller carburettors, riders just tuned their engines around the new rules. In fact, with the small carbs, within a few meetings we were actually going faster, because we were getting more grip.

Above: With my 1978 World Pairs partner, Gordon Kennett and (below) chasing Ivan Mauger, the man who I beat in a run-off to decide the gold medal in Poland.

England pride

Anyway, Gordon, myself and team manager John Berry got to Poland and discovered that every tyre Gordon had with him was cut – it didn't matter in the British League but this was against FIM international rules and I don't think John was too impressed at Gordon's lack of professionalism. We all knew the rules – Gordon and I had even won the semi-final at Debrecen, Hungary earlier in the season – but obviously Gordon had either forgotten them or didn't take any notice of the regulations. I had five tyres with me – enough for me to do five rides and then there was the option to turn them round, although I didn't plan on doing that anyway. I just had five wheels with a new, uncut tyre on each, ready to race. Good job I did! The way around Gordon's problem was for us to us to share my tyres, but turn them around after each race and use the second edge.

We hit another snag in practice when it was obvious that Gordon's Weslake bikes weren't quick enough, so he had to use my second bike in the meeting itself. Bob Dugard, whose Eastbourne track was closest to the Weslake factory at Rye in Sussex, always ensured that his riders – either for Eastbourne or White City – had more Wessie engines than anyone else. It was supposed to be a pairs meeting in Poland but the English duo weren't exactly sharing the burden this time. The only thing that wasn't mine about this England pairing was Gordon himself! He was sharing my tyres and now my bike too.

Anyway, I ended up scoring 15 points and Gordon weighed in with nine (Ole Olsen was the top individual scorer with 16). We tied on 24 points with the New Zealand pairing of Ivan Mauger and Larry Ross, who scored 12 points apiece. It came down to a run-off between Ivan and myself to decide the championship.

Ivan pratted about so much before the run-off, it was untrue. I was a bit nervous and I didn't have a new rear tyre, so I borrowed one from Ole Olsen, who obviously didn't want the Kiwis to win! We went to the start, where Ivan then turned round and then went back to do something to his bike. I was a bit surprised that Ole should lend me a tyre to beat Ivan . . . .and I was even more confused when Olsen then appeared to lend his bike to Ivan!

We went back to the start, only for Ivan to turn round again and go back to the pits for a second time, where someone produced a different bike for him to ride. Maybe Olsen's bike wasn't good enough for him, or it had only been brought out as another delaying tactic, while the mechanics were rushing to fix Ivan's own bike.

We were on two minutes to get back to the start and then, to delay things a few seconds longer, they took the front wheel out of Ivan's bike on the track. The original two minute time allowance went completely out of the window – the referee just forgot about it, or he chose to.

But Ivan's psychological warfare went on far too long for it to have an adverse effect on my preparations or nerves. He did get to me for a little while but his messing about just continued for what seemed like an age, so I just switched off from it in the end and my concentration held. John had absolute faith in me and told me before the race that I could beat Ivan.

And then came the last attempt by Ivan to put me out of my stride. Just as we were about to be pushed off from the pits, his good friend and business manager, Peter Oakes, walked very close by me, turned round and whispered in my ear: "You know Ivan's never been beaten in a run-off, don't you?" It was ever such a clever move by Peter, another part of the Mauger psychological strategy and typical of the mind games that he played on a lot of riders through the years. Obviously, given the pressure of the situation, it didn't dawn on me until later that Ivan *had* previously lost a run-off for the 1973 world title to Poland's Jerzy Szczakiel. Ivan tried every trick in the book to win races and most times it worked for him.

Not this time, though. As luck would have it, I made the perfect start and never put a foot wrong for four laps. England were World Pairs champions for a fourth time and, despite all Gordon's previous problems, we'd got through it all. As I came back to the pits gate afterwards, Peter Oakes was the first person I saw, so I just looked at him and, with a big smile on my face said: 'He has now!'. As parting shots go, they don't get any more satisfying than that, but Ivan and Peter were good about it and offered us their congratulations. I think Larry Ross was the sickest man in Poland that day – he was in tears and so upset at losing out on what he hoped would be his first FIM gold medal.

To win my third pairs title by beating Ivan (who was also going for a third pairs win) in a run-off, gave me more satisfaction than any of the two previous pairs successes I'd shared with Louis and Collins.

The big Vojens con trick

I thought I had a good chance of breaking the record I shared with Anders Michanek by winning the World Pairs for a fourth time in 1979 – but Michael Lee and I were cheated out of a run-off for the title at Vojens, where Ole Olsen controlled everything.

Ole Olsen has had many roles at Vojens, including that of 'referee' for the 1979 World Pairs Final.

England pride

I think I was about fourth in line to be Mike's partner – I even withdrew from the semi-final in Landshut, where I was due to partner Gordon Kennett – but there must have been injuries to a couple of the other contenders because I suddenly got a phone call from John Berry to say I was needed in Denmark. For some reason, John had so much faith in me and I don't know why because I never rode for him at Ipswich. He asked me if I could do a job and, having just changed from Weslake to the new Godden engines, I thought I could. But I can remember saying to him: 'There's got to be someone better than me', but he reckoned there wasn't.

> **"Jancarz, who was on the outside, right up against the fence, actually snatched second place by six inches – it was clear to everyone who saw it. But Olsen was very clever. A few yards short of the line, he looked back, thought that Nielsen had second spot in the bag and just stuck his arm up in the air, as if to claim the victory before he'd even crossed the line"**

I rode pretty well in the first half of the meeting – I even did Olsen from the back – but I went from second to last in the first race after the interval and couldn't work out why. I thought that perhaps the track had got slicker and I was no better than mediocre in the second half of the meeting. It was not until I got home, and was cleaning the bike, that I found out that the back end of the frame was broken, down by the footrest. That accounted for why the bike didn't grip in the latter part of the meeting like it did in the first half, but it was wet and mucky that day and no matter how much we cleaned the bike between races we didn't notice the crack.

Michael was good to ride with and he came really came into his own in the second half of the meeting, when we almost did enough to win the title.

We needed the Poles to do us a big favour in their last ride, against our biggest rivals Denmark. We had a word with Edward Jancarz before the race, urging him to beat the home favourites, Olsen and Hans Nielsen.

Jancarz, who was on the outside, right up against the fence, actually snatched second place from Nielsen by six inches – it was clear to everyone who saw it. But Olsen was very clever. A few yards short of the line, he looked back, thought Nielsen had second spot in the bag and just stuck his arm up in the air, claiming victory before he'd even crossed the line. Norwegian referee Tore Kittilsen had been conned by Olsen but because Ole was his mate, he gave him the benefit of the doubt and awarded the race 5-1 in the Danes' favour. ITV covered the meeting and even their studio presenter, Dickie Davies, couldn't believe that Jancarz had been robbed.

It was the biggest con in speedway that I've ever been involved in.

The World Cup win at Landshut, followed by their World Pairs victory in 1979, was the making of Denmark as a world speedway force. It was the first time they had even reached the World Team Cup Final but all the FIM gold medals – for team, pairs and individual – would become almost their sole property throughout the 80s. After England's grand slam under Booey and Thomas in 1980, Denmark's toughest competition came from Bruce Penhall, who won the individual crown in 1981 and '82, and his fellow Americans.

Bruce Penhall leads Michael Lee and Chris Morton. Mike was very much influenced by the Yanks.

The Californian influence

There is no doubt that the Americans were good for British speedway in the 70s and 80s. Scott Autrey was the forerunner in 1973 and every one of them who followed him here was a character in his own right. They did their own thing – we all know most of them took drugs – and that was their choice. The drugs thing was a culture shock for a lot of us in this country but to the Yanks, it was a way of life since childhood.

We didn't need drugs in speedway, though, it was already dangerous enough. If you're riding under the influence – of whatever – I assume it gives you a manufactured sense of courage, or why else would you take it? You don't want to be riding against that as well as the rider himself, wondering just how far they are prepared to push the limits. The way I looked at it, a rider who was using drugs wouldn't be worrying about himself – or others around him – as much as he would if he wasn't taking them.

It did concern me now and again, although I can honestly say that I never knew of either Bruce Penhall or Dennis Sigalos taking drugs . . . but I knew full well that many of the others did.

With Dennis Sigalos, who was nicer than Penhall.

Whether Penhall and Sigalos dabbled in substances away from speedway, I don't know. But Shawn and Kelly Moran, Cookie (John Cook) and Bobby Schwartz . . . it was a known fact that *they* were involved with drugs.

The thing is, they were bloody good riders and you could never knock their riding skill. And actually, I did think they were safe riders 99 per cent of the time. They had their own ways of riding and different styles but double World Champion Penhall and Sigalos were the most outstanding two.

I liked some of them as people, but not all of them. I thought Penhall was really cocky. I didn't know him well, we never really hit it off as acquaintances. We'd pass the time of day but then I'd sit back and watch him putting himself around so much, thinking to himself, 'look at me, I'm Bruce Penhall'. That's just my personal impression of him and no doubt there will be many who saw him differently to me. I know that he and Peter Collins had a really good relationship, so maybe I'm wrong about Penhall.

While I could appreciate his technical skill on a bike, I thought he always bought everything he possibly could to make his bikes the best – he wasn't like the rest of us, money was never an object to him. Even if the rest of us, who were trying to keep pace with him in the early 80s, couldn't really afford to buy the best gear, we still bought it because we knew we had to. But with Penhall, he never even had to think about the money he spent on his stuff. He just got the best available.

Dennis Sigalos was a nicer person than Penhall but he didn't have the 'front' that Penhall had and he appeared more shy and retiring. On the other hand, Schwartz had the front but didn't have the same ability as the other two. Whereas Kelly and Shawn Moran gave the impression that they were just in it for a joke.

The American team certainly knew how to psyche out the English boys a lot of the time when we met in a Test series. They knew all their happy-slappy behaviour in the pits wound us up and that's why they did it all the more. I should think that all the camaraderie was typical of them anyway but they seemed to make a point of doing it even more when they came together on English tracks to race against us. We'd sit on our toolboxes thinking, 'look at those bleedin' prats', but, all credit to them, their antics worked to their benefit.

I never found it easy to make friends and if I didn't like someone in the beginning, that would be the end of it. But, of the Americans who raced here, I always got on all right with Schwartz and Kelly Moran in particular.

Bobby Schwartz, Dennis Sigalos and John Cook.

SIMMO

Kelly was, of course, a notoriously big drinker. I rode for Wimbledon at Eastbourne one Sunday afternoon and he turned up for the meeting pissed, having just flown in from the States. He came up to me in the pits before the first race and his breath stunk of whisky. He started three races but never got further than the first corner before falling off each time.

All the Wimbledon riders were concerned about Kelly's condition – it was clear to us that he was pissed out of his head – and, as captain, I reported him to the referee. The ref called for the track doctor to give Kelly a breathalyser test but the doc – obviously employed by Eastbourne boss Bob Dugard and too frightened to do anything to upset him – declared that there was nothing wrong with him. Funny, but Kelly was too far gone to take his last two rides.

The fun-loving, hard-drinking but very likeable Kelly Moran.

That was Eastbourne for you – you'd *never* get the better of Bob, no matter what.

I was riding for Wimbledon and had passed my 36th birthday when John Berry and his new co-manager, Eric Boocock, recalled me to the England team for the 1982 Test series against the USA and Denmark. I was honoured to be asked back and I don't think I let anyone down by scoring more points than my younger team-mates and top-scoring with 13 against the fast-emerging, full-strength Danes at Hackney. I was still around for England when Wally Mawdsley took charge in 1983, although Carl Glover turned more to youth the following year.

My final senior appearance for my country was in the sixth, and final, Test against the USA at Swindon in September 1985. The Yanks had already clinched the series and I was 39-years-old, way past my sell-by date, and the oldest rider still competing in the senior league at the time. It was good of John Berry to recall me, especially as just a couple of weeks earlier I'd actually applied for his job!

The job I always wanted

I always fancied a crack at the England manager myself and officially applied for the job near the end of the 1985 season, when I was winding down my riding career at Swindon and the national team was going through a poor spell before Berry – who had three different spells in charge – finally turned it in and emigrated to Perth. I had been publicly critical of my old manager, who had clearly lost his enthusiasm for the job as well as the sport in general.

Having done a good job as captain for a long and relatively successful period, and served an apprenticeship as team manager with Crayford and Hackney in the National League for a few years, I thought I had a lot to offer as manager of England, I could have been quite good at it, and I would have relished the challenge of taking us back to the top again.

But we'll never know if I'd have been a success at it. The time when I would have been best suited to the role would have been around about the period when I had the big bust up with Bill Barker at King's Lynn. Over that, I was banned by the BSPA for five years from holding any official position in speedway and by the time that ended I was more or less out of the picture anyway.

Still, I can look back on my days as an England rider and captain with a lot of pride and plenty of satisfaction. When I rode for my country it was more about pride rather than money and being able to say that you were one of the best seven riders in the country – because there were a lot of good English riders who didn't win many caps in the 70s. We got close to winning the BBC's Sports Personality of the Year team award on more than one occasion. Looking back, it was brilliant to be part of those teams and the great speedway era in which I rode.

"When I rode for my country it was more about pride rather than money and being able to say that you were one of the best seven riders in the country – because there were a lot of good English riders who didn't win many caps in the 70s"

With four consecutive World Team Cup winners' medals, three World Pairs victories (with different partners) and 80 international caps to my name, I have a lot to be happy about.

I was 39 but still gave Sam Ermolenko a good run for his money on my last-ever Test appearance.

Keeping PC at bay on the Godden in the British Final at Coventry, 1979.

ENGLAND RIVALS

I WAS both fortunate enough – or unfortunate, whichever way you look at it – to ride with and against a few of the all-time England greats in the 70s and 80s. Here are some of my thoughts on four of them . . .

Peter Collins

PC and I got on really great, a relationship best illustrated after I got the new twin-carburettors going very well in 1976.

I obtained them from Bruce Cribb, who was the first to get a set together but he was unable to get them going well enough on his Weslake. He had the idea but couldn't follow it through, so I took a set of twin carbs off him and they went very well for me from day one. I won the British Final using them and didn't need to touch them again. In fact, I used them right through 1977 as well.

At the time, we were limited to a 34mm carburettor, but no-one said we couldn't use two smaller carbs together. I used two 28mm carbs, which worked much better than one measuring 34mm. It had a double effect of giving me more pulling power off the corners and a lot more top speed.

Some riders got the twin-carb set-up to go well for them while others didn't. PC was one who wasn't happy with his – even though he'd used them to win the 1976 World Final, he still reckoned mine were better than his. Dave Nourish tuned Peter's bikes but apart from a bit of work Weslake did for me, I prepared my own machinery.

To give you an example of how friendly PC and I became, I loaned him my carburettors for his use in the 1977 World Final at Gothenburg. That's how well we

England pride

Not a car boot sale but the pre-meeting parade at Belle Vue's Golden Apple meeting, 1977.

got on. Funnily enough, it was only last year that Peter said to me that he'd never really thanked me properly for lending him my carburettors for that final, although he added that he never really understood why I did so!

The reason I did was that I'd been injured in the British Final, we were mates and he had a good chance of winning the 1977 World Championship. As I was out of the reckoning anyway, it didn't matter to me who won it, so why not Peter again? He did brilliantly to finish runner-up to Ivan in terribly wet track conditions in Sweden and but for the handicap of riding with a serious leg injury, he could have won back-to-back World Finals.

We never fell out, although there was probably a bit of envy on my part at times because no matter how good anyone else went, PC always seemed to get most of the glory. I think one of Peter's mechanics said once in conversation, when asked who was the better rider out of Peter and myself: 'PC is the better speedway rider and Malcolm's the better motorcyclist'. The way I saw it, I was equally as good as him at speedway and probably a better all round motorcyclist! Since his early youth, Peter has only really ever done speedway seriously, whereas I've also ridden a lot of grasstrack and trials.

"We never fell out, although there was probably a bit of envy on my part at times because no matter how good anyone else went, PC always seemed to get most of the glory. The way I saw it, I was equally as good as him at speedway and probably a better all round motorcyclist!"

People say that while I always looked so easy on a bike, as if I didn't put myself out to win races, I never looked as spectacular as PC always did at his peak. Other people interpreted this view as me not being all that bothered but, believe me, I wanted to win as much as anyone.

'Tiger' John and me, World Pairs champions at Eskilstuna, Sweden, 1976.

John Louis

I suppose it was inevitable really, given the intense East Anglian rivalry between my team King's Lynn and John's Ipswich Witches, that we would have our fair share of on-track clashes in the early 70s. And I guess the most famous were probably our Golden Helmet battles in the summer of 1974, when the 'Tiger' was flying and I was still trying to break out from Bettsy's shadow.

My nomination as a challenger for the Helmet, which then carried some real prestige and was contested on a monthly basis, gave me a great chance to make a big impact and a name for myself. John was the winter holder of the Speedway Star-sponsored helmet and then successfully defended it against Ray Wilson and Peter Collins before we met at each other's home tracks in June.

We had won one race each in the first leg at Ipswich but on about the third lap of the deciding race I knew I had no chance of passing him so I just rode straight into him. I deliberately knocked him off. We both came down but the race was rightly awarded to John, so he won the first leg at Ipswich by 2-1.

The second leg at King's Lynn took on a very similar pattern. John and I again won a race each before I was leading the third heat and he ran into me on the pits corner, causing us both to crash. We were laying on the track, it was tit for tat, but in that surreal moment we probably became friends. We shook hands immediately and decided there and then to agree that we wouldn't try to knock each other off again – and we never did. We were able to step outside the natural rivalry between the Stars and the Witches, which meant so much to the fans of both clubs, and realised that we were England team-mates and friends with a lot in common.

In the deciding third leg at Hackney, I couldn't get near enough to him in either race to knock him off, even if I'd wanted to, so John retained the headgear for another month and went on to beat Dag Lovaas (Hackney) and Ole Olsen (Wolverhampton), before finally losing his grip on the Golden Helmet to Newport's Phil Crump in the last month of the season.

When I next got the chance to challenge for the Helmet, more than a year later, Louis was the match race title holder again! I was at Poole by then, but he still beat me at home and away.

I got on fine with John, just as I did all the other England riders in my time. John Louis has been Mister Ipswich Speedway since day one and it's super that he is still going strong there and working as hard as he is in the interests of his home town track.

John leading PC at the 1976 British Final.

SIMMO

Billy Sanders is outgated by DJ and myself during the England v Australasia Test at Swindon, 1979.

Dave Jessup

We always had a sort of love-hate relationship – one minute we got on, the next we didn't. We're both Kent born and bred but we were opposites when it came to spending money on our bikes and other equipment. I spent a lot, wasting plenty, but he'd spend next to nothing!

It wasn't just lack of money that cost Dave possibly World Championship glory at Wembley in 1978 and again in 1981. He was also drill-happy – if a piece of his bike could possibly be drilled, he'd drill a hole in it! I told him once: 'Just give up eating for a day and your bike will still be as light as you want it to be and prove more reliable too'. The jubilee clip that broke on him at Wembley in '78 was drilled and, not surprisingly, it just fell apart.

I also felt that Dave tried to copy me in everything I did – and I hated it when people copied me. If I rode grasstrack, he rode grasstrack; if I rode trials, he would ride trials, and it got on my nerves.

His love of golf is well documented but it was me who took him out for his first ever round, at Deangate Ridge public course in Strood, near where we both lived. He wore borrowed golf shoes and borrowed this and that – he looked absolutely horrendous. We used to play there two or three times a week for a while but because Dave wanted to be very good at golf, he persevered with it and he's become a bloody good golfer. My best handicap was 14 but Dave had his sights set on becoming professional and had a sand bunker especially built in his garden.

He wasn't a real racer, he was a trapper, and five times out of 10 his gating ability was down to great anticipation – he was very good at anticipating the tapes. I remember him coming to Swindon for a Test match, I think it was against the USA, on one of the first GMs. It was so fast and from that day on, we all had to have the Italian motor.

Dave never got out of shape on a bike, he always looked in control and once he

England pride

got in front you couldn't get by him. He obviously had a great speedway career when you add up all his FIM gold medals for team and pairs. He could have won the individual world title too – if only he'd not cut corners with his equipment and hadn't drilled the arse off everything!

But I come back to how mean he was and can offer a great example from an incident that happened in the winter of 1973. We were both riding trials on our sponsored Bultacos and we'd do different things to them to try and make them go that little bit better than the rest. Well, Dave had the bright idea of filing away the slide on the carburettor, which he thought would make it run a lot cleaner on the bottom end.

His filing away of the carb obviously didn't work for him but rather than throw that one away and buy a new one, he bodged it together with Araldite and hoped it would hold in place. Anyway, Dave came over the top of the hill to where me and four or five others were parked at the bottom, ready to start the next section. We were chatting away, weighing up the next bit of the course, when we suddenly heard this almighty crash. We looked round and saw that Dave had hit all our bikes – he physically bent one bloke's bike so badly that he had to pack up riding that day.

What had happened was, as Dave came over the top of the steep hill, his bit of Araldite had fallen out of the carburettor slide, jammed the throttle wide out and sent him hurling at high speed down the hill towards our bikes. He just couldn't stop and he broke his leg – all for the sake of buying a new £2.00 carburettor slide!

We had to carry him out of the woods on a big sheet of corrugated iron. It was quite serious, forcing him to miss the start of the season at Leicester, but he obviously didn't lose his mean streak as the years went by!

My guess is DJ liked the look of my latest leather jacket and decided to get one for himself.

Before a Test against Australasia at Ipswich, 1978. Left to right: John Louis, Tony Davey, Terry Betts, myself, Michael Lee, Gordon Kennett, Peter Collins and Dave Jessup.

Michael Lee

He was his own worst enemy throughout most of his career. Contrary to what Michael claimed in his interview with *Backtrack* magazine last year, he completely wasted his career and the chance he had to dominate and win more world titles than the one he won in 1980.

I think he was badly influenced by the Americans, particularly Kelly Moran who I saw as his worst influence in his younger days. I know Michael still says that the Americans didn't lead him astray but if it wasn't them, then who else was it? Certainly no-one in the England camp. I think he's just being loyal to his American mates by saying that.

Although I can understand why he was drawn to the 'fun-loving' Americans and why he described us English blokes as 'boring' by comparison. While we wanted to be speedway riders the Ivan Mauger way, perhaps Michael preferred to do it the Bruce Penhall way? Not that Penhall was in to drugs that I know of, but he was more of a party animal and us older English blokes weren't. Penhall could party but did he take drugs? He didn't around speedway, I know that much, so why did Michael feel that he needed to?

I don't think Michael was able to cope with winning the World Final at such an early age. Maybe if he'd won it later on in his career, when he might have been more mature, he would have gone on to have enjoyed a more successful career and coped with the pressure much easier.

But he has no-one to blame for his downfall but himself. He was the one who was caught with cocaine in his car – nobody else. No-one put the drugs there, did they?

But he went straight from winning the speedway world title in Sweden to winning the World Longtrack Championship the following year.

I was a law unto myself at times but Michael just thought he was above everyone and everything. He couldn't accept discipline in any way.

I spoke to his father, Andy, about it a few times and he'd just shrug his shoulders and say: 'Well, it's Michael's life' and he'd let him get on with it. Maybe Andy

England pride

could have done more to have helped his son? I know John Berry tried hard to try and change Michael but nobody could. And I don't think being at King's Lynn was necessarily part of his problem. He went to Poole in 1983 and nothing changed, did it?

Michael's ability was phenomenal, especially as he shouldn't really have been a speedway rider. People say that I was too tall to be any good but Michael was much taller than me – he really created his own style. That tells you just how good he was on a bike. I saw him when he first came to King's Lynn in 1974 and even if he was a bit harem-scarem, he always looked quick and had his dad behind him. Andy was a major influence and ensured Michael always had top equipment.

Michael followed on from me in several ways. Apart from taking over from me at Lynn, he came to Poole after I left and his two British Championships followed in the two years after mine.

He had a couple of bad injuries to his back and neck that interrupted his career and couldn't have helped him.

I rated Michael a better rider than Peter Collins, because he was a better starter. He could race and he could pass, and they had the same ability on a bike, but Michael made a lot, lot more starts compared to PC. And that makes all the difference in the really big meetings.

He never offered me any drugs, though. The only time I saw him doing anything untoward was when he appeared to slip something into Dave Jessup's bottle of orange in the pits. I say orange, but DJ was so mean that it was more like water because he'd diluted the orange so much! When DJ was out for a race, I saw Lee sneakily unscrew the top and do something to the bottle but someone must have told Jessup because he tipped it away before he next went to take a sip. Michael was probably just messing around, I don't know.

Whenever I think of Michael, I just shake my head and think to myself what a waste of great ability.

Although quite tall for a speedway rider, Michael still had a neat and very effective style of riding.

169

Even when you were out in front of Kenny, as in this shot from a Wimbledon v Halifax clash at Plough Lane, you knew he would always fight until the finish.

Kenny Carter

I rode with him a little in my latter days with England, when he was the rising self-proclaimed national No.1 and I was very much the Old Boy of the team. He was out for one thing and one thing only – himself.

He was probably the most single-minded speedway rider ever, or certainly in my time, and he totally believed he would be the best in the world. Was he too obsessed? Can you be too driven? Ivan was also very driven, although he was obviously able to control it.

You had to admire the way he overcame such bad injuries and still went out and won races, but he was also like a canon waiting to explode. And in the end he did in very sad and tragic circumstances.

Kenny couldn't control his emotions at all, and would let off at anyone and everyone around him when things were going against him. I think because he got away with being badly hurt so many times, he didn't give a shit about crashing – and Chris Pusey was another who was like that. If there was a gap, you could be sure that Kenny would go for it, whether he took you out in the process or not.

There was too much going on between Kenny and Bruce Penhall, but Carter was the only loser in that battle. He should have realised that if he didn't win one race against Penhall, he could win the next. But he had to win every time and it just doesn't happen. You only had to watch their infamous heat 14 clash in the 1982 World Final to see that it was going to end in tears. He just wanted to stuff Penhall, whereas Penhall just wanted to win.

If Carter had won in the Los Angeles Coliseum that night, I don't think he would have gone on to dominate speedway for long. He would have burnt himself out very quickly, because that was the nature of the guy. I don't think he had the temperament to have stayed at the top. I don't believe Kenny could have won a World Final unless he did everything absolutely right and things also went wrong for his main rivals. Michael Lee could have put 10 very good races together at any given time, but Kenny could always blow a fuse . . . especially if there was an American in the race.

It's a great shame, but he was his own worst enemy in the same way that Michael Lee was. I don't care what anyone says, to be able to go as fast as Kenny did and to be as good as he was, you have to have quite a lot of ability. He had ability as well as a screw loose.

I beat him once while I was guesting for Eastbourne against Halifax by tricking him at the gate. I just let the clutch go slightly and, being so hyper, he just went through the tapes. He came back afterwards and gave me a bit of verbal, but when he calmed down he agreed that I'd taught him a useful lesson.

"Kenny couldn't control his emotions at all, and would let off at anyone and everyone around him when things were going against him. I think because he got away with being badly hurt so many times, he didn't give a shit about crashing – and Chris Pusey was another who was like that. If there was a gap, you could be sure that Kenny would go for it, whether he took you out in the process or not"

Riding for England always meant a lot to both of us.

SIMMO

On a crisp morning in February, 1978, I was invited to be part of the Golden Jubilee of British Speedway celebrations at Hackney. I was proud to be asked to appear in an exhibition match-race with my fellow former England captain, Belle Vue legend Jack Parker.

But there was an interesting twist in that Jack rode my four-valve Weslake, while I was mounted on a pre-war Douglas bike.

Jack, who used to dominate the old Golden Helmet match-race series, was around 72-years-old when we met up at Waterden Road that day, but I couldn't fail to be impressed by his enduring enthusiasm for speedway.

Hackney promoter Len Silver introduces Johnnie Hoskins before the jubilee meeting.

172

Golden Jubilee of British Speedway

And now for something completely different . . . I've got to admit, the vintage Douglas bike I rode at Hackney on that historic day took a lot of getting used to. I tried to put on a show for the fans, with a bit of leg-trailing, but the bike wasn't exactly suited to the slick conditions. Give me a Weslake any day.

Jack still looks the part, while I struggle to get to grips with the old Duggie.

11

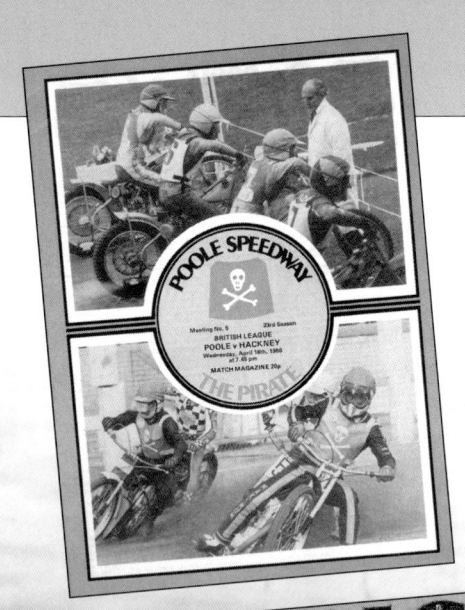

SIMMONS SACKED IN RACE ROW

HUNG OUT TO DRY

SIMMO

WHEN the end came for me at Poole it was very acrimonious and nothing like how I would have wanted to say goodbye to the club where I'd spent the best six years of my career and enjoyed the adulation of the fans.

The 1980 season was all but finished when my home track staged a low-key best pairs meeting on October 1 featuring all the Pirates and several other riders, mostly from local tracks. It was a nothing meeting really, an end-of-season filler with not even any prize money at stake, but the night of the Sheba World (Travel) Best Pairs will forever be remembered as the end of the line for me at Wimborne Road.

The Sheba travel agency were one of my sponsors – and they certainly got some unexpectedly big publicity from their involvement in that infamous meeting.

Now, after 26 years, I can reveal the full story behind my sensational sacking that provoked a supporters' rebellion and led to my sudden departure from the Dorset track where I'd enjoyed my biggest successes in speedway.

Having won two of my first four rides, I trailed in third behind Reading's John Davis and his partner, Malcolm Holloway of Swindon, in my last outing. Their 5-1 ensured they went through to a run-off for the title against the USA duo of Ron Preston – a Poole favourite – and Shawn Moran. My partner, Neil Middleditch, finished behind me at the back, just as he had all night.

Yes, I'll admit it . . . despite my denials when the story hit the local and national headlines, I can honestly say now that I didn't try to win my last ride.

This is what *really* happened...

John Davis approached Neil and myself before our last programmed ride and said that he and Holloway needed a 5-1 if they were to equal the points total of the American pair, Ron Preston and Shawn Moran. He asked if we'd do them a favour by keeping out of the way when we met in the next race. I wasn't keen to drop any more points but as Neil (who hadn't scored anything at that point) and I couldn't win the meeting – in fact, we finished last – it seemed a reasonable request. After all, John was Neil's best mate and a good friend of mine – we were England team-mates and had travelled the world together over numerous years. I was happy to do him a favour and so was Neil. It certainly wouldn't be the first time – or the last – that someone had finished behind an opponent who was in greater need of points in the closing stages of a meeting.

I then said to John that we needed the agreement of Poole promoter Terry Chandler, so John, Holloway, Neil and myself grabbed Terry and informed him of the proposal. He was not particularly happy about it – mainly because he'd rather have seen the local favourite, Preston, win the meeting with Moran.

It was then suggested by John that him and Holloway should beat Middlo and

Hung out to dry

Poole 1980, my last season with the Pirates. Back row, left to right: Peter Prinsloo, Danny Kennedy, Ron Preston, Vaclav Verner and myself. Front: John McNeill and Neil Middleditch.

Terry Chandler . . . couldn't handler the pressure from irate supporters.

myself in the next race, to give them the run-off they wanted, but that Davis and Holloway would not stop the American duo from winning the decisive, last race. This was agreed by all parties concerned.

I said to Chandler that if he wasn't happy with those arrangements, then we'd forget it and Neil and I'd just do our best as normal. But he agreed that the plan sounded OK . . . and just left the four of us to get on with it.

His attitude soon changed, though. At the end of the race, with Davis and Holloway having collected the 5-1 they needed and myself placed third, some of the crowd

177

got a bit hostile and shouted accusations of 'fix' and 'fiddle' from the stands. I thought I'd made it look good enough but they obviously sensed something was up. Crucially for me, I don't think Chandler could handle the pressure of the situation once the irate ones among the crowd started to direct their anger towards him.

In the run-off, Preston beat Davis, with Moran third to clinch victory for the Americans, just as we'd all discussed in the pits beforehand. But, the next day, Chandler announced through the media that I'd been sacked. I received confirmation of the shock news in a telegram.

While Chandler didn't quite go as far as to publicly state that I'd cheated or thrown the race in question, the implication of skullduggery was clear from the media coverage that followed.

> "I had done Davis and Holloway a favour, but not behind Chandler's back. He knew how things had been worked out between the riders in the pits, but when the shit hit the fan he subsequently denied it. It certainly wouldn't be the first time – or the last – that someone had finished behind an opponent who was in greater need of points"

Five years after the Poole furore, John Davis, Neil Middleditch and Malcolm Holloway together again in much less controversial circumstances.

Fair enough, I *had* done Davis and Holloway an unpaid favour for a mate, but not behind Chandler's back. He knew how things had been worked out between the riders in the pits, he was there when we spoke about it, but when the shit hit the fan he subsequently denied it.

Most of the Poole fans were up in arms at my sudden dismissal. Mrs Janet Hughes, a Poole supporter since 1948, immediately set up an SOS (Save Our Simmo) campaign and gathered up a petition containing more than 2,000

Hung out to dry

Remember when speedway used to be back page news in the tabloids.

signatures from Poole people demanding my reinstatement. They had collected most of them when they came to see me compete in the Wimborne Whoppa grasstrack meeting a few days after the pairs event at Poole.

At the Pirates' next home match, against Swindon, many fans demonstrated their anger by calling for the removal of Chandler and waving banners supporting me. One read: 'Simmo's Magic, Chandler's Tragic!' while another less complimentary placard said: 'Chandler is like a kipper – two faced and no guts!'

I had also intended going along to the meeting, to have it out with the management and hopefully resolve matters to my satisfaction, but was warned by police not to turn up in case my presence incited a riot among supporters.

After all the adverse publicity surrounding Poole Speedway, and no doubt feeling the heat himself, Chandler decided to 'explain' more fully his reasons for sacking me. At first, the way the press presented the story, it all centred around his anger at what was described as a "last race incident" but in a statement released to the local press a few days later, he gave 14 reasons detailing why he had decided to sack me. These ranged from claims that I had refused to attend certain meetings; had feigned injury to miss others; walked out of a meeting at Wolverhampton; refused to accept the offers of machinery from team-mates; and had accepted an open booking at Hackney which clashed with a Poole function.

It was all lies apart from the invitation I accepted to ride at Hackney. If Poole Speedway chose to stage its end-of-season dinner and dance before the end of the racing season, how could they expect me to turn away the chance to earn a few extra bob with the a long winter just around the corner?

Of the acrimony surrounding the Sheba pairs meeting, Chandler was quoted as saying: 'Due to an exchange of comments and a statement made by Malcolm Simmons to me before heat 15, the result of the race and the comments afterwards, I considered this the last straw in a long line of unsatisfactory behaviour.'

I knew I had the backing of most of the fans and the way they rallied round me after my sacking thrilled me. It proved that they thought more of me than they did of the promoters. Their tremendous show of support didn't save me from the sack, though, and even the national press covered the story, which made back page news in the *Daily Mirror*.

I still don't understand why I was axed and yet nothing, as far as I can gather, was ever said to Neil Middleditch about it

Do I regret the conversation in the pits and my agreement not to get in the way

179

Shortly after I was sacked, John Davis became a Poole rider – here he is with Middlo and myself before a Poole v Wimbledon match in 1981.

of mine and Neil's two opponents that night? Yes, of course I do, given how things turned out.

I expected Neil to speak up publicly in my defence but he never did. And I was very disappointed that John Davis declined my request to publicly admit what we'd discussed, and agreed to, in the pits on that fateful night. And to this day, neither John nor Neil has spoken up for me over that incident, even though all three of us – along with Malcolm Holloway – were equally to blame.

Five, if you count Chandler. But Reg Fearman's gopher denied that any such agreement had ever taken place.

I'd been well and truly hung out to dry.

The great irony was that as soon as my sacking was announced, Poole named the rider they wanted to replace me as their new No.1 . . . John Davis! JD went on record at the time as saying that he wasn't prepared to leave Reading for Poole unless I remained with the Pirates. Nevertheless, he did join them the following winter, before I'd sorted out a move to Wimbledon. Perhaps this was all part of a pre-planned plot to try and oust me from Poole Speedway?

The whole unsavoury affair hurt me deeply at the time, and I still regret the circumstances of my departure from the club that saw the very best years of my career between 1975 and '80. I loved riding for the Poole people and had wanted to stay there until my racing career finished.

My career with Poole took a big turn for the worst in the summer of the previous year, when the Knotts sold the speedway promoting rights and their whole interest in The Stadium, including greyhound racing, to Reg Fearman. There had been

Hung out to dry

rumours that Poole was going to be sold, so I sought out Charles Knott to see if he would confirm what we'd heard – I thought we had that good a relationship that he would confide in me. He said 'Yes, it's true,' and when I asked who was taking over, he said the name I didn't want to hear: "Reg Fearman".

I told him immediately: "I don't want to be here – I won't ride for Fearman." I didn't like him and always vowed that I would never ride at one of his tracks – Reg also had interests in Leicester and Halifax at the time, having previously sold his stake in Reading. He was a former BSPA chairman, with a wealth of experience, but he wasn't my cup of tea.

Charles wasn't pleased with my reaction to his news about the impending management takeover. He pointed out to me that if I refused to ride for the new management, it would wreck his whole deal and he was adamant that I remained part of his sell-on package. I felt let down and hit back at him by saying I thought he was out of order for not having given me and the rest of the Poole riders the opportunity to move elsewhere, by letting us know what was going on behind the scenes. This was the first, and only, time that I ever fell out with the Knott family.

The takeover deal went through in July, when Fearman took control and appointed Chandler, a former Reading second half rider and Poole's clerk of the course for the previous few years, as his promoter to run the day to day operation. Although I stayed for the rest of '79, I put in for a transfer at the end of the year. But Fearman, like most promoters who'd been round the block a few times, knew my weakness for money and by offering me a couple of grand more than I'd been on the previous season, I agreed to stay on for a sixth season.

While I was better off financially, Poole Speedway wasn't what it was as far as I was concerned and I know others felt the same way. The family atmosphere had gone and, as I said, I didn't want to be riding for Reg Fearman. In all the years I'd known him, Reg had never done me down, or stitched me up in any way, but I'd just taken a general dislike to him. My enthusiasm at Poole waned after he and Chandler took over and that probably showed a bit in my riding, as my average slumped from 10.77 in 1978 to a fraction over nine points a match the following year.

I went on the transfer list again at my own request midway through 1980 but, once again, no move materialised and I continued to ride for Poole, although Neil Middleditch was given the captaincy.

Maybe I should accept some responsibility for my ultimate fall-out with the new management, as I didn't really give them a chance from the start. My mind was made up and, after the Knott family went, I no longer enjoyed being there as much as I had done under the old regime.

From my perspective, it seemed that Fearman's problem with me was that I was Mister Poole Speedway and he wanted to be. But he knew that he never would be the main man there while I was still around as his No.1 rider. The management wanted me out and, after what happened at that ill-fated best pairs meeting at the end of 1980, I'd given them the perfect excuse they wanted to get rid of me.

A couple of weeks after I was dismissed, the Poole promotion asked the BSPA not to accept me as the club's representative at the British League Riders' Championship

SIMMO

One occasion when I was happy to acknowledge Reg Fearman.

Despite the wishes of the Poole management, I took my place in the 1980 BLRC alongside Gordon Kennett and Scott Autrey.

> "I would like to think that the vast majority will accept that I did a lot more good than harm to Poole Speedway and believe me when I say that I always rode for the Pirates with pride. And I was very proud, too, when the *Dorset Daily Echo* conducted a readers' poll in 2004 and I was voted second to Tony Rickardsson as the Greatest-ever Poole Pirate of all-time"

a few weeks later but I had every intention of taking my place at Belle Vue. I'd earned the right to be there by topping the Pirates' averages for the sixth consecutive season.

I *did* represent the Pirates at Hyde Road and, on the pre-meeting parade, who should be one of the guests of honour introduced to all 16 riders but . . . Reg Fearman. He went down the line, shaking the hand of each rider in turn, and when he got to me I just turned my back on him. I wouldn't acknowledge him at all.

The whole episode had overshadowed all the many good things I'd done with Poole, where I enjoyed legendary status and, hopefully, still do.

I don't know how the Poole fans, who were supporting me then, will react when they read these admissions. Possibly some will feel a little betrayed that they backed me 100 per cent when I was sacked for 'fixing' a race that really was of very little consequence. I hope that they prefer to recall the many happy times when I led the team to victory or gave them pleasure with a race win or match-winning performance.

I would like to think that the vast majority will accept that I did a lot more good than harm to Poole Speedway and believe me when I say that I always rode for the Pirates with pride. And I was very proud, too, when the Dorset Daily Echo conducted a readers' poll in September 2004 and I was voted second to Tony Rickardsson as the 'Greatest-ever Poole Pirate of all-time'. There is no doubt that the six times World Champion deserves his No.1 status in the all-time rankings at Wimborne Road, although I was delighted to poll only five per cent less votes than the Swedish superstar.

It was just such a great shame that my association with the team and the town had to end the way it did.

Hung out to dry

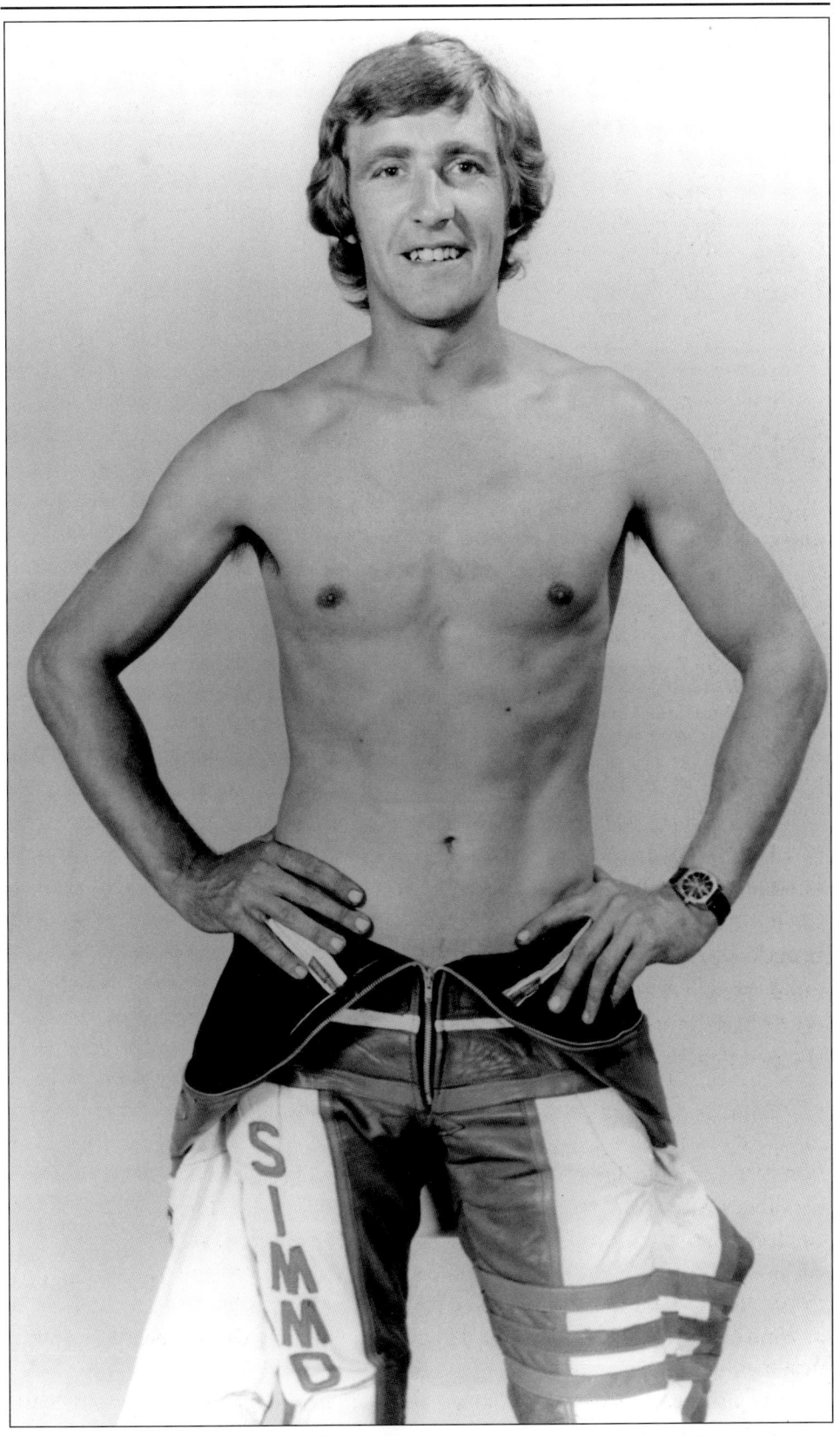

Not even the great Tony Rickardsson has appeared as the Daily Mirror's 'Page Seven Fella'.

12

DO ME A FAVOUR

Simon Wigg and I weren't laughing when we were caught up in the race-fixing 'scandal' of 1984 – and each ended up with a year's international ban and a fine.

MY admission, in the previous chapter, that I deliberately didn't try to pass my two opponents in that best pairs meeting at Poole will undoubtedly horrify many speedway purists and others who like to think that no such shenanigans went on in my day.

It's an unwritten rule among speedway riders, promoters and administrators that any whiff of wrongdoing is swiftly swept under the carpet. It's like speedway's own code of *omerta*.

But let me say right from the start that I'm absolutely sure that very little or no race fixing exists in speedway today. It never has done in bread and butter league and cup competition anyway, as far as I know.

But at ordinary individual meetings, and under the old World Championship formula, when we had to progress through various qualifying rounds to reach the one-off World Final . . . well, there was quite a lot of ducking and diving going on as riders asked for, and gave, favours depending on their circumstances.

And anyone who denies that this happened was either living on a different planet or just won't admit the brutal truth.

Of course I'm not saying that speedway was riddled with widespread corruption or that bribery was rife among the riders. Far from it. What I am talking about is a simple scenario where one rider says to another: 'Look, I just need a point or three to reach the next round of the World Championship, so can you please do me a favour and stay out of my way around the first corner? You don't need the point(s) in any case, whereas I do. And by the way, here's 20 quid for your trouble'. It's not a bribe in my eyes. It's just a way of covering potential loss of earnings.

Sometimes, favours would be given without money changing hands – for example, it was considered even more of a crime to beat your team-mate in an important individual World Championship qualifier if you were already through to the next stage and he desperately needed any help you could give him. That's not being crooked. It's looking after your mate, showing a bit of loyalty to a friend in need. I'm sure that Joe Screen rightly kept out of Mark Loram's way when his fellow Englishman was about to clinch the 2000 Grand Prix series, although the nature of the GP series itself means that it is nowhere near as open to abuse as the old World Championship qualifying system, culminating in the one-off World Final.

You won't hear or read about riders admitting to these things but, believe me, they *did* go on in my time – and I should know.

For example, in most of the second-half finals I've ridden in around the country, the points money was split equally between all four riders. That's not the same as buying and selling points and, in many cases, it was probably the best race of the night anyway. I know I still wanted to beat Terry Betts whenever we met in the

Do me a favour

second-half as King's Lynn riders, regardless of who was paid what, but the split payments thing made the promoters happier because they didn't want their own riders killing themselves to be top dog.

The first point I ever bought was from my old West Ham captain, Ken McKinlay. We were contesting the same World Championship round at Halifax and I had around six or seven points after we'd all taken four rides. Ken came up to me before my last race and, in an almost matter of fact way, said: "Do you want to get through to the next round?"

"Of course," I replied.

"It'll cost you a fiver then," he added.

Ken had already qualified from the meeting, so he moved over and let me take second place for the two points I needed to be sure of joining him in the next round. That was it, done and dusted. I handed over five pounds to him at the end of the meeting, or the next time I saw him at West Ham, and we both went home happy to have qualified.

To me, it was part and parcel of speedway and typical of what went on in the World Championship year after year.

Speedway historians have claimed in print that some of the most famous World Finals were decided after two or more riders reached a 'deal' in the pits before a crucial race, going back to the earliest days of the World Championship in the late 30s and early 40s. In 1951, they tell me that Jack Biggs would have been crowned World Champion at Wembley if only he'd 'paid off' his last race rivals, but he was either too stubborn, proud or confident to do so. Biggs needed just one point from his last scheduled ride to clinch the title, but he finished last behind two other riders, who had no hope of winning the meeting, and then blew it completely by finishing last in the run-off for the famous winged wheel. Maybe Jack slept with a clear conscience that night, but I doubt that he got any sleep at all after letting what would have been his only world title slip through his hands, all but for the sake of seeking a favour when he needed it most.

After a couple of seasons in the sport I was aware of the fact that small amounts of cash changed hands as riders bought a point here and there. I was aware of it but until that day with McKinlay at Halifax I'd not been involved in it – I wasn't good enough to have been before then. I would never have thought to have gone up to Ken and ask a favour, because he was so much better than me. But he had obviously looked more closely at the programme than me and . . . well, a fiver's a fiver.

To get through to the next stage of the World Championship at such a young age was very good for me, and I saw nothing wrong in buying a point to make absolutely sure I got there. And all these many years later, I still don't regret my actions.

That was my first dealing but it was by no means the last. In my whole career I'd say that I have not sold a point to an opponent, in an individual meeting, more than a dozen times. I know it's not right but it happened.

A lot of the time, it was more a case of the rider concerned guaranteeing his passage to the next round. Chances are, he would have beaten the other bloke he'd bought the point(s) from anyway. It's like taking out an insurance policy to protect yourself against an unforeseen misfortune, a slowing engine or another mechanical mishap that can ruin everything.

That's what I did in my last ride of the British Final that I won in 1976. I was the best rider at Coventry that night, head and shoulders above the rest, and had won all of my first four rides. But in my last race, I got halfway round the first corner and my clutch started to slip. I could smell the clutch burning and was on tenterhooks whether I'd finish the race and win the championship. As luck would have it, it held out and I went on to complete the biggest victory of my career. But if the clutch problem had got worse, and I'd lost a little speed, at least I had the peace of mind to know that the blokes behind me would slow up a bit and not bust a gut to go racing past me. They had nothing to gain and I had it all to lose, so I had a quiet word with them before the crucial heat.

I'm not talking here about thousands, or even hundreds, of pounds changing hands in shady corners of the pits. The 'pay off' for the rider who did the favour would more often than not be no more than the same money they could have collected from winning the race.

And can anyone who saw me win the 1976 British Championship with an emphatic 15-point maximum honestly claim now that I didn't deserve to win the once coveted title at Coventry on that night?

Or that I didn't deserve to at least be runner-up to Peter Collins in the World Final at Katowice later that same year? On that occasion, before my last ride, I had a quiet word with Anders Michanek and asked him to stay out of my way, as there was still a chance that I could win the title if PC messed up badly in his last race. 'Mich' was only in the rerun of heat 17 as meeting reserve after the Russian, Valeri Gordeev, had been excluded but I'd always got on well with him and thought nothing of asking him for a little bit of co-operation when I needed it most. Mich liked to be alone a lot of the time and wasn't exactly popular with a lot of the other riders, some of whom used to take the piss out of him for being so precise – like wearing gloves when unloading his bike and that sort of thing. But I never did make fun of him and I think he respected the fact that I respected him.

Michanek was very unlucky not to have qualified for the World Final as one of the 16 starters, having won the title two years earlier and finished runner-up in 1975, so I knew he was very capable of beating me

Anders Michanek was happy to stay out of my way.

Do me a favour

Wiggy deserved his place as the sole Englishman in the 1984 World Final.

at any time. I didn't offer, or pay him, anything for keeping out of my way – he finished second behind me – and I would've done the same for him.

It didn't matter in the end, although I'm sure that had he needed a bit of help, PC would have said to Ivan Mauger, before heat 20, what I'd said to Mich a few races earlier. Ivan had helped to set PC on the path to glory when they were team-mates at Belle Vue years earlier, so I'd have been an idiot to think that Ivan would have done anything to stop Peter from becoming World Champion. As it happened, PC could afford to settle for a place behind his old mentor in Chorzow before snatching the gold medal. I am certain World Finals through the years are littered with similar such instances of favours.

Occasionally, the stakes did go higher and big money changed hands. The most I was ever offered to deliberately not try to win a World Championship race was £1,000. But on that occasion I was also offered TWICE AS MUCH to beat the rider concerned by a representative for a national federation – after I'd lied to him that the rider had just offered me double what he'd really promised to pay! So I was effectively in a no-lose situation, although I did genuinely race for it and, in that instance, pocketed a grand from the rider who beat me fair and square. So there's another example of the best rider coming out on top regardless of his 'insurance policy'.

> **"Occasionally, the stakes did go higher and big money changed hands. The most I was ever offered to deliberately not try to win a World Championship race was £1,000. But on that occasion I was also offered TWICE AS MUCH to beat the rider concerned by a representative for a national federation – after I'd lied to him that the rider had just offered me double what he'd really promised to pay!"**

The most famous case of alleged race fixing in British speedway was in May 1984. The Speedway Control Board was forced to hold a tribunal hearing at the RAC's Belgrave Square headquarters in London the following March after the *Sunday People* ran a series of sensational articles alleging race-fixing and corruption in the sport. *The People* had sent undercover reporters to entrap a few selected riders and Wiggy and myself were the prime targets for their 'sting'.

The tabloid rag's most damning accusation was that I had helped Simon to reach the British Final of the World Championship at Coventry by fixing a race in the semi-final at Oxford, where a shoulder injury caused him to struggle badly all night and narrowly miss out on the eighth, and last, qualifying berth,

I just about made it through to the big meeting at Coventry but, at the age of 38, I knew I had no realistic hope of getting much further along the championship trail. My bikes weren't going well and I was right off form, so I was happy to stand down and let Wiggy take my place. He was a 24-year-old England international who was really going places and, as I said, it was only his shoulder injury that prevented him from qualifying direct for the British Final in the first place.

After I feigned illness to let Simon into the Coventry round, he went all the way to the '84 World Final, where he did well to score nine points as England's only representative. That fine sixth place achievement in itself vindicated my decision to

No-one, apart from the British fans, said a word against Bruce Penhall when he deliberately – and blatantly – let three fellow Americans beat him in a World Championship qualifier at White City in 1982.

Do me a favour

accept the payment of a couple of thousand pounds that reached me via Simon and one of his main sponsors.

Although the SCB tribunal found Wiggy, myself and Mark Courtney (who allegedly received fifty quid from Wiggy at the British Final) not guilty of bribery and corruption, we were found guilty of 'conduct prejudicial to the sport'. Wiggy and I were also both banned from the World Championship for a year and fined £1,000 plus £900 costs each. Courtney was initially banned from riding until May 1 of that year, fined £200 and ordered to pay £200 costs.

Ironically, I would not have received a penny from Wiggy or anybody else if only Kenny Carter hadn't torn up our carefully planned script and won the vital heat 20 in question at Oxford. Wiggy, who rode in agony with his shoulder strapped up, had it all worked out in the pits before our last race. He knew exactly in which position Kenny, John Louis (who had already qualified for the next round) and myself needed to finish in our last ride to ensure we all got through to the British Final. And it was all going to plan until Kenny came charging past myself and then Wiggy, who almost fell off, with Kenny going on to win and Louis at the back. As John stood to lose the most for coming last, I thought the three of us chipped in to compensate his loss of earnings, to the tune of £250. That's how I remember it anyway – Wiggy and myself paid Carter and I thought he paid the full amount to John.

Tragically, Wiggy and Kenny are not here to confirm or deny my version of events from 22 years ago, but I phoned John recently, just to check my facts, and he remembers that night at Oxford completely differently to me. He insists he was not involved in that race fix in any way and received no payment whatsoever. John says that the reason he missed the start and was running last in that decisive heat was due to the fact that he had just started wearing glasses under his goggles. He says that they misted up badly on the start line in that race, caused him to miss the start and, on a track that was wet and mucky, there was no chance of him passing anyone.

If that's how John remembers it, so be it. In all fairness, he was the only one of us who appeared before the tribunal who was completely exonerated of any wrongdoing. I just can't help but wonder why those glasses didn't steam up in his previous four races that night! Still, no-one can question the immense contribution John Louis had made to British speedway and Ipswich in particular.

Kenny had himself ridden the qualifying round at Oxford despite being in great pain from a broken leg that he had encased in a special oversized boot. After we came back into the pits to ask him what the hell he was playing at, he just shrugged his shoulders and mumbled something about the track conditions getting worse and how he was worried about falling off and risking further damage to his leg. He said he'd been getting in all sorts of trouble by riding so slowly at the back and had to get a move on. That was Kenny all over – he could lose the plot very easily! Wiggy was devastated and that's why he needed me to withdraw from the next stage through 'illness' to reopen the door on his World Championship hopes.

Again, I realise that many of you reading this will be horrified by the events I've just described but I've been as honest as possible here and I couldn't see anything wrong in what we did.

What's more, I still don't regret it.

I couldn't see how what happened at Oxford, and my dropping out of Coventry for Simon Wigg's benefit, was any different to what the four Americans concocted in their last ride of the Overseas Final at White City in 1982. On that occasion, Bruce Penhall made no secret of his intention to cruise round behind his three fellow Californians to ensure they all qualified for the next stage of the World Championship that year. Penhall, who misjudged the mood of the British fans by blatantly pulling wheelies at the back, was booed by the crowd and visibly shocked by their reaction.

But no-one at *The People* screamed that Penhall should be banned, as Wiggy and I were two years later. What was the difference? What was the harm in us doing what we could to enhance the chances of England producing another World Champion? I made Penhall right for what he did to help his three compatriots – we just made it look better than he did!

Wiggy's problem was that his fine efforts in scoring nine points in the Gothenburg World Final only added further fuel to the *The People's* claims. By reaching the World Final he'd made their story even bigger than it already was. Simon had been naive to allow the reporters to get too close to him, having befriended him in the guise of newspaper journalists from Sweden who turned out to be investigative reporters hell bent on blowing the whistle on speedway.

I must admit, though, those arseholes from *The People* were very convincing actors, or liars to put it another way. I invited a few of them around to my place for a cup of tea and a chat one afternoon, on the pretext of giving them an interview about drugs in speedway and how I was totally against it. I was happy to talk to them on that basis. Later on, they would turn off their microphones and say something like, "how about that time when you did this or that . . . ?" and I'd go: "Yeah, 'course I took a hundred quid off him for that." I'd got to know them over a period of weeks and started to trust them – not suspecting that they still had hidden tape recorders running. And to help convince me of their motives, they even got me to talk on my home telephone to some guy in Sweden who was claiming to be their boss. He sounded genuine enough but the truth was, they had pulled off an elaborate scam and those of us riders caught up in it had been done, hook, line and sinker.

Of course, when we were hauled before the Speedway Control Board on Monday, March 15, 1985, we totally denied all *The People's* published allegations. We had been conned by the paper's reporters into making confessions but, faced with their serious allegations, our only way out was to turn everything around on them and say to the Board that we knew we were being misled and that we deliberately told *The People* hacks lies to set them up with stories. It was a load of bollocks but, thankfully, SCB chairman Michael Limb and the three other 'jurors' believed us.

With insufficient evidence to throw the book at us, the SCB had to be seen to be taking some serious action, so Wiggy and I were both banned from the following year's World Championship, which, at my age and stage of career, didn't really matter much to me. The 12-month international speedway ban was a much bigger blow to Simon, although I was glad to see him turn that setback into a major positive by winning his first of five World Longtrack Championship titles in '85.

Do me a favour

John Louis, seen here in action at the 1976 Inter-Continental Final, firmly denies receiving any money from *that* race at Oxford. John was the only rider completely cleared by the SCB tribunal in 1985.

The two grand I received for giving up my British Final place to Wiggy was recovered by the SCB, who made me pay up £1,900 in a fine and costs, in addition to the 12-month ban. But to be honest, it was a pretty frightening ordeal to go through and I seriously feared, right up until the day of the tribunal, that we might even have been banned for life. I would have been devastated if that had happened, because the punishment would not have fitted the crime.

The two people we owed most thanks to for getting us off the hook were Ivan Henry, the former Arena Essex co-promoter and main sponsor of Danish star Bo Petersen, and the professional barrister he got to represent us at the hearing. We were very lucky to have them on our side.

I know people will question my morality and accuse me of 'selling speedway out' – and June, too, has been appalled to hear about some of the things I've been involved in – but I can still sleep at night. I can say, hand on heart, that I have never been involved in anything untoward in league matches or team meetings for club or country – only individual events. Oh yes, and that bloody best pairs meeting that brought to an end my career with Poole.

Like it or not, that's just the way it used to be. But I realise that's not going to mean redemption for me.

13

BACK ON TRACK

Wimbledon 1982 – back row, left to right: Alan Mogridge, Brad Oxley, myself, Anders Eriksson and Cyril Maidment.
Front: Dave Jessup and Kai Niemi.
On bike: Roger Johns.

SIMMO

IF anyone thought that my sacking by Poole would be the finish of me as a top flight rider, they would be proved wrong. I signed for Wimbledon in 1981 and had four happy years with the Dons – two of them as a No.1.

On my first return visit to Poole with Wimbledon, I orchestrated a superb 41-37 BL victory for the Dons, set a new track record when I beat the Pirates' new top man, Scott Autrey, by 40 yards and would have scored a maximum 15 points had I not team-rode and finished just behind my partner, Kai Niemi, in the race that swung the match our way. Victory at the south coast track tasted all the sweeter because Wimbledon were virtually a six-man team, operating the rider replacement facility for the injured Dave Jessup.

And in my second season at Plough Lane, I even earned a Test match recall with England, at the age of 39.

Wimbledon was my first choice, I'd always enjoyed a lot of very good meetings there, and with Larry Ross wanting to join Belle Vue, it all fell into place. I dealt with Cyril Maidment, who would automatically refer all financial deals to his bosses at the Greyhound Racing Association (GRA), who ran speedway and everything else that happened at the well appointed south London stadium. I think I had to accept a lesser up front payment of £8,000 in my first season with the Dons but I was just happy to be there.

My period with the Dons in the early 80s was probably the most boring of my career – devoid of controversy and nothing out of the usual ever happened – but it was an enjoyable time for me and I loved the Plough Lane track. John Forster always prepared the track superbly and even if the weather did its best to spoil things, you could rely on him to turn it all around and provide a raceable surface in the space of an hour. There were times when we rode in the wet and yet the surface was still unbelievably good, although he was probably helped a little by the tarmac base, laid for the benefit of stock cars, before the bends were later laid within the stock car circuit.

The shape itself was completely different to what it had been when I became West Ham's cup hero there in 1965. In those days the circuit was much longer, more pointed in the corners and not an easy track to ride. You could even say it was one of those trick-tracks. I'm not sure when the shape changed drastically but they made the circuit shorter and, although it still wasn't easy to ride, I loved it nevertheless. You had to be able to use your head and, if the surface was spot on, there were so many different ways to ride it.

The only thing against Wimbledon is that gate four was always so much better than the three other starting positions. It must have been the only place in the country where, as captain, if you won the toss, you chose gates two and four in heat one.

Back on track

I think the big advantage gate four had was down to the fact that they used to put the stock car fence posts in around that area, where it was that little bit softer, and grippier, than the rest of the starting grid.

It was a pleasure to turn up at Wimbledon – everything, from the GRA-owned stadium itself to the car park and the dressing rooms – was all quality. Even when Wimbledon's track was very wet, it still looked good, whereas over in east London, Hackney's track was often like a quagmire in the early heats. No matter how much you got onto Len Silver about it, he just kept watering away. You wouldn't be able to see a thing if you were behind in the first four races but for the rest of the night it was superb. Well, it was good until Len Silver's latter days in charge at The Wick, when it became too banked and provided only one racing line – right out next to the fence.

I didn't do as well as I'd hoped in my first season in the red-and-yellow, my average dropping below nine points for the first time in 10 years. I suppose a factor in this could have been my experimentation with the new single-cam Jawa, which I was the first in England to try. Weslake and, to a lesser extent, Godden engines dominated in those days, just before the Italian GM burst onto the scene in 1983, and Jawa knew that they had to come up with something more competitive than their double-overhead cam motor that was used almost exclusively by their two works sponsored riders, Ivan Mauger and Ole Olsen.

Those DOHC Jawas were a beast to ride – big and heavy. I recall an example of how difficult they were to manoeuvre when Olsen and I rode in an individual meeting at Ipswich one night. My Weslake had packed up and Ole offered to lend me his Jawa for one race, which I was pleased to do. But did I struggle on it . . .

The Weslake was so much easier to handle by comparison – you could shut off the throttle and virtually do what you like with it, it was very responsive. But the Jawa was all about top-end speed – and you had to keep it at that level, because the second you shut off it didn't want to go forward again. It was quicker than the Weslake, but only at top speed, and it was so much harder to ride.

I remember coming back into the pits after the race and saying to Olsen: "You're a much better rider than I thought!" To be able to ride the DOHC as good as he did, compared to the user-friendly Weslakes most of us were using, was some feat. I wondered how much better Ole would have been during that period if he'd ridden a Weslake but he and Ivan remained very loyal to Jawa when very few riders were prepared to ride them as the four-valve revolution got underway in the mid-to-late 70s.

I'm sure the long-term relationship between Jawa and Ivan has been great for both parties. In fact, thanks to an extraordinary agreement the highly astute Mauger struck with the Czech company 27 years ago, he still receives two brand new Jawa bikes from the factory every year – even though he has retired from competitive racing and now only rides at his training academies and when making special guest appearances. Ivan revealed to me when I met him last year that, just before he won the last of his six individual world titles, in Poland in 1979, he had gone to Katowice seriously contemplating abandoning the Jawa to use the new Godden

Kai Niemi and me clocked up a lot of vital 5-1 heat wins – this time over Belle Vue's Larry Ross.

GR500 machine instead. Evidently Ivan told the Jawa people before that final that their engine was no longer competitive enough at this level. After an exchange of views and plenty of wheeling and dealing, Ivan eventually agreed to stay faithful to the Czech motor . . . .on condition that if he used their engine in the World Final, and won it, the factory would provide him with a brand new Jawa speedway and longtrack bike every year for the rest of his life!

The Jawa representatives must have thought they had nothing to lose when they struck that bizarre agreement with Ivan, who was then 40-years-old and in the twilight of his illustrious career and certainly not among the favourites to win the 1979 World Final. Of course, he proved almost everyone wrong yet again that day and now he can look forward to two brand new gleaming Jawas turning up at his doorstep for the rest of his days. What a super deal and typical of Ivan's negotiating powers!

A couple of years later, Jawa sent a mechanic over from Czecho with the new, single-overhead cam for me to try out on their behalf and I was immediately impressed with it. I first used it in a private practice spin at Wimbledon but when they asked me if I'd be prepared to ride it in the second half of the next meeting, I told them I'd use it in the main match itself. I scored 11 points out of a possible 12, and knew then that Jawa was onto a winner with their new SOHC engine. It had the speed of their twin-cam unit but the easy handling characteristics of a Weslake, though quicker than the English engine because the new Jawa I tested was an overhead-cam model. It also had that trusty Jawa reliability about it. The trouble was, there were very few of those engines about at the time – it was very much in the development stage when I tested it – although I got a semi-sponsorship deal from Jawa in 1982.

Before Jawa completed their development of their SOHC, I reverted to the Godden that I'd first tried in 1979, when my old grasstrack rival Don Godden first launched his new creation. At that time, I'd become disenchanted with Weslake engines, which kept breaking down and were losing the popularity they'd enjoyed

Back on track

in the previous three years. I rode the GR500 for the first time at Halifax, where I'd led every race for a few laps but struggled to finish one, which turned out to be a carburettor problem. Apart from that, I still say the Godden I used at the fast, steeply banked Shay track that night was the quickest upright engine I ever rode. It was so fast in a straight line, although Don then changed some of the characteristics to make it more of a speedway engine. It had lots of top speed, but not a lot else, and at Halifax that was ideal.

I phoned Don before I left the west Yorkshire track and arranged to meet him back in Kent in the early hours of the following morning. He took his engine back, did a few things to correct the carb problem, and it went fine after that.

I found the Godden a lot heavier than Weslake, which meant changing my riding style quite a bit. The GR500 used to run past the corners, so I had to learn to turn that little bit earlier.

Don enjoyed great success in the World Championship through Hans Nielsen, on speedway, and Simon Wigg, on the longtrack – although the German tuner Hans Zierk actually supplied and prepared Wiggy's engines on the continent. But the biggest problem with the Godden was Don himself – you couldn't tell him anything. After riding his complete bike for a number of weeks, I reported back to him with the advice that the engine was too wide and ever so top-heavy in terms of weight distribution. I suggested to him that he should narrow the top of the engine, because my legs were hanging out too wide, and lighten it. He wouldn't have it at first but, about 18 months later, he produced a much narrower and lighter model. Where Don was concerned, I soon learned not to tell him anything – I'd merely suggest certain ideas to him and then walk away. Then a couple of weeks later, I would find that my suggestions had become his ideas!

I did go back onto Weslake, the engine I enjoyed riding the best and on which I had most success. The works factory tie-up I had with them was the most lucrative and successful sponsorship deal I ever had.

Getting back to Wimbledon, they were a good bunch of blokes. I used to get on well with Eddie Jancarz and it was sad, years later, to hear of his battles with the booze after he quit riding and returned to Poland. I knew he liked a drink, but obviously nothing like to the extent that eventually killed him in 1992. Half the time he seemed to be back in Poland fulfilling either club or international commitments but whenever he was with us, he was good for the Wimbledon team.

I never did like Colin Richardson – I found him arrogant, someone who thought he was so much better than he really was. Brad Oxley was as silly as a sheet but he was all right, a young American who had come over to London and didn't look as if he'd ever been outside Costa Mesa in his life before! Although he improved a lot, I think he realised he was never going to be the next Penhall. Brad now runs the Costa Mesa track, where his father, Harry, first made his name running speedway in southern California during the 70s and 80s.

Roger Johns was our captain and if Bettsy was Mister King's Lynn, then Roger was Mister Wimbledon. He was there a hell of a long time and I thought him a very underrated rider – probably even by himself. I don't know why he didn't keep improving and reach a much higher level but I guess some nasty injuries took their toll, especially the broken leg he suffered one night at Poole.

Roger Johns' younger brother, Peter, didn't promise to become much better than a reserve at BL level but he made a great decision when he chose to go down the road of engine tuning and now enjoys a fine reputation as one of the top tuners in the business. I've heard lots of good things about Peter's work – he tunes engines for Leigh Adams and they don't come much better than him.

The problem most tuners have is that no matter how impartial they would like to be, they inevitably end up giving a better service to one rider in particular. I found that, too, when I started to tune engines for several riders. Another problem is that the feedback you get from your riders is often negative – "that engine Simmo did for me was awful," was a typical comment – but they never bother to tell you, or others, when the motor you've prepared for them has got them maximum points. I'm sure that most tuners found this and, because I didn't want the grief any more, I stopped doing engines and went back to riding.

I still get on well with the popular Dutchman Rudy Muts, another who spent some time living at the Simmo homestead. It was Rudy who got me and some friends of mine interested in karting – we used to go to the Buckmore Park track just down the road from me at Maidstone. We all agreed that no-one would buy anything better than the karts we already had, as we were all at a certain level and just having good fun. But Rudy went back to Holland and returned with a super-fast engine, which meant he was suddenly beating us all out of sight.

Being naturally competitive and not wanting him to put one over on us, we then all had to go and buy better engines to try and keep pace with Rudy, so what started out as a bit of harmless fun turned much more serious and competitive. Did I say harmless fun? One day I came up fast behind him and accidentally shunted him off the track and the impact broke his collar bone! Rudy decided he didn't want to play with us any more, he took his toys back to Holland, and our karting sessions ended there and then.

I think Rudy now earns his living chauffeuring around ex-FIM supremo, Jos Vaessen, in their native Holland. June and I met up with Rudy at Collier Street grasstrack the other year. He was over to help the Dutchman, Maik Groen, who rode for Somerset Rebels.

It was disappointing to finish bottom of 16 BL clubs in 1981, so I welcomed the arrival of Dave Jessup to ease some of the pressure on me the following year, when the Dons climbed to 11th place. While I didn't like the idea of him taking some of the glory away from me, I had a better season for DJ's presence. Having said that,

Rudy Muts knows how to have serious fun.

Back on track

when you're averaging only eight points a match, as I was then, there isn't much glory to be had anyway!

I think Kai Niemi and I must have won 20 matches in last-heat deciders in 1982 and '83. Kai liked to ride the inside line while I preferred the outside, so we were well suited as a pairing.

Individually, I grabbed a bit of the limelight by winning the Laurels meeting from Erik Gundersen – one of the oldest and most traditional meetings in speedway history – at the end of '82.

My second season with the Dons saw me experimenting again – this time as the first British tester and user of the new American Carlisle tyre, imported by my old friend Barry Briggs, who now lives in the States. It was much wider, and had a softer rubber compound, than the Dunlop tyre we were using in the BL at the time and was the grippiest thing I'd ever used – the first time I tried it, I couldn't even get the bike into a skid. But it was such a smoother ride and, after taking a meeting or two to get used to it, I soon rated the Carlisle very highly. It gave me a major advantage for a little while, until everybody else started using them.

In speedway you are only allowed one size of tyre – 350mm x 19 inch wheel – and these were the dimensions imprinted on the side of the Carlisle. I'm not sure what metric system they use out in the States but you could see, just from looking at one, that they were much bigger than anything else on the market. I don't know how Briggo got away with it! Of course, Barry raved about them when he first brought them out, as he does with everything he's ever involved in, but the Carlisle really did work – and work very well. It was just a shame that other riders realised how good they were, so my initial advantage was soon lost.

I don't know why the BSPA eventually banned the Carlisle, because I didn't share the views of those who said that they were dangerous. People were blaming a spate of nasty crashes – notably, the death of Reading's American Denny Pyeatt at Hackney in 1982 – on the new tyre but I found that they gave me a much more controlled ride than what I'd been used to.

Ole Olsen was the chief advocate of reducing the size of the tyres we used on safety grounds. Through his strong Jawa connections, he worked with the Czech manufacturer to reduce the Barum tread depth, which Carlisle couldn't – or wouldn't – counter.

Olsen, who had the support of the FIM, believed that by reducing the depth of the tread, our tyres wouldn't grip the surface as much, so it would produce the effect of slowing down the bikes. By this time, tracks were getting much slicker and, much to Ole's dismay, we soon re-tuned our engines to suit the shallower treads . . . and were going faster than before.

They changed the rules to ban the Carlisle, who weren't prepared to change their moulds, and yet the Barum we used over the next couple of years was pretty dangerous and horrendous to ride before the people back at the Czech factory found the right formula. They were unpredictable, whereas the Carlisle was an easy, consistent ride and you had the confidence to go out wide and into the dirt. But when the small treads came in, you were better off riding round the inside, because

SIMMO

John Titman lapped up Carlisle tyres.

With John Davis and 'mad' Kelvin Tatum.

the early Barum didn't hold you up in the dirt to be found further out on the track. The Carlisle also lasted longer so, while they were a little more expensive than their rivals, riders got more use out of them and, therefore, better value for money.

As with the vast majority of new rules surrounding bikes and equipment, it became largely pointless. The riders who were at the top before regulations were altered invariably remained there after any new legislation was brought in.

One rider who benefited from the Carlisle tyre more than most during my time at Wimbledon was team-mate John Titman. I can honestly say that John was a bigger scratch-arse than his fellow Aussie Phil Crump, who I rode with at Swindon in 1985, and Dave Jessup! John would collect up all the old Carlisle tyres, crate them and then send them back home to Oz. Fair play to him, though, he built a very good motorcycle business for himself at home in Brisbane, which I believe is still going strong today. John's bikes never looked sparkling but his engines were always top class and he scored a lot of points throughout his successful BL career.

The team improved even more, up to sixth place, in my third season at Wimbledon when Kelvin Tatum started his speedway career. He was nutty, an absolutely loony! When he first started he had no finesse and would just race flat out from start to finish. He was scoring points but Christ, he was frightening to watch.

It got to around mid-season and I asked him to come out on to the track with me after the meeting, so that I could show him the best way round Plough Lane. I told him not to try and pass me, but to just follow me everywhere I went on the track. It was a case of teaching him how to ride the track smoothly, to pick the right lines to be able to pass people without getting into trouble or crashing. He'd been riding it flat out, a bit hit and miss.

For example, the Wimbledon riders had a knack of passing opponents on the inside coming out of the second turn, as the away riders tended to drift too wide on the exit to the corner. I needed to show Kelvin the finer points, such as how

Back on track

A brave (or foolish?) move by me to try and go round Kelvin and Exeter guest Stan Bear, 1984.

> "I didn't think then that he would go on and establish himself as England's No.1 within a year or two and he was, in fact, our only World Finalist at Bradford in 1985. One thing he always had going for him, though, was an ability to absorb information and learn very quickly. He was one of the few English youngsters I came across who was willing to take notice and I knew that if I told him something, he would go and try it"

to go in wide and chop back on the line, and I think he appreciated my advice at that very early stage in his career development. I could see he was hungry for it and wanted to go places, which was why I took a keen interest in him. I'd known the Tatum family name from my early grasstrack days, when I used to ride against Kelvin's father, Martin.

Kelvin took on board everything I did and you could see the improvement in him after our private coaching session together. He was very unfortunate to break his thigh early in his second season but still showed the courage and character to come back and raise his average by slightly more than a point, to just over seven a match, which was some going considering his inexperience.

I must admit, I didn't think then that he would go on and establish himself as England's No.1 within a year or two and he was, in fact, our only World Finalist at Bradford in 1985. One thing he always had going for him, though, was an ability to absorb information and learn very quickly. He was one of the few English youngsters I came across who was willing to take notice and I knew that if I told him something, he would go and try it. He had intelligence on and off a bike.

It was good in a way that he came to speedway absolutely raw, having only previously ridden moto cross, whereas most youngsters come into it having practiced for years and have already established a certain style of riding, which is often not a good one. It's so hard to change people who develop bad habits and faults at any stage but Kelvin didn't have a style and it was therefore easier to teach him. He only needed a few tips and hints and we all know how successful he has been in his career on both speedway and longtrack. He became ever so neat and polished on a bike, totally different from the wild kid I first saw in our Wimbledon days. I like to think I contributed in some way to what he has achieved and I take my hat off to him.

John Davis, who followed me from Poole to Wimbledon and finished the 1984 season pushing me all the way at the top of the Dons' averages, seemed to have it all but never quite made the final leap into the world class bracket. As I said in the England chapter, John did a great job of covering for me in the 1977 World Team Cup Final, and he was called up for the World Cup Final again nine years later, but he didn't quite cut it at the very highest level. He was a good rider, but not exceptional.

John's biggest problem in my eyes was that he worried too much about the other riders in his race – I don't know if anybody else noticed, but whenever he was in front, he was always looking behind him to see where the others were. He was a very good trapper but he would never ride his own race. I tried to tell him this time and again but he would carry on making the start and then concern himself with looking around for the opposition. There were times when he would try to run me out wide but, more often than not, I'd just turn back underneath him and go past. He wasn't dirty, but he would always try and move you over.

One thing I will say for John Davis, though . . . he was the best at getting himself sponsorship, almost on a par with Ivan Mauger. John pushed himself forward so well, he knew how to get himself noticed and liked the attention. I thought he worried more about fame and image than actually riding and winning races, for no one had a better looking van, with about six pairs of flashy leathers hanging up inside, than John.

Perhaps it didn't help his cause that he was relatively well off and didn't need to win races to put food on the table for his family. His father, Harry, who always looked after John's engines so well, had money and John obviously never went short. But, then again, nor did Bruce Penhall and he won the ultimate prize twice. I can only come to the conclusion that John didn't have the same ability as Bruce and it was really this that stopped him from becoming a genuine world class performer, capable of winning a World Final.

Crayford calling

I was still riding for Wimbledon in 1983 when Terry Russell, who had bought the promoting rights at Crayford from Ladbrokes, asked me if I wanted to become his team manager. I got to know Terry through Andy Galvin, a promising Wimbledon and Crayford junior who spent quite a bit of time at my place, where I'd help him out with his bikes. Terry idolised Andy for some reason and supported him through his Sabre office cleaning company. I also knew that Terry had bought Dave Jessup's big house at Hoo, so there were a couple of connections before I really got to know him well. We were friendly rather than friends.

Terry and I used to live fairly close to each other – he was later based in Upper Shorne (the posh bit!) and I was at Lower Shorne – and we were chatting one day when I mentioned to him that I fancied becoming a team manager. He invited

Back on track

With Terry Russell and Barry Thomas at Crayford, 1983. I enjoyed being the Kestrels' team manager and learned a lot, but one thing I never did achieve was to turn Thommo into a good gater.

me along to Crayford and, knowing I could fit it in with my Wimbledon riding commitments – Crayford were one of the few tracks that raced on Tuesdays – I took up the challenge.

Team managing didn't come easily to me and was more difficult than I'd imagined it would be. At first, I thought it was basically a case of keeping a programme up to date and then telling a rider when he was in or out of a race. It was a major learning curve and I soon realised that I was dealing with seven individuals who all had to be handled differently. For instance, Andy Galvin was in his first full season of NL racing with the Kestrels and he was one who regularly needed a kick up the arse to get the best out of him.

Alan Mogridge was another youngster in his first full NL campaign at Crayford and I ended up seeing plenty of Moggo again when I went on to manage and ride for Hackney from 1984. Moggo was Moggo – he could be brilliant one minute and then absolutely rubbish the next and I distinctly remember telling him at Hackney one night that he'd never make a speedway rider as long as he had a hole up his arse! I told him he was useless, far too inconsistent to make anything of himself in the sport. But, fair play to him, Moggo is still riding now for Stoke in the Premier League, at the age of 42, and still going pretty good, too.

In 1984, when the Kestrels moved lock, stock and barrel to start a new era of NL racing under Terry and Dave Pavitt at Hackney, I went with them, still combining my riding for Wimbledon with team management duties. The next exciting youngster to burst onto the scene was Paul Whittaker and he's one that I'm really surprised didn't make it big. Paul was so good at the age of 16 but he had a number of bad crashes that took their toll on him.

Andy Galvin also had everything going for him – probably the best sponsorship of

205

any NL rider in the country, the best this and the best that – but not the best attitude towards racing. I think everything was too easy for him. He had one really good year with Hackney but he never progressed from that. He could have gone a lot further had he dedicated himself to speedway.

Trevor Banks was another who I came across at both Crayford and Hackney. I didn't only know Trevor well, I actually rode against his father, Monty, on the grasstrack many years earlier and had also ridden many times against his late brother, Graham. Grasstrack always came first for Trevor but he was a good trapper at speedway and did well for Hackney and, later, Milton Keynes.

Alan Sage, another product of the Kent youth motorcycle scene, gave Crayford loyal service but, despite spells with West Ham and Ipswich, he never made the breakthrough at top level. Alan seemed to have everything – he was certainly good to watch from a style point of view – but he lacked speed.

Crayford had their highest-ever finish – third, behind champions Newcastle and Mildenhall – in my only season as team manager of the Kent club and having helped guide Hackney to fourth place the following year, I suppose I did OK in my early years of management.

"I should have switched to the National League when Wimbledon and Poole did"

Cyril Maidment was always my team manager at Wimbledon but Maido wasn't a Ronnie Greene, more a Tony Lewis, and he wasn't a good team manager. But he was Wimbledon Speedway through and through and a very nice bloke too. I would've been happy to have stayed at Wimbledon until I finished riding but at the end of 1984, when I'd regained the No.1 spot in the team after Jessup returned to King's Lynn, the GRA decided that the club would be better off dropping into the National League. By then the senior league was showing serious signs of struggle and, overnight, the BL had lost five tracks. It made sense for the Dons, who were already down on crowds, to switch to the NL, where they would benefit from more local derbies against teams like Hackney (who had made the same switch the previous year) and Arena Essex, plus matches against other southern-based teams like Eastbourne and Canterbury, in the 19-strong NL.

Roger Johns, Mike Ferreira and Jamie Luckhurst had the right idea when they chose to drop down a division with the Dons in 1985, guaranteeing themselves a lot more meetings even if they were on less money than they had been in the BL. I'd known what the National League was all about, and could see what a good environment it was to race in, from working part-time as team manager at Crayford and Hackney.

Even my beloved Poole, where it all went pear-shaped and Reg Fearman's company went into liquidation in 1984, had to revive itself as an NL track, under the new management of Mervyn Stewkesbury, in 1985.

I should have switched to the National League when Wimbledon and Poole did but I was persuaded to stay in the top flight for one final year . . . at Swindon.

14 SWINDON SHAME

CONSIDERING I didn't really want to be at Swindon, or anywhere else in the British League by 1985, I thought I did OK for the Adver Robins. Come the latter part of the season, though, I was finding it harder and harder in top flight company. I was still scoring points as the third heat leader, behind the Danish star Bo Petersen and former Australian No.1 Phil Crump, but it was becoming an increasing struggle.

Weighing on my mind, too, was the fact that Hackney promoter Terry Russell had offered me a very good deal to drop down into the National League with Hackney. Good? It was twice as much as I was earning for Swindon in the higher league. I already knew everyone associated with the HL1 Kestrels very well, having been their team manager the previous season. I could see what a good thing those riders had going for them – lots more meetings than we were getting in the rapidly shrinking BL and, more often than not, on tracks that were much better prepared than a number of the senior circuits.

I knew of Terry's offer and was fully aware of his plans for 1986 midway through the '85 season with Swindon, so it's fair to say that I had one eye on joining the east London track the following year. I had no intention of walking out on the Robins before the season had finished, though. The averages – which govern team strengths at both BL and NL level – wouldn't have allowed me to make the switch at that time anyway.

The averages, with a maximum upper limit, are meant to ensure a fair equalisation of teams throughout the leagues. In reality, it is just a way of forcing the better run tracks to release riders to weaker opponents who, in many cases, didn't have the same professional outlook and ambition as those clubs who had to let riders go.

For the handful of riders who, like me, wanted to drop down a grade, the BSPA threw in an extra obstacle. The average achieved in the BL would be converted and increased to calculate our worth in the NL. This posed a major problem to me in that my Swindon average was going to be too high for Hackney to fit me into their line-up. The BL members of the BSPA didn't like the idea of losing riders to what they considered the inferior division and this rule was as good a deterrent as any to prevent riders from dropping down a league.

But I had my heart and mind set on joining the then thriving National League and, rules or no rules, no one was going to stop me. There was only one thing for it, I

SIMMO

Swindon Robins, 1985. Left to right: Richard Vowles, Per Sorensen, myself, Phil Crump (on bike), Bo Petersen, Ari Koponen, Gordon Kennett and David Smart.

had to reduce my Swindon average quickly. With only about a month of the season left, it was brought to my attention that I needed to start dropping more points – and fast – if I was to be accommodated in Hackney's 1986 team. I was advised that I needed to finish the season with a BL average of less than eight points a match. After scoring 10 (paid 11) points from four rides in our home win against Wolverhampton on October 5, I faded badly. In my next four BL matches for the Robins, two at home and two away, I scraped just 12 points from 15 rides. I wasn't trying any more, it's as simple as that.

With just one league match to ride, the, rearranged BL match at Blunsdon against King's Lynn on October 26, I still hadn't quite reduced my average enough. It meant I went into that finale against my former club knowing that I couldn't afford to score a point if I was to get my way and sign for Hackney. It wasn't even as straightforward as that, though.

I had to take all four of my programmed rides, too! Zero points from, say, two races wouldn't have reduced my average sufficiently, whereas my figures would tumble a lot more by recording four straight noughts. So for the first time in my life I went to a meeting hoping I wouldn't score a single point.

Now I admitted earlier that, probably on about a dozen occasions throughout my long career, I've bought a point or two here and there to ensure qualification through World Championship rounds, or asked for a favour and then reciprocated in return. I repeat, I saw no harm in that. I was racing as an individual, not as part of a team.

What I did that night at Swindon, though, was totally wrong and I still feel guilty about it today. It's the only time I've not tried for my team and I know that I let everyone at Swindon Speedway, and the Robins' supporters, down by deliberately

Swindon shame

trailing last in all four of my rides against my former club.

I don't expect any credit for such unacceptable behaviour but, take it from me, it's not as easy as you might think to finish behind three other riders, especially when you still need to be competitive enough to convince your team manager that you're worthy of being given all four scheduled outings! I couldn't afford to be dropped from any of my rides.

In my first ride I broke the tapes. In my second I suffered 'engine failure' – so far so good . . . or bad, if you look at it the other way. In my third ride I was battling for the lead when I literally fell off on the pit corner and slid into the fence. At least it looked as if I was trying and having a go for the team.

Three rides and no points – just one more to go and it would all be over. Job done. Thankfully, I wasn't dropped from my fourth ride, in which I again finished at the back, and that was the end of my one-year stint with Swindon. I don't think anyone at Swindon knew for sure what I was up to, although the fans gave me some flak for an uncharacteristically poor performance against Lynn and I suspect that Richard Vowles half guessed what was going on with me in our last match. He had every right to expect more from his second heat leader – as I was by that stage with Crumpie out injured – and I let him down that night. I was gutted really, although I was very relieved that at least Swindon had won the match, 46-32, and also collected the aggregate bonus point.

Looking back, apart from that last meeting and my scores dropping away from the start of October, I thought I served Swindon reasonably well. I was fast approaching 40-years-old by then, the oldest rider competing in the top flight, but I still averaged a fraction under eight points a match – and that might have been as high as nine if I hadn't done what I did at the end. I scored three maximums, while our No.1, Bo Petersen, managed only one more than me.

That last meeting also worked out well for the Swedish rider Jimmy Nilsen, my 18-year-old opening race partner, whose 10 points against the Stars meant he achieved the minimum 6.00 CMA he needed to earn himself a work permit for the following season. I can honestly say that I helped Jimmy to get through his first season in Britain, allowing him to win a lot of races. He was one of Sweden's best, young talents at the time – on a par with Per Jonsson who went on to win the 1990 World Final – but with Jimmy, it got to the stage in the end where he thought about things too deeply. He tended to allow little setbacks to get to him too easily, especially as he got older.

The Finn, Ari Koponen, was another who didn't fulfil his potential. He moved with me from Wimbledon, so I knew what he was capable of, but he'd beat someone really good one night and the next he'd finish behind a novice. I couldn't understand it. I also knew Martin Yeates well from our time at Poole. A quiet lad, Martin would take some catching if he hit the front but he spent all his best years in the National League being a big fish in a smaller pond . . . which is where I ended up.

I don't think Alun Rossiter ever put his heart and soul into racing enough to make much of an impact. He could probably have been a lot better than he was but he pratted around too much all his career really. While I could understand 'Roscoe'

The immaculate Bo Petersen, who had the best of everything – thanks to his main sponsor.

becoming a pub landlord, I wouldn't have imagined that today he'd be the Swindon promoter – appointed, ironically, by Terry Russell.

It was a shame for Richard, though, who was already having a tough time and had just about lost the plot by then. He seemed on the verge of a nervous breakdown at one stage, he kept threatening to quit and seemed to go from one stressful situation to another in his attempts to make Swindon a success. I wasn't surprised when his health suffered and he walked away from speedway soon after I moved on.

It was a shameful way for me to end my one and only season with the Wiltshire track, because I'd enjoyed myself there right up until the last month of the season. The track was badly prepared at times but conditions improved after Richard brought in Neil Street as team manager. As well as giving the riders the benefit of his vast experience and knowledge, Streetie also advised on track preparation.

Bo Petersen was the ultimate professional. I think he must have had more new bikes than any other rider in the world at that time, courtesy of his brilliant sponsor Ivan Henry. If Bo missed a start, he'd fit a brand new clutch for his next meeting. A new clutch used to cost three or four hundred quid but it didn't matter to our Danish star – he had the ever-faithful Ivan to pick up the bill. A lot of people were surprised when Bo decided, at the end of that season, to retire from British speedway and return to Denmark to make his money manufacturing boats.

Crumpie was usually one step behind Bo – he'd be there buying all the good stuff that Bo chucked away! Crumpie was a bit of a scratch-arse, never buying anything new. His mechanical set up was brilliant, as you'd expect with someone like Neil

Swindon shame

Street tuning his engines, but you could never accuse Phil of wasting much money on aesthetics.

There was never anything wrong with the stuff that Bo discarded – it was just his frame of mind and the fact that he was spoiled rotten by a great sponsor. Essex-based Ivan supplied Bo's cars and vans and drove him to all his meetings in England. I once asked Ivan – who subsequently had a year as co-promoter with Terry Russell at Arena Essex – how much it cost to run the American-made van that he provided for Bo. He couldn't say for sure but he reckoned it cost him £85 in petrol to get to Swindon and back! I think Ivan even brought Bo a cup of tea in bed each morning! Bo was a very good rider, though. I had some great races with him, especially at Hackney.

I loved Phil Crump. I lent him my bike for a big World Championship qualifier at White City and while I thought that perhaps the English riders in the meeting wouldn't be impressed with my lending a bike to an Australian, I thought 'so what?' I'd do anything for Phil and he was the same with everybody else. He missed the final few weeks of the 1985 season after requiring another operation on his troublesome scaphoid but he was a class act and I liked him being around.

Ironically, a report in *Speedway Mail* more or less accused the Swindon management of conspiring to reduce my average for their benefit, so that I'd fit more easily into their team for the following season. But all the time it was Hackney, and myself, who stood to gain from my end-of-season shenanigans.

I'd been completely selfish at the end of my time with the Robins when I only had thoughts of joining Hackney and an exciting, new era of NL racing. I thought I'd served British speedway very well until then and I'd reached the stage where I wanted to enjoy a few years making life a bit easier for myself.

Jimmy Nilsen – seen here with Cradley's Jan O Pedersen – was another whose average worked out just right.

15 FLYING HIGH AGAIN

AFTER 22 years of continuous top flight racing, I was back where I started in 1986 . . . in the second tier of racing at Hackney, where it all began for me on the shale in 1963.

Except I didn't look at it as a backward step. The National League, with 20 tracks compared to the dwindling 11 that lined up in the British League that season, was very much the place for an old hand like me to be. I knew I'd be good enough to score plenty of points at the lower level and, as I said, I was on even better money than I'd been on in the top flight with Swindon the previous year.

From riding just once every seven days, at times, in the BL, I was suddenly racing four or maybe even five times a week. There was a much greater variety, too. Instead of facing teams twice home and away, as I did with Swindon, the NL had enough tracks going to ensure they only had to meet each other once at home and once away. Instead of going to Oxford four or five times a season with the Robins, I was racing at places as far afield as Exeter and Edinburgh, on tracks that I'd never been to before like Berwick, Mildenhall, Milton Keynes and Birmingham.

Being the elder statesman of the HL1 Kestrels team meant I had a lot to offer the up and coming youngsters around me and I relished the responsibility that co-promoters Terry Russell and Dave Pavitt gave me. They expected big things from me but that was the kind of pressure I welcomed anyway. While Hackney had done well since the new promotion brought NL speedway to Waterden Road following the closure of Crayford in 1983, finishing fourth and fifth in the final table, they had lacked an out and out No.1 who would be virtually guaranteed to score double figures in every meeting. To fit me into their line-up on my assessed 11.50 average, Russell and Pavitt had to sacrifice three riders from their 1985 team under the maximum 45-point limit rule, with Paul Bosley, Alan Mogridge and Trevor Banks the ones to make way.

Apart from forgetting to turn on my fuel tap in a race at Milton Keynes, the '86 season started very well for me. I went 25 races before dropping my first genuine point, to Berwick's Steve McDermott, who was very determined to beat me. In fact, I probably brought the best out of most opponents eager to put one over on me.

The BSPA were certainly determined not to let me have things my own way for too long. King's Lynn promoter Martin Rogers shrewdly tried to exploit the rule that allowed BL clubs to call upon NL riders as No.8 replacement for an injured or absent team member – and I enjoyed some good 'doubling up' between Hackney and Lynn. Or at least I did before the BSPA suddenly dreamt up a new rule that prevented the likes of Dave Jessup, Paul Woods, Mark Courtney, Les Collins and myself from riding in both leagues. The promoters argued that we were putting the novices, who were then filling all the reserve berths in the top grade, at an unfair

Flying high again

From Robins to Kestrels . . . Hackney 1986. Left to right: Richard Pettman, myself, Barry Thomas, Gary Rolls, Carl Chalcraft, Andy Galvin, Paul Whittaker and, a year before his league debut, Mark Loram.

disadvantage but in my book they were just being petty.

The 'Old Hands' were good for the NL, because we improved the quality of the racing and also showed the existing, younger NL riders what they needed to do to get better.

When I made up my mind to drop down into the NL, it wasn't with a view to doubling up between the two divisions, as some promoters clearly thought. But once King's Lynn phoned me up and asked me to be their No.8, to be used as cover, I wasn't going to turn them down. The extra bookings – and earnings – were, of course, most welcome. I came to the conclusion that the BL track bosses who eventually blocked me from riding for Lynn were just jealous that Martin Rogers had his smart idea before they did. Some people wondered why my previous club, Swindon, hadn't snapped me up as their No.8 but, as I say, King's Lynn were first off the blocks.

It was good to go back to Lynn and enjoy myself again without the pressure of thinking I had to score a lot of points, although I averaged more than eight in five League Cup matches at the start of the season before the BSPA stepped in with their rule of convenience.

I've got to say that dropping down a division was good fun and fairly easy for me. I didn't feel any pressure, which meant I was winning most of my races. I liked everything about the set-up, having known Terry Russell for some years and been his team manager at Crayford and Hackney in 1983 and '84 while I was still riding for Wimbledon.

I got to know the Hackney riders very well during my time as their manager. As any good team boss will tell you, riders have to be handled differently, you can't treat them all the same way. Some needed mollycoddling while others needed a kick up the arse. For example, I wouldn't shout at Paul Whittaker because I knew that if I did, he'd go even worse than before. Paul just needed a quiet word in his ear to get him going well again. Bo Petersen and Richard Knight, who both rode under me when I became co-promoter at King's Lynn, were opposites. You could never shout at Bo, whereas Richard would only respond to strong words and being told that he could do so much better. I have always said to riders, and even my former mechanic Ken Beckett, that whatever is said during the meeting ends when the meeting itself does. You can't allow things to fester and that's how it always worked with me.

One rider I just couldn't motivate, no matter what, was Barry Thomas. I'd talk to him before a race at Hackney and he'd nod his head in agreement with me, but then he'd just go out and do his own thing as usual. I could never get through to him. As for helping him to become a better gater, forget it. No-one could ever help Thommo in that respect. Barry would go as fast as anyone, especially around Hackney, and it's such a shame that he never applied himself to make better starts – he could have gone to the top.

Chris Morton is another classic example of a brave, fast racer who never learnt to trap. I don't care what he says, you can learn to gate – but you have to learn how to do it early on in your career. Mort was a bit like me – he couldn't cheat at the start, whereas his Belle Vue team-mate and good mate, Peter Collins, could. PC had great anticipation at the tapes and would often be on the move before the tapes even flickered. The best thing that ever happened to me in speedway was when they brought in the rule that said you couldn't move an inch at the start without being excluded. Mort would have gone further in his career if he had moved to a smaller track, where he would've had to learn how to gate. The trouble is that Mort – and PC – never had to make starts at Belle Vue – they'd pass you no matter what you did to try and keep them at bay.

Paul Hurry is also pretty fearless but he has always listened to too many people. I once spent a whole day with him at Rye House, teaching him how to make starts and finding the right clutch plates to suit his set-up, and he looked like he'd finally cracked it. But then at his next meeting, after chatting to one of his team-mates and telling him what clutch plates he had in, he decided to change them before even trying them in a competitive race. I'd wasted my time on him. He never listened to anyone, including his own family, who told him he needed to lose weight. I think he was about 13 stone most of the time, whereas I remained at 10st 7lbs throughout most of my career and only went up to 11 stone at the end – through age. You're at such a disadvantage by being overweight – that extra two or three miles per hour can be crucial.

Terry Russell offered me a great deal to sign for Hackney – but he couldn't get me on the coach to Exeter.

Hackney was one of the most

Flying high again

professionally run tracks in the country, although I didn't always go along with the idealogy of my promoters. For instance, Terry used to have this big thing about us all having to travel together on the supporters' club coach to our farthest away matches. I went on a Northern tour with them once and it seemed to take days, so just before we were due to go to Exeter I told him: "I'm not going to Exeter by coach – not for you or anybody else!" I had a nice, new van that Hackney had supplied me with and couldn't afford the extra time I knew it would take for a coach to get from East London to Devon and back. He kept insisting that I had to go with the rest of the team, so I said: "We'll see."

I enjoyed the more relaxed atmosphere of the NL, including a happy return visit to Wimbledon and this win over Roger Johns.

On the morning they were about to leave, I phoned up and said I wasn't ready to go yet – I think they were setting off at something ridiculous like 10 o'clock – because I was still working on my bikes. Obviously, I had everything ready and just told Terry this to get out of the coach trip, which I knew would be a nightmare. He warned me: "You'd better be here in an hour, because that's when we're leaving," but I never did turn up.

> **"He had the hump with me big-time . . . and he had the hump a whole lot more on the way home, when the back axle went on their coach and it broke down!"**

Anyway, they set off for Exeter and took Christ knows how many hours to get there, while I reached the County Ground by van in about a quarter of the time. I had six rides in the match and won them all, plus my second half heat and final, and then loaded up and went home. Terry was still annoyed and told me that he wouldn't be paying me any travelling expenses, because I'd gone there off my own bat. I told him: "Stick your f****** travel money. Who gives a shit…I've just got 24 points!"

He had the hump with me big-time . . . and he had the hump a whole lot more on the way home, when the back axle went on their coach and it broke down! Apparently, the coach had to be towed to a garage to be repaired, which meant they had to hire another one to get them back to London. I'm told that Terry turned to his co-promoter Dave Pavitt and said: "That Simmo . . . he's come down 'ere, got an 18-point max in the match, cleaned up in the second half, then he's pissed off home without us and now he's f****** laying in bed while we're sat here, at the side of the A303 at two o'clock in the morning, cold and wet and with a broken down coach!"

I just laughed when I heard what had happened . . . but Terry never did pay me those travelling expenses to Exeter! He's probably still got the hump about it today!

The only major setback in my first season at Hackney was a broken collarbone sustained in July when someone speared me at Long Eaton. It was the most serious

215

Mark Loram didn't have my ears when he first started, in 1987.

My final season and still mixing it in world class company – this time Cradley's Jan O. Pedersen.

Flying high again

injury I'd had for years and it took me a long time to recover from it fully. Without me to spearhead the side, we struggled, let some silly points slip at home and Terry was disappointed that the youngsters didn't emerge as well as he hoped.

I returned to action before the end of the season and was pleased enough to finish my first NL season with nine full and one paid maximum and a 9.70 average as Hackney's No.1 – but the team dropped down to 13th place.

My only mistake at Hackney was a big one – I should never have moved back up into the British League with them in 1987. The money was still good, and not wanting to increase my travelling distance to home meetings, I stayed there for a second season.

It was a very costly mistake by the promotion, too. Terry had decided to quit at the end of 1986 and hand sole control to Dave Pavitt. Dave did his best, bringing in my old World Pairs partner John Louis to manage the team, but he reportedly lost £30,000 that year in the top flight, where we were nowhere near as successful a team and the cost of BL speedway was becoming astronomical. Going back up was certainly a big mistake for me – I was going as fast as I had done the previous year but I was up against the world's best again and could no longer win as many races as before. From 25 BL, League Cup and KO Cup matches, my average dipped to just 5.40 and for the first time since 1964 I failed to record a top flight maximum.

To add to my problems, I broke my left shoulder in the second half in a crash involving my Kestrels team-mates, Allan Johansen and Andy Galvin. The Dane, Johansen, fell off, I laid my bike down to avoid him and although Andy laid his bike down too, he let it go and it hit me in my shoulder, which dislocated on impact. It was the same shoulder that I bust in Germany 10 years earlier, which ruled me out of the 1977 British Final and left me with about only 75 per cent movement in the joint since that crash. I still can't raise my arm to its full length now but I can continue to move it to either side, so it never physically affected my riding to any great degree. I'd previously had a couple of operations on it and damaging the same shoulder again at Hackney didn't do me any favours.

My 1987 season virtually ended there and then, which was a pity as it meant I was unable to ride in my own Silver Jubilee meeting at Hackney on August 9 to commemorate my 25 years in the sport. In addition to the riders who competed in a four team tournament, I also invited along a few 'Old Boys' for a series of nostalgia races – my old mate Terry Betts, John Louis, Martin Ashby, Roy Trigg and Bert Harkins all squeezed themselves into leathers again and I was ever so grateful to everyone who turned out for me that day.

The Hackney riders were disappointed at how the track surface had deteriorated that season, with Simon Wigg – our new No.1, on loan from Oxford – typically outspoken. It was a bit like riding on ice most weeks, they could never seem to get enough dirt onto the track. The shape had also changed, so there wasn't as much passing as the fans had been used to at The Wick and crowds dropped accordingly.

The decision to take Hackney back up into the British League was a big mistake all round. Almost as big a mistake as my decision to go into partnership with Bill Barker at King's Lynn . . .

16 WHO'S THE FRAUDSTER?

THEY say you should never go back, and my return to King's Lynn as a new co-promoter in 1988 was fraught with problems. It ended very acrimoniously, just before the start of the 1989 season, when I had a big bust up with my business partner, Bill Barker, and an unwelcome home visit from the fraud squad.

Yet it all looked so attractive when I followed up an advertisement I saw in *Speedway Star* in November 1987, which basically read 'Track For Sale – so you want to be a speedway promoter?'. I phoned up to find out more details and, to my delight, it turned out the ad had been placed by Martin Rogers, who was looking to sell up after five years as sole promoter at King's Lynn in 1968, when he was then the Stars' announcer and PRO, before becoming general manager of the Littlechild-Crane empire in 1973. In 1983, he became the sole promoter at Lynn, having taken over at Leicester three years earlier. He also spread his interests into the National League with Peterborough and in 1987 helped to organise my Silver Jubilee meeting at Lynn (the other one was at Hackney) to mark my 25 years as a rider. But, by 1988, he'd just about had enough and Oz was in his sights.

From memory, I think Martin's company, Quailmist, was around £60,000 overdrawn at the bank and he wanted that covered by the sale, plus an extra 20 grand for riding assets and the promoting rights. I didn't have that sort of money, or any kind of cash to put in, so I contacted Bill Barker, who'd become a friend after we'd first met by chance when our kids attended the Medway Roller Skating Club in Rochester. He didn't have that much money either but he did own a house that we could use as collateral, so we went into partnership under the existing company name. As with the previous promotion, we rented use of the stadium from the owners, Norfolk Speedways, run by Cyril Crane.

My only previous business experience was the Shorne Speed spares service I ran with Dave Jessup before I became co-promoter at Lynn, but me and DJ never made any real money out of it. Dave persevered on his own, though, and still provides the same good, albeit expensive, service for riders today at tracks like Arena Essex and Rye House.

I had responsibility for the signing of riders, dealing with the riders, team

Who's the fraudster?

Me and Bill Barker welcome Allan Johansen to King's Lynn, 1988. The smiles soon disappeared.

management and liaising with the press as our club spokesman, while Bill looked after the day-to-day business side of the operation. Bill didn't have a clue about speedway, and I was never any good with money, so it made sense to divide our responsibilities in this way. He also ran the commercial side – well, he was a very good bullshitter, wasn't he? – and never stopped trying to raise money through advertising, sponsorship and God knows how many other fund-raising projects.

With the permission of our bank, we took over Martin's existing overdraft and, I think, agreed to pay him his 20 grand in one thousand pounds a week installments from turnstile revenue.

My first signing was Lance King, the American star and World No.3 from 1984, who joined us on loan from Cradley Heath. We also did loan deals to bring in Allan Johansen, after Hackney went back to National League in 1988, and my old England and Wimbledon team-mate John Davis. I must admit, when I signed my old mate, John Davis, I thought I could inspire him to produce a little bit more than he had done previously, although maybe it was too late in his career by then for me to have much effect on him. He was still a bloody good trapper and I thought if I could just keep on at him all the time, encouraging him and offering little bits of advice here and there, that he would finally realise his potential.

We retained Richard Knight, who had been No.1 the previous year, and Aussie international Stephen Davies, who was also part of the Stars team that had struggled and finished bottom of the British League in 1987. Youngsters Adrian Stevens and Roger Horspool were also still around and we completed our team by persuading Bo Petersen, my former Swindon team-mate, to come out of retirement.

We had planned to use Mick Poole but he suddenly went out of the equation when Petersen's main sponsor, Ivan Henry, made it known to me that his man was ready to make a comeback. I felt sorry for Mick, who had flown from Australia to ride for us, and felt bad when I told him that we wouldn't fit him in after all. I got him sorted out at NL Peterborough, where he established himself as the No.1 over the next few years, but I still didn't enjoy doing the dirty on a rider like that. Understandably, Mick wasn't happy with me at the time but I spoke to him about halfway through the season and was pleased to hear that he was happy riding for the Panthers.

At first I told Ivan Henry we couldn't afford Bo but, after a lot of soul-searching and a lot of pressure from Ivan, we finally agreed to take a gamble on signing the former World Finalist from Denmark. Bo's wages were very high – I seem to recall it was something like £250 per meeting guaranteed, plus about £40 or £50 per point, which was a lot of money in those days. I can't remember whether we also paid him a signing-on fee, but we probably did. Bill and I reckoned that the extra Bo cost us would hopefully be covered from a more successful team pulling in more supporters. Although not ultra-strong, I thought it was a side competitive enough to challenge for a top three place, a fair line-up considering it was our first season as promoters.

But, in hindsight, I was wrong to do the Petersen deal – it crippled us financially. Bo averaged 7.26 points from 30 matches, scoring no full maximums and only one paid, and didn't justify his high earnings. More disappointingly for me, he didn't even look too interested for half a season.

Even so, we still managed to pay off Martin Rogers completely before the end of the season, and Bill and I were well into clearing our debt at the bank, but Petersen's financial package drained us, especially after the promising early season crowds soon dwindled to around the 2,000 mark. The Italian, Armando Dal Chiele, made a good impression when he arrived in September but we were scrapping at the wrong end of the BL table by then and eventually finished ninth out of 11 teams. Only Ipswich and Bradford were below us.

When Bill and I formed our partnership, it was on the clear understanding that I would be employed by the company 12 months of the year – I couldn't afford to give King's Lynn Speedway everything from March until October and then have no income come the winter. I'd had more than my fair share of those worries throughout my racing career and I wanted more stability in my life. I also thought I could do a good job of promoting.

But when Bill and I sat down to have a chat and reflect on our first season, he said that the company couldn't afford to pay me a salary during the close season. I'm sure that there was enough money in the kitty to pay me but he just didn't want to part with it. I think we'd originally agreed that I'd be paid £200 per week in the winter – and it wasn't as if I would be sitting on my arse all day, every day,

John Davis and Richard Knight.

Who's the fraudster?

doing nothing to help the running of the club. I planned to be up at Lynn a couple of times a week, doing work that needed to be carried out on and around the track, and also hopefully run some training schools that would benefit us long-term.

When Bill reneged on our agreement, it left me struggling financially, even though I did run a couple of training schools there. Anyway, early in 1989 we started to talk about a possible team for the forthcoming season and one of the considerations was Steve Regeling, the Aussie international who'd previously ridden for Lynn but who had spent the '88 term starring on loan to Exeter in the NL. I took a call from Exeter boss Colin Hill, who wanted to turn the loan deal into a permanent move, and I did the transfer on that basis. I received a cheque for £2,000 from Exeter Speedway, made out to myself, and paid it into my personal bank account.

In my eyes, the two grand Exeter paid covered the winter wages I should have received as per my original agreement with Bill, but he didn't like that idea and we had a big fall-out. He called in the police, accusing me of defrauding our company, and after a succession of big rows about it I ended up having to hand over the £2,000 to him and resign from the company.

Bill couldn't see that I'd sold a rider we had no intention of recalling to ride for us in 1989 and, at the same time, raised the money to fund my wages that winter – the wages we'd agreed I would be paid when we first set up the company. He argued that the Regeling money should have been paid into the club, to help pay off debts. Bill had previously been in the building game and I think he expected me to go out and get a job to tide me over until the speedway season started again.

He never went into how he earned *his* money during the close season – he didn't work but was in control of all the track's finances. Maybe this tells another story?

Looking back, I can see now that I handled the situation wrongly. Maybe if I'd sold Regeling and then consulted Barker about retaining the £2,000 fee for myself, in lieu of wages, he would have considered it, or at least agreed to me keeping part of the money for myself.

As I said, I had no involvement in the financial running of King's Lynn in my year with Bill Barker, and that included knowing nothing about how he handled the monies raised from selling 'King's Lynn Bonds' to our supporters. These were not businessman, just ordinary working class supporters, who gave Bill thousands of pounds to help finance the continuation

> "He called in the police, accusing me of defrauding our company, and after a succession of big rows about it I ended up having to hand over the £2,000 to him and resign from the company"

Steve Regeling's fee was at the centre of a big row.

of the track they loved. I think one couple even gave him up to 20 grand! I'm not sure what happened to all their money but I wouldn't have been happy, if I'd been them, when he was eventually forced to pull the plug on the business. It wasn't the first time I thought Bill was being 'creative' with figures.

In August 1987, Bill had taken care of the money generated by my Golden Jubilee meeting at Hackney. All the riders rode for expenses only, while the staff and St. John's people gave their services free of charge. The stadium rent was reduced by half especially for the occasion, and we had a fair sized crowd, but when I went to Bill's house to collect my money from the proceeds of the meeting, I was dismayed to receive only £3,000. Even when I questioned the final amount he handed over, as usual, 'Billy Bullshit' had all the answers to convince me that that was all I was due. Perhaps I should have called the cops on him that day and possibly spared us all the fiasco that would shortly ensue at King's Lynn.

I thought the bond scheme he conjured up was no more than a con. We had rows about it because, as I saw it, our fans were being fleeced and I felt for them. They were handing over their hard-earned money to Bill but what were they getting in return? – not even a discount on admission or anything else. They were keeping King's Lynn afloat simply because Bill would threaten to close the track because of the deteriorating economic climate that engulfed British speedway by the mid-to-late 80s. I didn't think those threats by him were fully justified either but they continued for a long time after I left.

Sure, the sport was enduring very tough times and there came a point, during the winter of 1988-89, went I publicly expressed my fears for the future of the British League, which had shrunk to just nine tracks for 1989. Sheffield had closed and, much more significantly, our local rivals Ipswich had switched to the second division (NL) under the new management of Dave Pavitt and John Louis, who took over from Chris Shears. Most of the tracks had seen better days but I still felt that King's Lynn had a future and, despite the disappointments of my first season on the other side of the fence, I did enjoy it.

Another problem with Bill is that I had the feeling that he resented me getting all the glory while he was obviously working hard behind the scenes. I got the impression that, having introduced him to speedway, he got a taste for it and wanted me out of the way. He slated me all the way through it but I've never said anything about what went on at King's Lynn during our time together. Until now.

Another Hammering

After my unsavoury departure from King's Lynn in February 1989, I spent a couple of months working part-time – three days a week – for the Roy Francis Motorcycle dealership in Maidstone, where I repaired and delivered motor bikes. Roy was a long-time sponsor of mine through my trials riding exploits – he also probably felt sorry for me, although we still see each other regularly now and remain good friends.

I can't remember whether I approached Arena Essex or their promoter, Peter Thorogood, phoned me, but we soon sorted out a deal for me to ride for the

Hammers in 1989. Roy agreed to sponsor me again, and I think Arena provided me with transport, but it wasn't a particularly good financial deal and I only earned according to my points return. There was an incentive for high scoring but certainly no guarantee.

I rode 16 official matches for Arena, averaging 7.68, and enjoyed it until I got injured on a northern tour. I wasn't riding that good, and had lost a bit of confidence, when my so-called team-mate Rob Tilbury stuck me in the fence at Middlesbrough. He came into the turn so hard and, thankfully, I just managed to get off the bike before hitting the fence at Cleveland Park. I remember laying on the track, my foot hurting like hell, and a Boro fan leant over the fence and said: "Get up, Simmo, laying there making out you're hurt. You're a better actor than Richard Burton!" I certainly wasn't feigning injury.

Richard Burton in action for Arena Essex.

I'd ripped all the ligaments in my ankle and stopped off to see Dr. Carlo Biagi at the Peel Hospital in Galashiels, on our way to Edinburgh, where the team was racing the next night. I was unfit to ride at Powderhall and after trying again at Stoke the next night, I pulled out and never rode for Arena again. I didn't want to get hurt by brainless riders like Tilbury again and decided to pack up riding speedway.

I remained retired until the new King's Lynn promoter, Keith 'Buster' Chapman, who took over from Barker at the end of 1992, persuaded me to ride again midway through '94 . . . in the senior league! I'd been working for Buster as his track man, preparing the Saddlebow Road – or should that be Norfolk Arena? – circuit for him each week. I kept a speedway bike in the shed at the track and sometimes, after work, I'd get it out and have a play for a few laps. I just couldn't resist it. Buster came up from his Essex home one day, saw me riding round on my own and said: "You're as fast as most of the riders in my team – you'll have to ride for us!"

Buster could always talk a good game and he's never changed. He used to ride a bit himself as a junior and second-halver in the early 70s and to listen to him you'd think he'd been World Champion! But, in fairness, he always delivers on a promise and I'm delighted that he and his son Jonathan have done very well to keep King's Lynn Speedway still going strong today – not only as promoters but as stadium owners, having subsequently bought it from the Littlechild family and reopened as King's Lynn Knights in 1997. It can't have been easy for them at times but Lynn is still a very viable Premier League outfit and one of the best tracks to ride.

I think Buster bought my registration off the BSPA for about one hundred quid, so he wasn't exactly taking a big financial risk on me! My first meeting for my old club was at . . . Arena Essex! Buster supplied me with a brand new Jawa bike, which I hadn't even seen until he brought it to the Thurrock track for me to ride that night! I was quite apprehensive about it all but, as luck would have it, the meeting was rained off, so I could take the bike home with me and set it up to my personal requirements.

One of my few matches for Lynn was at home against Coventry and I can remember trying hard to catch Hans Nielsen, even looking like I might actually pass him round the outside. Of course, I didn't overtake the Main Dane – I was 48-years-old, for Christ's sake! – and after I came back into the pits, my old mate Terry Betts laughed at me and said: "What the f*** do you think you're doing, Simmo, trying to pass Nielsen!" Bettsy was always taking the piss out of me but he was right to question my sanity this time.

I rode in only a handful of matches after the rain-off at Arena before I finally accepted that I was out of my depth. It was fine for me to play around at King's Lynn but this was the first division, serious business, and I was way past my sell-by date. It was silly of me, I wasn't on the pace and it was no longer worth the struggle to score even one point. The sport had moved on and I'd lost touch with it. I found that I'd lost my starting ability and that meant I could never win races again.

It was the hardest decision I ever made to finally stop riding – it's in your blood and so hard to give up. That's why I deliberately didn't go and watch speedway for a few years afterwards, so that I wouldn't get the urge to try it one more time. I always said to myself that if I ever felt a little bit scared of racing, I'd stop there and then, and I've got to admit I was a little bit frightened riding those few meetings for King's Lynn in 1994. In that respect, the decision to stop was quite easy.

I was pleased to accept Buster's later offer to become the team manager at King's Lynn in 1997 and continued to combine the role with that of track manager. I found track maintenance relatively easy – it was a case of using all my experience in speedway and tips I'd picked up from watching how others did the job. As well as Lynn, I'd also prepared the tracks at Rye House and Hackney for a while in the early 90s. Ronnie Russell – Terry's big brother – took over at Rye and he got me involved there. Ronnie's favourite saying to me was always the same: "I don't care what you do with the track, but I don't want dust." Never mind my work with the hosepipe and sprinkler, with the River Lea running right alongside the stadium, there were occasions when Ronnie had more than his fill of water!

I used to arrive at the Hoddesdon track at 5am on a Sunday but it didn't matter how much you flooded the

The Rye House track under water – at least there's no dust.

Index

Hedge, Trevor 32, 34, 44,
Henry, Ivan 193, 210, 211, 219, 220
Hill, Colin 221
Holden, Kevin 17, 102, 103, 105
Holmqvist, Hasse 54
Holloway, Malcolm 176-178, 180
Horspool, Roger 219
Hoskins, Johnnie 53, 172
Howes, Derek 225
Hughes, Geoff 44
Hughes, Janet 178
Humphreys, Bob 71, 80, 83, 84, 103
Hunter, George 76, 78, 79, 120
Hunter, Jan 44
Hunter, Norman 29, 32, 33, 35, 37, 44, 47, 49, 52, 55, 57
Hurry, Graham 236
Hurry, Paul 214, 225, 236

Jancarz, Edward 142, 157, 199
Jansson, Bengt 125
Jansson, Tommy 87, 117
Jarvis, Brenda 55
Jarvis, Fred 30
Jarvis, Glen 30
Jarvis, Sid 30, 31
Jenkins, Lee 243
Jenkins, Michael 240
Jenkins, Scott 243
Jessup, Dave 14, 93-95, 97, 118, 121, 142, 148-151, 153, 166-169, 195, 196, 200, 202, 204, 206, 212, 218, 229
Johansen, Allan 217, 219
Johns, Peter 200
Johns, Roger 195, 199, 200, 206, 215
Johnson, Alan 27
Johnson, Fred 27
Jonsson, Per 209
Julian, Chris 46, 84

Kennedy, Danny 177
Kennett, Gordon 14, 21, 22, 131, 139, 153-157, 168, 182, 208, 250
Kilby, Bob 58, 117, 119
Kittilsen, Tore 13, 157
King, Lance 219
Knight, Richard 214, 219, 220
Knott, Charles (jnr) 100-103, 180, 181
Knott, Charles (snr) 100
Knott, Jack 100, 103, 180, 181
Knott, Jimmy 100, 103, 180, 181
Koponen, Ari 208, 209
Knutson, Bjorn 39, 40

Laessing, Ted 71,
Langfield, John 76, 79,
Lanning, Dave 39, 44, 47, 52, 54, 130
Lee, Andy 168, 169
Lee, Barry 48
Lee, Michael 13, 14, 97, 108, 116, 138, 146, 152, 153, 156-158, 168, 169, 171, 236, 250
Leonard, Brian 45, 47, 49, 51, 52, 55
Lewis, Tony 100, 101, 103, 108, 206
Littlechild, Alan 71, 81-83, 96, 241
Littlechild, Maurice 56, 57, 60-64, 70, 73, 80-82, 85, 92
Littlechild, Violet 62, 82, 92, 96
Lofqvist, Christer 150
Louis, John 13,14, 95, 99, 113, 116-118, 122, 126, 131, 133, 139, 142, 144, 147, 150, 151, 154, 156, 164, 165, 168, 191, 193, 217, 222, 229, 250

Lomas, Tony 76, 77, 79,
Loram, Mark 186, 213, 216, 227, 228, 231
Lovaas, Dag 165
Luckhurst, Jamie 206
Luckhurst, Reg 30, 31, 34, 35, 39, 40, 45, 235

MacDonald, Chris 15, 246
Maclean, Brian 27
Maidment, Cyril 195, 196, 206
Malmqvist, Olle 55
Mauger, Ivan 11-15, 21, 39, 74, 77, 90, 109-113, 118, 130, 142, 154-156, 170, 189, 197, 198, 204, 228-230, 234, 246, 247, 250
Mawdsley, Wally 143, 144, 160
Maxted, Brian 235
May, Richard 102, 107
McDermott, Steve 212
McGillivray, Les 54
McKee, Colin 32
McKinlay, Ken 37,40-42, 44-46, 47, 49, 52, 54, 55, 105, 187
McMillan, Jimmy 76, 78, 118
McNeill, John 177
McQueen, Steve 67
Michanek, Anders 90, 93, 113, 132, 148, 149, 156, 188
Middleditch, Ken 104
Middleditch, Neil 101, 102, 104, 108, 176-181, 227
Middleton, Garry 108, 109
Migro, Con 14
Miles, Graham 53, 54
Mogridge, Alan 195, 205, 212
Mole, Tony 225
Moore, Ronnie 13,16,
Moran, Kelly 159, 160, 168
Moran, Shawn 159, 176, 178, 236
Morrell, Les 226
Morton, Chris 116-118, 120, 122, 123, 129, 147, 152, 158, 214, 229
Morton, Dave 117, 119, 229
Morton, Wal 31, 34, 39,
Mourinho, Jose 145
Muckley, Gary 225
Mullarkey, Kelvin 104
Müller, Egon 132, 142, 235
Muts, Rudy 200

Nicholls, Scott 227-230
Nielsen, Hans 13, 153, 157, 199, 224
Niemi, Kai 195, 196, 198, 201
Nilsen, Jimmy 209, 211
Nordin, Gote 60
Norris, David 229
Nourish, Dave 129, 162
Nygren, Olle 45,

Oakes, Peter 65, 155, 156, 229, 250
Ochiltree, Charles 54
Olsen, Ole 90, 93, 94, 111, 113, 117, 118, 135, 139, 152, 155-157, 165, 197, 201
Oxley, Brad 195, 199

Palmer, Bill (grandfather) 23
Palmer, Nan (grandmother) 23
Palmer, Ray 228
Palmer, Tommy 228
Parker, Jack 172, 173
Parker, Mike 31, 32, 33, 34
Parker, Shane 225

Pavitt, Dave 205, 212, 215, 217, 222, 225
Pedersen, Nicki 139, 231
Pedersen, Jan O 211, 216
Pendlebury, Craig 104
Penniket, Geoff 32
Persson, Bernt 132
Petersen, Bo 193, 207-211, 214, 219, 220
Pettman, Richard 213
Penhall, Bruce 157-159, 170, 190, 192, 199, 204
Piddock, Martyn 70
Plech, Zenon 104, 150
Poole, Mick 219, 220
Potter, Mick 246
Poyser, John 32,
Pratt, Colin 40, 70
Preston, Ron 107, 108, 176-178
Price, Tommy 37, 38, 39, 54, 56
Prinsloo, Peter 177
Pusey, Chris 76, 77, 78, 79, 119, 120, 171, 235
Pyeatt, Denny 201

Read, Titch 32, 34,
Reeves, Eddie 32, 43, 83,
Reinke, Steve 112
Rembas, Jerzy 129
Regeling, Steve 221
Richards, John 144
Richardson, Colin 199
Richardson, Lee 228-230
Rickardsson, Tony 182, 183, 227-233, 234, 235
Roger, Bert 25, 27
Roger, Bob 25
Roger, Cyril 25, 27
Rogers, Martin 96, 212, 213, 218-220
Rogers, Martin (jnr) 218
Rogers, Lin 218
Rolfe, Ronnie 32
Rolls, Gary 213
Rolls, George 225
Ross, Andy 53
Ross, Larry 21, 155, 156, 196, 198
Rossiter, Alun 209
Rushbrook, Trevor 52
Russell, Ronnie 224, 225
Russell, Terry 204, 205, 207, 210-215, 217, 224, 225

Sage, Alan 206
Sampson, Peter 32
Sanders, Billy 125, 142, 166
Schwartz, Bobby 159
Screen, Joe 186
Shears, Chris 222
Sheene, Barry 85
Shirley, Alan 247
Shirra, Mitch 147
Sigalos, Dennis 158, 159
Silver, Len 32, 144, 145, 149-151, 172, 197
Simmons, Barry (step-brother) 27, 244
Simmons, Irena (step-mother) 27,
Simmons, Jack (grandfather) 23
Simmons, Mabel (grandmother) 23
Simmons, Margaret (mother) 23, 24, 25, 26, 27, 30, 244
Simmons, Sandra (nee Wood, ex-wife) 11, 55, 56, 63-65, 68, 79, 94, 95, 240-244
Simmons, Tony (father) 11, 23-27, 30-32, 243, 244, 245
Sjosten, Christer 101, 102, 104, 105, 108
Sjosten, Soren 105
Smart, David 208
Smith, Don 39, 49, 50, 51, 52

Smith, Pete 100-102, 106
Sorensen, Per 208
Stapleton, Graeme 76
Stewkesbury, Mervyn 206
Stevens, Adrian 219
Stevens, Stan 51, 55, 70
Street, Neil 112, 210
Stripp, Lew 71, 76,
Surtees, Jack 23
Surtees, John 23
Sweetman, Tommy 32
Szczakiel, Jerzy 156

Tatum, Kelvin 202, 203, 237
Tatum, Martin 203
Teodorowicz, Teo 43, 48
Tilbury, Rob 223
Titman, John 202
Tkocz, Andrzej 40, 108
Trigg, Roy 54, 109, 217
Thorogood, Peter 143, 222
Thorpe, Dave 248
Thurlow, Peter 92, 93, 96
Thomas, Barry 41, 205, 213, 214
Thomas, Ian 147, 157
Trott, Reg 40, 41, 42, 45, 47, 52
Turner, Ian 71, 80, 81, 83, 92

Valentine, Ron 112, 113
Vassen, Jos 200
Verner, Vaclav 105, 177
Vowles, Richard 208-210

Wassermann, Hans 132
Watson, Craig 231
Weedon, Alf 62, 245
Wiesbock, Alois 234, 235
Whitmore, Ken 81
Whitmore, Linda 81
Whittaker, Paul 205, 213, 214
Wills, Dave 48, 103
Wilson, John 245, 246
Wilson, Ray 13, 82, 95, 113, 142, 148, 149, 151, 165
Wilson, Reg 120
Wimmer, Frank 247
Wigg, Simon 111, 185, 190-193, 199, 217, 225, 236
Woods, Paul 212
Wooster, Julie 39
Woryna, Antoni 55
Wright, Billy 41
Wyer, Doug 118, 120-125, 134

Yeates, Martin 104, 108, 209
Young, Jack 48

Zierk, Hans 199

RETRO SPEEDWAY COASTERS
Great gifts at any time of the year!

Drinks will never be the same with our black baize-backed aluminium coaster/beer mats (89mm x 89mm) featuring speedway's all-time greats pictured in nostalgic black & white (names in red type).
A simply sensational souvenir of glorious days gone by.
Available to buy in three different series sets of six coasters, or individually.

LEGENDS SERIES – Ivan Mauger, Barry Briggs, Ronnie Moore, Ove Fundin, Peter Craven, Freddie Williams.

70s SERIES – Malcolm Simmons, Peter Collins, Michael Lee, John Louis, Anders Michanek, Ole Olsen.

80s SERIES – Bruce Penhall, Erik Gundersen, Hans Nielsen, Kenny Carter, Simon Wigg, Sam Ermolenko.

ONLY £2.99 PER INDIVIDUAL COASTER
OR £15.00 FOR FULL SET OF SIX

Order by post (cheque/PO payable to Retro Speedway) from the address below or phone our Credit Card Hotline.
Add £1 **Europe** or £2 **Rest of World** per order. Allow 21 days for delivery.

retro SPEEDWAY

103 DOUGLAS ROAD, HORNCHURCH, ESSEX, RM11 1AW
Credit Card Hotline 01708 734 502

RETRO SPEEDWAY LOVERS!

If you loved watching speedway in the 70s & 80s, then you'll love BACKTRACK magazine – the glossy, A4-size, bi-monthly from the same publishers of this book. Every issue is crammed with exclusive interviews and features on your favourites from the past. It costs only £16 a year (6 issues) to subscribe in the UK. Or if you like to go back even further in time, try our quarterly VINTAGE SPEEDWAY MAGAZINE covering the pre-war to 70s period. It costs just £12 a year (4 issues) for UK subscribers.

Other speedway-related books from Retro Speedway...

WIGGY: SIMON WIGG IN HIS OWN WORDS
By Gareth Rogers
Published November 2005
272 pages, softback, £15.99

"The measure of the man is that the tributes resemble a who's who of track racing. This is a unique speedway book about a unique speedway person"

CONFESSIONS OF A SPEEDWAY PROMOTER
John Berry reveals the truth about speedway in the 70s & 80s
Published November 2004
256 pages, softback, £14.99

"Explosive, emotive, pulls no punches"

– Speedway Star magazine

SLIDING INTO HELL
A raunchy speedway-based novel by John Berry
Published November 2005
256 pages, softback, £8.99

Look out for these new books coming soon...
TOMMY JANSSON: Legend Who Died Young
To be published late June 2006
BOOEY: Around in Circles – The Eric Boocock Story
To be published late July 2006
MORE CONFESSIONS by John Berry
To be published late October 2006

These books, *Backtrack* and *VSM* can be ordered from Retro Speedway by post (P&P FREE in UK) at: **Retro Speedway, 103 Douglas Road, Hornchurch, Essex, RM11 1AW, England.**

Credit Card Hotline: **01708 734 502.**
Or via our website: **www.retro-speedway.com**

SIMMO: SPEEDWAY HONOURS & MILESTONES

WORLD FINAL RECORD

Individual

1975	Wembley, England	10 pts	5th
1976	Katowice, Poland	13 pts	2nd
1978	Wembley, England	10 pts	5th

Team Cup

1973	Wembley, England	8 pts	1st
1974	Katowice, Poland	8 pts	1st
1975	Norden, Germany	11 pts	1st
1977	Wroclaw, Poland	3 pts	1st
1978	Landshut, Germany	8 pts (top)	2nd

Pairs

1976	Eskilstuna, Sweden		1st
	(Simmons 10, John Louis 17)		
1977	Belle Vue, England		1st
	(Simmons 13, Peter Collins 15)		
1978	Katowice, Poland		1st
	(Simmons 15, Gordon Kennett 9		
	– Simmo beat Ivan Mauger in a run-off)		
1979	Vojens, Denmark		2nd
	(Simmons 9, Michael Lee 15)		

Other major titles

1976	British Champion (at Coventry, England)	1st – 15 points maximum
1976	Internationale (at Wimbledon, England)	1st – 15 points maximum

BRITISH LEAGUE RECORD

Year	Club	Matches	Total Pts	CMA	Year	Club	Matches	Total Pts	CMA
1965	West Ham	40	274	6.85 (	1981	Wimbledon	44	475	8.37
1966	West Ham	37	235	6.14	1982	Wimbledon	43	420	8.75
1967	West Ham	41	305	7.09	1983	Wimbledon	48	395	7.86
1968	K. Lynn	18	188	9.40					
1969	K. Lynn	40	340	8.14	1984	Wimbledon	50	457	8.38
1970	K. Lynn	37	307	7.58	1985	Swindon	40	330	7.90
1971	K. Lynn	38	401	9.21	1986	Hackney	38	400	9.69
1972	K. Lynn	37	349	8.35		K. Lynn	10	69	6.73
1973	K. Lynn	39	485	10.26	1987	Hackney	25	131	5.40
1974	K. Lynn	38	401	9.78	1989	A. Essex	16	146	7.68
1975	Poole	33	372	10.40					
1976	Poole	35	417	10.17					
1977	Poole	28	326	10.26					
1978	Poole	39	439	10.77					
1979	Poole	32	305	9.03					
1980	Poole	28	289	9.39					

Note: The above figures relate to all official league and cup fixtures.

Malcolm began his speedway career in 1963 for Hackney in the Provincial League (second division) before moving up into the National League (first division) with West Ham the following year.

In 1965, Malcolm won the BL championship, KO Cup and London Cup with West Ham.

Figures courtesy of *The Complete History of the British League*, edited by Peter Oakes.

Love and tears

Six Day Trials, where Eric Boocock has been up to compete in the pre-65 class in recent years, when we had walked about a mile out into the moors to enjoy some of the most remote scenery. Apart from us, there was only one other person on the moor – a gentleman who was coming in the opposite direction. As we passed each other, I just said "hello" and he replied: "Hi, Simmo!" and continued walking. June and I just looked at each other and burst out laughing. We were in the middle of nowhere, hundreds of miles from home, and a total stranger somehow recognised me. I think June was impressed!

A few years ago, I taught June how to ride . She was trying to learn on a 250 Fantic trials bike when she got into a little bit of trouble by the sea wall at Shorne. If she'd been going another five miles per hour faster, she might have disappeared over that wall! She's done really well, though, and has become a very competent motorcyclist.

Mind that wall, June!

I just wish June and I had got together much sooner than we did. She's as straight as a die and says what she thinks – in fact, she is appalled by what I've told her about the part I played in race-fixing and other scams I got up to over the years before we were together. She's kind, caring of others and works hard at all times – sometimes I get on her nerves when I tell her that she works too hard. We share most things and I also help out a bit with the cooking. I cook most of the meat we eat on our barbecue – even in winter. And yet before June and I met, I'd never done any household chores.

One of June's best qualities is that she is brilliant with money, which is a Godsend to someone with my track record. I can earn decent money now running the Southern Wheels repair and rebuild business that I operate from our home. June looks after my books, does all the invoicing, paperwork and tax returns, which leaves me to do the practical stuff out in the workshop. The business has grown well since I started it, on a more casual basis in 1997. It's one of those businesses where people who needed their wheels fixing would take it to an old boy down the road. Well, now I've become that 'old boy down the road!' June encouraged me to develop the business and it's going really well. I'm happy to run it as a one-man band, with vital administrative back-up from June. I don't want to take on anybody else to help out and love the fact that I just walk out our back door and go straight into work.

I have the best partner anyone could wish for in June and I think we complement each other very well. We have a thriving business, we own our own home in a nice part of Kent and we don't owe anyone a penny – not even the taxman!

And that is the honest truth.

Competing in the 2004 staging of the pre-65 Scottish Six-Day Trials event – watched by Mick Grant and Dave Thorpe, with June the closest onlooker to my left. I hope to be back there next year . . .

Park last year and another, quite recently, at Lydden, Kent. I was quite happy to finish 12th out of 25 riders in one race – there is no age limit – and I'll get better with time. I've now added a 250 Ducati bike to the Cotton to ensure I remain properly equipped. It suits me now because the races are somewhere between seven and 10 laps duration and it's not as physically demanding as grasstrack or trials. Yeah, I still get that adrenalin rush, I still think I'm one of the best starters out there! They all come by me afterwards but that doesn't matter. It would do me in if I couldn't ride bikes.

It was when I popped into the chemist the other day that it finally hit me that I'd turned 60 years of age. I had my inhaler out to pick up a repeat prescription, when the lady the other side of the counter pointed out that I'd passed the age where I didn't have to pay the regular £24 per month prescription charge any longer!

June and I are still both very active, always doing something at weekends. How unbelievable is this . . . we were up in Fort William, Scotland, watching the Scottish

the size of the sprockets he had on the back and he went right through my bike and told me exactly what I needed. He then added: "I got to the final, unbeaten, then I checked everyone else's sprockets and the bloke who looked quicker than me had a 56 sprocket on, but he was on the outside gate, so I didn't worry about him."

Ivan's advice and information was spot on – I went from last to first in the final and had the crowd on their feet.

Ivan didn't only record what set-up he'd used that day some 26 years earlier, but he also knew what all the others riders in the final were using! And he knew all that from within half-a-minute of me phoning him. Naturally, I consulted Ivan and his wonderful history book for my next meeting at Marianske Lazne in the Czech Republic and every other longtrack I rode at thereafter. That just shows one of the many reasons why Ivan was better than all the rest of us.

Ivan couldn't offer us any help, though, when the brand new Mercedes van we drove to Germany broke down about five miles down the road from the track. We must have run over something that had then caused the diesel tank to split, so I had to clamber under the van, still in my racing leathers (there were no showers at Pfarrkirchen) to try and fix it. June was moaning that she had to be at work the next morning and we were still some 500 miles from the ferry to take us back to England. I lay on the ground for five minutes, thinking about what to do, and in the end I jammed a bit of wood up in the tank, siliconed all around it and then bound it with duck tape. I had to put on my race goggles in case diesel spilled into my eyes. But do you know what, I didn't change that diesel tank on the van for three months!

I won the two-valve championship in my first year with the longtrack vets, so the following year I decided I'd enter both the two-valve and the four-valve championship. We were only meant to be doing it for fun – we never got paid – so I got myself some sponsors to cover things like the cost of the ferry. At my first meeting in the second season of the veterans' longtrack, I won both the classes and was leading the championship, but that didn't go down well with my rivals or the German organiser, Frank Wimmer, who wasn't impressed with an Englishman running away with his events.

My rivals complained that I was taking it all too seriously, Wimmer listened to them and it was decided to chuck me out of the event, on the pretence that I was an ex-professional and therefore, according to the organisers, I shouldn't have been in it. They became jealous of my success but I was pleased with myself that I could still win races.

Nothing or nobody can stop me riding motorbikes for long. I still enjoy riding trials, where the course enables me to have a rest between each section of the course, and now I've been introduced to another new motorcycling hobby of mine.

Last year, Arthur Browning, the old Birmingham speedway favourite, got me into classic road racing. I met him at Brands Hatch, at the King of Brands meeting, and by the end of the day I was hooked. He rides in the 500cc class, but it's mega-expensive if you want to finish up among the front-runners. I compete in the 250 class, where the cost is less and the racing more competitive. I bought a 250 Cotton bike from Alan Shirley in Birmingham and since then I did one meeting at Cadwell

Still chasing that Golden Pheasant at Klein-Krotzenburg, Germany.

Wilson of Wilson Tarmac. I think he's tarmacked everybody's driveway in Kent!

It started out as a bit of fun but inside three meetings, I'd qualified for a final. After six, I'd won the final. I was riding all over the country and the fun bit turned to something a bit more serious.

In year 2000, I had backing from another grasstrack sponsor, this time Mick Potter, who provided me with a bike to use in an indoor speedway meeting at Bournemouth. It was the first time I'd sat on a speedway bike for about six years, but I scored double figures in my first meeting riding what is the only lay-down Jawa speedway bike with rear suspension.

It was while I was in Bournemouth that I got invited to enter the Veterans' Longtrack Series in Europe. Although I ridden the German grasstracks, I'd never tried longtrack so I was looking forward to racing on these vast, super-fast tracks. My first meeting in 2000 was at Pfarrkirchen – a well-known 1,000 metre sandtrack circuit. Blimey, was it long! I could hardly even see from one end of the track to the other and I could never have visualised such a daunting proposition. After two laps of practice, though, I got the hang of it and won the meeting on a bike that used to belong to Ivan Mauger and which he'd actually ridden at Pfarrkirchen way back in 1974. Ivan's old mechanic, Chris MacDonald, kept the bike in England and he sponsored me with it for the veteran longtrack series that year.

The old bike wasn't the only useful help from Ivan that day. Here's a brief story that sums up perfectly the ultimate professional Ivan was, and still is to this day. Having ridden at this particular German track himself many times before, I asked Ivan's advice about what set-ups to use. "Any idea what gear is best around here?" I enquired. "Hang on a minute," he said. The line between Kent and the Australian Gold Coast went quiet for just less than a minute before Ivan returned to the phone.

He'd been to fetch his 'little black book' containing every gear ratio and other minute detail he'd noted down from every track he's ever ridden. He picked up the receiver again and said: "Pfarrkirchen, 1974, July, blah, blah, blah . . . temperature was 26 degrees . . ." He then proceeded to tell me what jet he had in his carburettor,

Love and tears

when June first phoned my father to try and bring us back together, his first question to her was: "Does he still smoke?" My father never smoked cigarettes or drank alcohol – and he hated me smoking.

I used to smoke 40 fags a day from about 1985 until when I stopped riding speedway. Before that, I was probably smoking between 20 and 30 a day all the time. I always smoked untipped cigarettes like Senior Service but, after a great struggle, I finally stopped completely six years ago. I tried those Nicotine patches but found that I was actually still smoking while wearing them, so they didn't work! The tablets under the tongue helped me more and I got to the stage where I was only smoking about four in the morning – the time all smokers enjoy a fag most. That routine went on for a couple of months until one morning I just woke up and didn't fancy a cigarette anymore. I can walk into a smokey bar now and it doesn't bother me, other than the fact that too much smoke affects my breathing.

I wish I'd never started smoking – but it was a lad's thing to do. Also, being the rebel that I was, the fact that my father was so dead set against it made me want to smoke all the more! I never smoked pot or touched any sort of drugs. The nearest I came to taking any stimulant was when speedway's longest-serving photographer Alf Weedon used to offer the riders little white pills in the pits before a meeting in the early 70s. Alf convinced me once that these pills were just the thing to calm my nerves before racing – he even told me that Nigel Boocock regularly had them off him. I said I'd try them once but they didn't made no bloody difference to me. It turned out that they were nothing more than Pro-Plus tablets – the kind of energy pills you can easily buy over the counter at any chemist, grocery store or supermarket today!

Smoking has had a damaging effect on me, though. Due to smoking heavily over a long period of my life, I've been diagnosed with COPD, which stands for Chronic Obstructive Pulmonary Disease. The most common of these incurable lung diseases is chronic bronchitis and emphysema. It's not lung cancer, but my lungs are badly damaged and cause me to get out of breath very quickly.

I'm treated as an asthma patient and have to take an inhaler four times a day. I get by but my breathing has got a lot worse in the last five years – now I'm hoping that there's some revolutionary new treatment on the horizon. I read in the *Daily Mail* that they are planning to start some medical trials soon where doctors basically insert lots of little things into the airwaves in your damaged lungs, and re-direct the air to the better parts of the lungs. It hopefully leads to a better quality of life so, provided I come through a CT scan that I'm scheduled to have soon, I'll be able to take part.

It was because I kept running out of puff that I had to give up grasstrack racing two years ago. I'd still been winning a lot of races until then but I found that I had to pull out of the race after just two laps because I was out of breath. It was a great shame because I hadn't lost that competitive streak or the urge to race, even if it was meant to be mainly for fun.

In 1995, Ian Barclay asked me to take part in the Golden Oldies meeting he was promoting at Salisbury, which I managed to win on a bike sponsored by John

The 1968 Speedway Beauty Queen still hasn't lost it.

taken much for us to fall out, because we were never that close, and we both just lost touch with each other over the years. It didn't bother me for years but it's a big regret to me now that so many years passed us by without contact.

When June and I finally got together, she obviously knew how I felt about Dad and wanting to make up with him. I wrote to him a few times, but never got a reply. June phoned him on several occasions, but he just didn't want to know. Dad adored Lisa but he never really took to Sandra and her family. I didn't mind June calling Dad to try and bring him and me back together. Despite June's best efforts, and some encouragement from his second wife Irena and their son, Barry, who I've not yet met properly, in the end Dad said he'd rather leave things as they were. He had his own life with his new family and didn't want the grief of meeting up with me again after so many years. And so I thought that was that.

Then, in February 2005, I had to undergo a prostate operation, in which the doctors said they had found some 'irregularities' – the medical staff didn't use the term cancer but said they'd have to do tests to establish all the facts. I admit, I immediately thought I had cancer and, consequently, felt really low and sorry for myself. Still feeling depressed in July, I wrote another letter to my dad, telling him that I could really do with seeing and talking to him again. He came up to the house to see me the next day. It was obviously a very emotional occasion, we both shed tears, and for the first time ever we sat down and really spoke about all the personal issues that had shaped my life from boyhood – about his early life with my mother, and why they ended up divorcing.

These were things I'd never known before and I found out more about the Simmons family from him that day than I'd ever done before. It was really good and now, even though he's 84, he occasionally drives up from Sittingbourne to see us in the Renault I helped him to buy.

Every time Dad and I see each other now, his parting shot is always the same: "I'm glad we've made up." So am I, Dad.

I was also very relieved that my PSA (Prostate Specific Antigen) reading has gone back down since I first went into hospital last year and medics have given me the all-clear, although I have to go back every six months for a check-up.

One thing June couldn't do for me was make me give up smoking. It was something I had to do for myself and it was bloody tough to finally stop. In fact,

Love and tears

An all too rare moment with James (left), who is pictured (right) having fun on his quad bike earlier this year.

her place on occasions, we're not close. I suppose it was inevitable that Lisa would take her mum's side after Sandra and I broke up but it's a shame that she doesn't want to have much to do with June and myself.

It saddens me all the more because it also means we have very little contact with my grandson, James, who is now seven-years-old and starting to show a keen interest in motor bikes – he's got a

Back with Dad, May 2006.

little quad he plays around on and I'd love to share those experiences with him. When I see him, which is only about four or five times a year, he doesn't really understand who I am, which is a shame but I won't give up trying to see more of Lisa, Paul and James.

June, who is three years younger than me, has the same problem with her youngest son, Lee, although her eldest, Scott, is fine with us. It's a pity others can't take a leaf out of his book and let bygones be bygones. Ironically, I used to be Lee's idol when he was a kid – he had pictures of me on his bedroom wall – but, sadly, he can't stand me now.

June couldn't do any more to try to bring our families together in harmony. In fact, it was thanks to her that my dad and I are now talking, and enjoying each other's company again, after some 20 years apart. Dad used to occasionally support me in the pits when I rode for Wimbledon in the early 80s – either him or my friend, Dave Brown, who I'd know from my Poole days, who helped out. Dave, who supported the Pirates, and his wife, Carol became good friends of mine and as they lived at New Addington, Wimbledon Speedway was quite handy for him.

But, for some reason, Dad and I fell out over something – I can't even remember what it was now and he can't put his finger on the problem either. It wouldn't have down to Rye House to meet me most days after she finished work as an accountant at a food company in Waltham Abbey, called Abbey View Produce Ltd.

Our affair came to a head in 1998, when June had a nasty accident at work, falling down some 20 concrete steps. She was taken to hospital and put in traction for a couple of days until her back improved. She was very fortunate not to break any bones but still had to spend a couple of weeks in hospital. Obviously, her husband and kids were regular visitors, which meant that I had great difficulty in seeing her. It was then that we agreed between us to come out and admit our affair.

As for the actual final act of leaving Sandra, I took the coward's way out and just left her a note. As I've said, she had her suspicions about June from years earlier but she didn't know that I was seeing her again from the mid-90s. I felt bad about leaving my wife the way I did but I didn't have the balls to front it out with Sandra. Evidently, I'm told that women will face these situations head-on, whereas men tend to take the coward's way out, which is exactly what I did.

Sandra did confront me quickly, seeking reasons for my decision to leave . . . although she only had to look at how we'd gone our separate ways over a long period for the answer to her question. We both agreed it was over and it was more upsetting for her because she was left on her own – in fact, she then moved in with our daughter Lisa and her husband, Paul.

After I left, Sandra slagged me off to our mutual friends and everybody else, claiming that I'd left her destitute and had taken every possession from our rented house, but that definitely wasn't the case. The rent was paid up to date and I can honestly say that I didn't take one bit of furniture from there to the little place June and I rented at Shorne, about four miles away from where I'd been living with Sandra. One or two of these friends soon saw for themselves that June and I were living a spartan existence in a place where we had a little camping table to eat from in the front room, a rented television, a bed and very little else. In fact, the only items I did take with me when I left Sandra were the cut-glass crystal vases and trophies that I'd won over the years in places like Poland and Sweden, plus one or two medals. All my old trophies were stashed away in the coal shed anyway – they weren't even on show indoors. I didn't take anything that affected Sandra's way of living.

Divorce can affect people in different ways, of course, especially when there are children involved. It's fair to say that Lisa just about tolerates me as her father and we're nowhere near as close as I'd like us to be. She's 38 now, old enough to know what life's about, and though I've tried hard to make it right between us, phoning and popping over to

An old picture with a young Lisa and Ken Beckett.

Love and tears

and establishing myself as one of England's top riders

My career was just taking off and I had to stay focussed on the big picture, trying to win the World Championship and become the undisputed No.1 rider I knew I could be at Poole. I had only one shot at fulfilling my dreams and I just had to go for it. I couldn't let June, or anybody else for that matter, get in the way of my driving ambition. I wasn't only riding in a lot more meetings all over Britain, but also representing my country in world finals and Test matches at home and abroad. As my career really took off, I no longer had the time to carry on an affair and our relationship petered out at that stage, although I know June wasn't happy with me at all for acting the way I did at the time. She understood, though, that I had to leave King's Lynn to get away from the shadow of Bettsy, as I've already explained earlier in the book. I went to Poole purely as a great career move for myself, not to deliberately get away from June.

When I joined Poole, I cut myself off from June completely and yet, ironically, signing for them helped keep my marriage going – even though Sandra wasn't keen on my move. June tells me that she sent me letters, addressed to me at both the track and at my home, but I can honestly say that I never received them. Whether they were intercepted, I don't know.

I missed June more than I could have imagined in my Poole years. In fact, it was probably around a year after I joined the Pirates that I thought about getting in touch with her again and, in fact, I drove up to Waltham Abbey, where she was living by then, to see her. I was driving quite near her house when I suddenly saw her pushing her two children in a pram, so I stopped some distance away and watched. June had stopped to chat to a girlfriend and she looked really happy. I thought to myself that no matter how much I thought of her, and really wanted to see her again, I just couldn't spoil that situation. I just drove off without speaking to her, without her even knowing I'd been there. In hindsight, I wished I had gone through with it and spoken to her, but I let it go and that's a shame.

The next time I saw June was in 1981, at her mum's house, when I popped in to say 'hello' to the family on my way to a meeting at Ipswich, although she doesn't remember that visit. There was no further contact between us until the early 90s.

Working up at King's Lynn for Buster Chapman took me away from home for three days a week and Sandra and I gradually drifted further and further apart. I'd go up there on a Wednesday and not return until Saturday night – we'd never previously spent so much time apart. I was also helping Terry Busch to prepare Hackney and then Ronnie Russell got me doing his track at Rye House. Sandra was doing her things with her friends and we were basically leading very separate lives.

It was while I was working at Rye House that I thought about getting in touch with June again. I phoned around a few people, including Allan Littlechild, to try and track her down but didn't have much luck until I looked up her mother's name in the phone book. I knew June's mum, Ruby, lived at Waltham Abbey, Essex and we were chatting away like old mates when I asked her where her daughter was living. She gave me June's number and it went from there.

It had been almost 20 years since our affair had ended but June started to come

I'M very happy to say that my life has changed fairly drastically, and very much for the better, since my partner, June, and I finally got together in 1999. It's the best thing I've ever done and I have no regrets about leaving Sandra.

To fully explain the break-up of my marriage to Sandra, I look back to the early 90s, when I was employed by Rye House, King's Lynn and Hackney to prepare and maintain their tracks. Actually, to explain exactly how June came into my life I have to go all the way back to the late 60s, when I joined King's Lynn and we met because she made up the riders' pay packets in the office at the end of meetings.

We soon became good friends and it remained that way for a number of months before we became romantically involved. Although we tried to be discreet and keep our relationship a secret for as long as possible, one or two people had an idea what was going on, especially Bettsy after I got him to drop me off at June's place one night! June's husband, Michael, was away at the time, so we made the most of the situation and spent the night together. We hadn't drawn the upstairs curtains when we went to bed, so imagine our surprise when, as we were about to get up the next morning, we suddenly saw the window cleaner at the top of his ladder. I'd tried to be careful not to be recognised but when the window cleaner knocked at the door for his money, he stood there with a silly smirk on his face and said to June: "I take it Mick's not in, then?" We'd been well and truly sussed.

Sandra, who usually accompanied me to home meetings, had an inkling that June and I had something going on, although she never confronted either of us about her suspicions. Sandra's best friend was Sue Betts, Terry's wife, and she didn't like June either. I would never have admitted anything had Sandra accused me anyway.

I would make an excuse to get out of the house – say I was picking up parts for my bikes or I had to go somewhere or other – and see as much of June as possible, which wasn't easy given that she was also married, lived in Bishop's Stortford, Essex and I was based down in Kent.

But when I got my transfer to Poole in 1975 I had to make a big decision: It was either June or my career? I had to decide which came first and I chose speedway. It was a very selfish and single-minded thing to do but I told her we had to stop seeing each other once I left King's Lynn and made a fresh start to my career. As much as June and I really thought a hell of a lot of each other and got on very well, we both had to face up to the reality that we were both married to different people and both had young kids. I would never have left Sandra until our daughter, Lisa, was old enough to look after herself, and June felt the same way about her two sons. What I didn't know at the time was that June's husband found out about our affair and started to give her a hard time while I was enjoying myself as the new Poole No.1

LOVE AND TEARS

18

England fears

attending one of my speedway training schools at Weymouth in the 70s!

There's hardly such a thing as grasstrack now, it's more or less died a death in England. There are no really major meetings and even Collier Street isn't the big event it was for many years. Meetings like the Lydden International in Kent and the Western Winner down in Exeter used to feature top internationals from all over Europe but now, apart from Kelvin Tatum and one or two of the leading Germans, the biggest meetings don't attract a class field. The promoters don't want to pay the best riders what they want to appear.

I love to ride grasstrack, though, and would still be doing it today but for health reasons, which I'll come to in the final chapter...

Back in action on the grass in October 1997 and (above) winning the Southern Centre 500cc Championship, September 1998. Only the effects of smoking forced me to give up grasstrack racing a couple of years ago.

Grasstrack star Paul Hurry could have done better on shale.

of the leading Germans who used to dominate.

I was never short of offers, and I'm ever so sure I would have been very successful on the continental grasstrack and longtrack scene, but no-one pushed me to do it and I just let the vast majority of those opportunities slide by. There is so much more to do and it's a limited lifespan riding bikes. I'm convinced that I could have achieved what Simon Wigg did as a multi-World Longtrack Champion in the 80s and 90s before his tragic death. But, stupidly, I only ever thought as far as next week and it's a big regret now.

I look back at how Michael Lee and Shawn Moran, both with very limited longtrack experience, still became world champions in the early 80s, while I was putting my feet up at home.

Wiggy was a bloody good speedway rider but if he'd curtailed his longtrack activities, he could have been so much better. I've said the same thing to Paul Hurry so many times, and it's too late now for him to prioritise. I said to Paul years ago, 'just leave grasstrack alone and concentrate on speedway and you'll be a much better speedway rider', because he does struggle on the shale at times and looks like a grasstrack rider. He's dominant on the grass but for what? . . . Twenty-five hundred quid? The World Longtrack and Grasstrack Championships don't pay big bucks these days but he could be so much more successful for Arena Essex now if he'd focused more on speedway.

I think Paul's dad, Graham, pushes him hard to maintain his success on the grasstracks and longtracks but at the expense of him fulfilling his obvious potential on shale. I'm showing my age here, but I vaguely remember Graham Hurry

> **"I was never short of offers, and I'm ever so sure I would have been very successful on the continental grasstrack and longtrack scene, but no-one pushed me to do it and I just let the vast majority of those opportunities slide by"**

England fears

been in place when he rode.

It remains to be seen if Rickardsson really does carry out his plan to quit speedway if he doesn't win his seventh world crown this year . . .

As for England and our world title prospects, I do fear for the future . . .

And as for domestic British speedway, I have a few serious concerns there, too. The top flight now calls itself the Elite League, but is it really elite? Some of the riders filling up Elite League teams are not even good enough to make the Premier League (second division) grade. And the problem is, the top two in every Elite team probably has the best equipment money can buy, so the others can't get near them. I think the Elite League has degraded itself as a product because the gap between the top riders and the lesser lights is too huge.

That's not good for television. I enjoy watching the Elite League coverage on Sky TV each week but the cameras can't cover all four riders at once – it's impossible for them to do so anyway, but even harder given the gulf in standard between the riders in most races – and all the empty gaps on the terraces don't do the sport any favours either.

The one thing I can't handle is the Golden Double tactical rule. What a load of rubbish that is. Matches are being kept artificially close and what many results don't tell you is that in three heats one team scored double their real points – a bit like handing Arsenal two goals after Chelsea have taken the lead! It's totally stupid.

The Premier League probably provides better racing than the Elite. The talent is more evenly spread throughout the teams and, as far as the promoters are concerned, it's more affordable to put on. Sheffield, for example, seem to have worked out that they are better being where they are in the Premier, knowing they wouldn't be able to attract sufficiently more fans to justify moving back up into the Elite division.

Grasstrack gone to pot

As my racing career more or less started on grasstrack, I suppose I should end this chapter by looking at the state of that sport, too.

It was Reggie Luckhurst who finally convinced me to give up grasstrack at the start of the 70s. I'd dominated the scene to such an extent that I went unbeaten for three years. The challengers – the likes of Chris Pusey and Brian Maxted – came from all over the country and they couldn't beat me. But Reg advised me: "If you're gonna be a good speedway rider, you've got to stop racing on the grass. Become a speedway rider and you can always go back to grasstrack later, when you will find it easier and be even better at it."

Quitting grasstrack was the best thing I did – well, giving up the English scene was. The stupid thing was, I should have gone to Germany most weekends and taken advantage of the rich pickings on offer there and at other European grasstracks, as many of the top speedway names did. There was really good money up for grabs – OK, I would probably have wasted it anyway! – but I didn't even bother to go for it. I was too bone idle and lazy. The few meetings that I did abroad, I won them – against the very best, including superstar Egon Müller, Alois Wiesbock and the rest

– and speedway riders never have stuck together on anything. To illustrate my point, I'll go back to a story surrounding the old Internationale meeting at Wimbledon. In the 70s, the top riders all demanded a guarantee to appear in the big open and individual meetings, plus their points money on top. We all had to negotiate our own guarantee, which would have been around £200-250, and probably against earnings in some cases. The World Champion would obviously command the highest appearance fee.

That all changed, though, when the BSPA, who promoted the Internationale every Whitsun Bank Holiday Monday, suddenly decided that no-one would be paid a guarantee from then on. That immediately sparked the riders into a mini revolt and a round of phone calls, in which we urged each other not to ride unless the promoters reverted to the guarantee payment we'd been used to. 'Stick it,' was the general consensus and I was happy to boycott the meeting.

Anyway, to cut a long story short, I went along to watch the Internationale that year and, apart from Ivan Mauger and myself, the rest all caved in and rode on the BSPA's terms. Ivan and I were both there to see just who would and wouldn't turn up and it turned out that we were the only two who had the balls to call the promoters' bluff. We were both dismayed that our colleagues didn't show the same resolve. That basically knackered the guarantee policy for us and was another prime example of speedway riders shooting themselves in the foot.

It's not the top riders who suffer most, though, when costs get out of hand, it's the second strings, reserves and juniors who can't afford to keep pumping thousands into their machinery, to keep up with the Jones's.

Take the biggest modern day innovator, Tony Rickardsson and his Penske frame. The word is that although Penske, who are based in Poole, won't go into mass production, his frame cost around £32,000 to develop. Now OK, say if Penske did start producing them and sold their speedway frame for £1,500, how is Joe Bloggs at, say, Rye House going to afford that, when he's used to paying around £400 for a frame now?

Rickardsson's frames, which remind me of the stiff JAP chassis we used to use but found too awkward, can adjust four ways – but how can a junior or lesser light be expected to keep pace with him and the other top boys? Even his GP rivals can't keep up with him! I spoke to Jason Crump last year and was very surprised that, at that stage, he hadn't hooked up with a frame manufacturer like PJ, who are based not far from him in the Midlands, and got them to develop a frame very similar to Rickardsson's. I advised Jason to get one of his pits crew to start secretly photographing what Rickardsson had and get into production as soon as possible!

Rickardsson says he's going to retire from speedway at the end of this season to go car racing, after trying to win his seventh world title and beat Ivan's record of six victories in the one-off World Championship era. Whether Rickardsson makes it seven this year or not, I still can't make a fair comparison between him and Ivan. How can you with any accuracy? They were both at the top in completely different eras of the sport. I'm not taking anything away from Tony as a rider, he's brilliant, but I'm sure Ivan would have won maybe 10 or 12 world titles if the GP system had myself. Apart from wearing my leathers over the top of my boots, I was the first BL rider to fit a rear wheel spoiler – a white disc that stood out from afar, with my name and those of my main sponsors' plastered across it. I used it in speedway from about 1975-76 but the only real benefit it gave me was when riding on the longtrack.

At 100mph, the spoiler would push the back wheel down and stop it from over-sliding. But those spoilers didn't make one bit of difference when used for speedway in England. I had a white fibreglass spoiler and then soon PC and a few others came out with one designed in the colours of the Union Jack flag, with a fancy glittery effect. But all they were really good for was providing extra room to slap a load more sponsors' stickers over our bikes!

I think today's bikes are detrimental to the sport. In the old days, the tracks allowed us to go faster and yet our bikes still remained safe to ride. But the bikes have now out-grown today's tracks – they're going so fast that overtaking is now so much harder on tracks that have hardly changed in size and shape since my day.

I'd also argue with anyone who claims that the lay-down engine is easier to ride than the old upright. They're not. The lay-downs are faster, though. Trouble is, everyone is paying twice as much money to make them go faster. The lay-downs are still designed to be fitted as uprights – no-one has yet designed a proper lay-down to . . . lay-down, but they're been modified to suit. They cost two or three times as much as the uprights to run and, once again, it's the riders who've been hit financially, as well as the promoters who pay their wages.

You can't blame the evolution of the bikes, and the subsequent spiralling costs, solely on the BSPA. They are just one governing body among many affiliated to the FIM. Ultimate responsibility for the development of speedway lies with the FIM but they won't step in and put the block on anything. I recall attending a meeting of top British-based promoters and riders at John Harrhy's place in the Midlands some 10 years ago, where we discussed how speedway bikes could be slowed down for the benefit of the sport. I came up with what I thought was a very straightforward and practical suggestion. I said that the carburettor manufacturers could make a throttle slide that was slightly longer than the standard one, which wouldn't allow a rider to achieve full throttle and, therefore, maximum power. That would immediately have the effect of slowing the bikes down.

If a rider happened to be racing in another country the next day, he could simply whip out the longer throttle slide and re-fit his FIM one for that meeting. It would have been easy for the machine examiners to police but my idea never got off the ground. They dismissed it because it was said that riders in Britain would simply 'tune around it', and then tune around it again when they rode abroad. I could see that argument but in this day and age, they've all got engines spread around different countries anyway.

I'm not pushing the use of either two-valve or four-valve engines, and we must accept that you can never stop the progress of technology, but today's bikes are not helping the entertainment level.

Of course, for change to come about you need the collective will of those involved

Jason Crump is posing the biggest threat to Tony Rickardsson's bid for seven GP titles.

in the past, a dirty rider, who rode like a dickhead at times. He caused so many unnecessary crashes but got away with it. But credit where its due – he can take exactly what he likes to dish out. I don't believe that he's a moaner in that respect, although I'm obviously not close to the GP scene and watch them all on Sky. Actually, June and I won £200 by backing Pedersen, each-way at odds of 10/1, to win the Slovenien GP earlier this year, so I can't knock him now. It has to be said that has developed into a much more mature and better rider, someone who now rides with his head.

The other thing I don't like about air fences is that they've cut the viewing down by about half. When I went to watch at Arena Essex last year and was stood up on the first turn banking, all I could see was the riders' shoulders and helmets, so the fences have taken away some of the spectacle of speedway.

So on grounds of both safety and spectator viewing, I think they should do away with air fences. If I was riding today I might look at it differently but, knowing that riders are taking even greater risks than ever because they believe the air fence will save them, is not right.

Safety standards, in general, have improved significantly since I started riding – even since I packed up in some cases. To think that we used to race, flat out, just inches from a line of metal lamp standards, would make many of today's riders shudder with fear. Those posts were lethal and thankfully the authorities finally got rid of them, albeit long after a number of riders were either maimed or killed after hitting them at high speed.

There are cosmetic things that have come in that I'm sure are nothing more than a gimmick – like the little pointed bit on top of the crash helmet. I don't know what it actually achieves. Having said that, I was never shy of using gimmicky things

Poole fans voted him the greatest Pirates rider of all-time in a local newspaper poll and I'm not knocking him for that. He was the best thing that happened to Poole Speedway at the time, the star of a very strong, all round team that won trophies, which is something the Pirates never did in my six years there.

How do I think Rickardsson and myself compare? I wouldn't say I was a better rider for Poole than him, but I think I did more overall for Poole Speedway than he did. Apart from their 1969 BL championship win, the Dorset club had been in the doldrums for a long, long time when I went there from King's Lynn in 1975 and I like to feel that I brought Poole back into the speedway limelight – and most of the publicity I generated there was good.

Funnily enough, I came very close to going back to Poole in 1994, when I spoke to promoter Pete Ansell about a comeback. I'd had a few practice spins and fancied the idea of returning to Wimborne Road, but my assessed average was about 0.02 too high, so they signed Craig Watson instead.

It's been suggested to me that Rickardsson doesn't possess the team-riding skills and awareness of an Ivan or myself. I don't know about that. I just believe that team-riding is a dying art in speedway anyway. It's become much more of an individual sport now.

When I look at the many changes speedway has seen in the years since I last rode, I have mixed feelings. For a start, I think air fences do more harm than good – riders are now taking too many chances. Mark Loram put it into perspective to me when we were chatting and he said: "We just go flat out into the first corner because we know that if we hit the air fence, we're not going to get badly hurt." I told him that I thought that was the wrong attitude to take but as he put it: "If you hit the fence and don't get hurt, you're usually back in the re-run."

Take it from me, if riders continue to adopt a reckless, gung-ho attitude, then someone will get badly hurt, or even worse, despite the absorbent qualities of the air fences we see at every GP and Elite League track now. I think riders are definitely taking more risks than ever before at the top level and that can only be attributed to the advent of the air fence.

One rider who has invited a number of his opponents to test the safety standards of the inflatable fence is Nicki Pedersen, the 2003 World Champion who was bang in form again at the start of the 2006 season. I think the Dane has been nasty

Nicki Pedersen can take what he dishes out.

SIMMO

Scott Nicholls and Lee Richardson – the best of British but not good enough to win the GP series.

fantastic offer like that! If it had been me, I'd have said: "I'll take 15 grand – and keep five for yourself!"

I felt for Crumpie a bit after he finished second to Rickardsson in the Grand Prix series three years in succession. You can put up with being runner-up once, as I was to PC in '76, but for it to happen again and again must have been devastating for him. Jason is definitely very good and he deserved to win the title in 2004, but the only way I can see him winning the GP consistently is after Rickardsson retires.

People can say that Crump is unfortunate to be around when Rickardsson has been in such great form, but it was the same for us with Ivan in the 70s. You just have to try and beat them somehow. There did, though, seem to be a lot more 10-point quality riders around when Ivan reigned and any one of us could've beaten him on the night if we'd had his mental attitude. He had it, we didn't, but we all had enough ability to beat him, whereas I wouldn't think there are that same amount of riders who are capable of beating Rickardsson today.

Mind you, I can't accept that the super-Swede was quite as brilliant as everyone said he was after his bizarre 'wall of death' ride round the fence in the 2005 GP at Cardiff. Countless television replays left the commentators, supporters and other observers gasping in disbelief as the six times World Champion was forced very wide around the first turn and then scooted along the bottom of the air fence – two-wheeling like a moto cross rider – to emerge in front down the back straight. It was a very unusual piece of riding but don't tell me it was purely an act of brilliance. It was more like pure luck!

To be honest, I lost a lot of respect for Tony when he claimed, afterwards, that what he did at Cardiff was the best corner he'd ever ridden in his life. Sure, he had skill. He had balls. But he also had 75 per cent luck. I mean, no-one could attempt to ride a corner like that and get away with – not even someone as talented as Tony, except he did it on that one occasion. It was more luck than judgement, though, and he couldn't do it again in another 100 attempts. I just wished he'd have admitted he got lucky at the time, rather than talk bollocks and take all the acclaim.

"When I look at the many changes speedway has seen in the years since I last rode, I have mixed feelings. For a start, I think air fences do more harm than good – riders are now taking too many chances"

I've met Tony only once – I congratulated him on winning his sixth title after bumping into him very briefly at Eastbourne at the end of last year. I didn't bother to introduce myself – he probably thought I was a supporter – and I just said to him: 'Well done, Tony'. The

Richardson is always moaning, offering some excuse or other – like his bikes were not going good enough or something else. I don't think he'll ever be any better than where he is now.

David Norris is never going to get any better than he is now either, while Dean Barker always says he's going to get himself fit at the start of every season and never does. It says a lot about the lack of genuine English talent in speedway today that, after around 12 league meetings at the start of the 2006 season, not one Brit had an Elite League average of nine points or more and only three – Nicholls, Simon Stead and Joe Screen – were in the eight-plus bracket.

But at the same stage in 1976, for example, John Louis and Peter Collins led the BL averages, while Dave Jessup, myself, Dave and Chris Morton and John Davis were all averaging 10 points a match and more.

But where do we look in England after Nicholls and Richardson? There are a lot of young kids about who have got the ambition to be the best, and Peter Oakes is working hard with his Under-15s Academy, but they have a very long way to go.

I see some of their comments and wonder sometimes if they've even been born. Someone said the other day that they'd had such a long season because they've done 80-odd meetings. In my best year, 1976, I rode in 138 meetings. Ivan did just a couple more than me that year.

I appreciate that the meetings we had didn't involve the same amount of travelling today's top riders face, commuting as they do between England, Sweden and Poland for league matches each week of the summer. I suppose 80 per cent of our meetings were raced in England, where we were riding on average four times a week. Having said that, we spent hours and hours driving up and down motorways in our cars, pulling along trailers, not in the luxurious motor homes the very top riders use now. Nigel Boocock worked it out once that for what he was paid at Coventry, and the hours he spent travelling and preparing his bikes in the workshop, he was earning 10 pence an hour! You wouldn't do it if it was a job, would you, but we never counted the hours spent in the workshop.

I would also argue that we rode in many more tougher meetings in the British racing calendar than they do today. Every track held its own big individual meeting at least once year, where Ivan and every other No.1 would compete against each other.

I think Tony Rickardsson would have been great in any era. He's just head and shoulders above everyone in everything he does – above them in attitude, equipment and sponsorship, before we even talk about riding ability – although he hasn't started the 2006 series well.

I heard a story that Rickardsson came to King's Lynn, when he was riding for the team there, and had a meeting with his sponsors – I'm not sure but he might have won his first world title by then. He met them at a hotel, put his briefcase on the table and simply said to them: "So what is your opening offer?" I think they offered him something like 20 grand for the season, so Rickardsson just shut his case and added: "Well, if that's the best you can do, there's no point in continuing this conversation," and off he went. It must be brilliant to be able to knock back a

Tony Rickardsson – would have been great in any era, but I lost a bit of respect for him at Cardiff.

Norrie Allen has earned Mark a lot more money than he would otherwise have had but he's obviously not been able to help him much with his riding, because he never rode himself. I think Mark needed someone else, in addition to Norrie, to accompany him to the big meetings. Norrie worked alongside Ivan for many years, and no doubt learned a lot in their time together, but he wasn't Ivan's mentor.

I'd question Mark's attitude, too. I was at Ray Palmer's motorcycle shop in Kent earlier this year when Mark was there with Tom Palmer, Ray's son who is a former junior rider at Arena Essex and great mate of Mark's. Mark likes a drink in the winter and they go out on the piss a lot together when they're not racing. To be fair to Mark, though, he will not touch alcohol within a month of the start of the season and when I last met him he said he was just starting his 'drying out' period!

After he won the GP in 2000, I asked him if he was enjoying it and he said: 'No, I bloody hate it, I'd much rather go down the pub and have a few beers with the boys'. He didn't want everything else that goes with being World Champion, so he seemed quite content not to win it again. But he could have won a second world title if only he was prepared to compromise his lifestyle and now that he's out of the GPs, I think he has regrets. Maybe his move to Ipswich this year will do the trick and see him regain his place among the GP elite, but I doubt it. It seems to me that he has too much else going on outside speedway – buying and selling cars and vans, which he says he enjoys doing. He doesn't need much more money, and that's where Norrie has been very good to him.

Mark will do his thing for Ipswich, and it will be worth going there to watch him win races from the back, but I'll be surprised if he can put it all together again and win back his place in the Grand Prix for 2007. I'd love him to prove me wrong . . .

Apart from Scott Nicholls, who else from England can possibly challenge the dominance of Tony Rickardsson and Jason Crump? No-one, as far as I can see. Lee

17 ENGLAND FEARS

ENGLAND ruled the world in the 70s but where are we in speedway terms today? Lagging some way behind Sweden, Denmark and Poland, that's where. These things tend to go in cycles but the future doesn't exactly look very bright for Team Great Britain and the riders that team manager Neil Middleditch has to pick from. We're clearly not producing enough young riders ourselves, while the Scandinavians continue to tap into their conveyor belt of talent coming through their youth mini speedway system that has been producing world champions for them since the 80s.

Scott Nicholls has got to be classed as the undisputed England No.1 in 2006 but only because there is nobody else offering a serious challenge to him for that title. Yeah, he's a good rider but he's not yet at a level where he's even going to win a Grand Prix, let alone become World Champion. He falls off too much – when do you see Tony Rickardsson or Jason Crump fall off anything like as often as Scott does? When there's big pressure on Scott, more often than not he'll crumble.

At times, Scott looks like he's wrestling with his bike and quite often the bike wins that particular battle. I don't rate him very highly. He's got good ability but not enough to become World Champion.

Our last World Champion was Mark Loram, in 2000. He is the PC of this era and I take nothing away from him for having won the GP title despite not managing to win a single round of the millennium year series. He produced the essential ingredient of what winning the GP series is all about – consistency. That was always my main strength and if the GP had been around in my day, I probably would have won umpteen titles. Certainly I believe I could have done in 1976 and 1977, despite my shoulder injury that ended my chances that year.

You can't knock Mark, he was a true World Champion. The way he rides, and the fact that he can't make consistent starts, I'd never thought him capable of becoming World Champion, so he deserves all the more credit for getting to the top. I'd travel to see him race anywhere, because he's worth watching.

Mark Loram – a true World Champion.

Who's the fraudster?

track, if the weather was hot it would be dry as a bone halfway through the afternoon meeting. I think we coped with things quite well, though. We didn't have much dust, but there was a bit of mud around at times!

It was a shame that Ronnie had to pack up promoting at Rye at the end of '93 but – with brother Terry's help – he bounced back again

Back at King's Lynn in 1997 as team manager of the new-look 'Knights'. Left to right: Bo Brhel, Simon Wigg, Paul Hurry, Shane Parker. Front: Shaun Tacey and Tomas Topinka.

and is now running Elite League speedway at Arena Essex. After Rye closed and they started to lay a stock car circuit there, I still kept popping in to the little Hertfordshire stadium because some of the track equipment I used at King's Lynn was still kept at Rye. When Tony Mole took over, he wanted to sell off all the track maintenance gear and he sold it to me at such a good price, that I made good money from it. I think the grader went to Hull Speedway, the tractor went to the Isle of Wight and other bits and pieces went somewhere else – all at a tidy profit!

Not that there was any profit to be made by the Hackney Kestrels promoting consortium of Derek Howes and his fellow shareholders, Gary Muckley and George Rolls, who bought the promoting rights from Dave Pavitt in 1991. I was working at The Wick on the night that thousands of pounds were stolen from the promoters' office, situated at the back of the pits.

Halfway through a meeting one night, a fuse box apparently blew and plunged the stadium into complete darkness. The root of the problem appeared to centre around a lamp standard, just behind the safety fence, that was causing sparks to fly everywhere. It took a little while to fix and, in fact, I was actually stood out by the safety fence, trying to solve the problem with the electrician and one or two others, when the money was snatched.

When the lights came back on, co-promoter Howes went back into his office and it was then that he discovered the money had been stolen. I couldn't believe it when he told me what had happened – I was just glad I'd been out by the safety fence when the thief struck, in full view of those in the immediate vicinity and the spectators. At least then no-one could point the finger of suspicion at me this time!

I have a bloody good idea who did nick the cash – and so did Derek Howes and most other people associated with Hackney in those days – but I can't prove it, so I'm keeping this one to myself. It was a big shame for Howes, who was already finding it tough enough to adapt from where he'd come from – a former souvenir track kiosk seller at Ipswich to running speedway at Hackney, with one or two others supposedly helping out. A former sports master at a Church-run school, poor Derek didn't really have a clue about running a speedway track and the theft of the takings more or less finished him and the club . . . until Terry Russell briefly revived the London Lions at Waterden Road in 1996, the last season of league racing at the track where my own speedway career began.

Although, in theory, I was there in '91 just to help Terry Busch prepare the track, in reality I was also Hackney's team manager. Even though the BSPA had banned me from being employed by a club in an official capacity for five years, after being forced to resign at Lynn, we found a way around the BSPA's block. Les Morrell was named in the programme as team manager but I was the one who made all the decisions about tactical substitutions and other team changes – through him.

Now where have I heard about the theft of speedway cash takings before?

Bill Barker's four-and-a-half years as promoter at King's Lynn ended soon after King's Lynn staged the 1992 Commonwealth Final round of the World Championship on behalf of the BSPA. All the turnstile and programme takings, around £26,000, was reportedly stolen from Barker's Kent home that night. For some strange reason, he changed his usual routine that night and instead of depositing all the money straight into the overnight safe at his bank in King's Lynn town centre, he took it home with him in his car to Kent.

> **"I took a lot of stick from bullshitter Barker through the press after our relationship ended so abruptly and acrimoniously in February 1989. The events had left another stain on my character but I knew the truth about what really happened between us"**

Barker claimed that burglars broke into his house overnight and ran off with the BSPA's money. No! Before you even entertain such scurrilous thoughts, I had absolutely nothing to do with this mysterious theft! I've since been told about the BSPA management committee meeting at which Barker faced a difficult grilling about the events of that fateful night when the Commonwealth Final takings went missing. Apparently, it emerged that Bill kept a dog at home but it had been a very hot night and he had left all the windows in the house open to let in some fresh air. It was also claimed by him that another reason he left the windows open all night was because the dog suffered from flatulence. Oh, and by the way, it was also deaf!

I knew who and what I was getting involved with when Bill and I became business partners. What no-one in speedway probably knew, when we became King's Lynn co-promoters in '88, was that Bill had previously served 18 months in prison for . . . guess what? . . . FRAUD! I took him on as a partner, *knowing* his background, and was obviously too trusting again for my own good.

I can't say I was sorry to see him forced out of King's Lynn soon afterwards, when the BSPA recouped most of their losses by selling off some of his riding assets. That says everything about where they thought the real blame for the missing money lay.

I took a lot of stick from bullshitter Barker through the press after our relationship ended so abruptly and acrimoniously in February 1989. The events had left another stain on my character but I knew the truth about what really happened between us.

Some three years later, those same people within the BSPA were left pointing the finger of suspicion straight at Bill Barker himself.